KV-144-454

PENGUIN BOOKS

HILL OF DESTINY

Dr Peter Becker has won international repute as an author and authority on African history, languages and cultures. Born of English parentage, he was reared in a Transvaal rural area where most of his childhood companions were Africans. His entire adult life has been devoted to a close, on-the-spot study of all African peoples, and this has called for countless research trips into all tribal territories bounded by the Cape in the south, the Zambezi River in the north, and the Indian and Atlantic Oceans.

Peter Becker's fluency in Zulu and related dialects, as well as his intimate understanding of tribal custom and etiquette, have earned him the unique privilege of witnessing, and indeed taking part in, closely guarded rituals and ceremonies, of attending tribal courts, of being admitted into royal villages and kraals of African Kings, Paramount Chiefs and other African dignitaries, and of acquiring first-hand knowledge of African occultism.

In recent times, Becker's researches have been extended to peoples beyond the shores of Africa, namely the inhabitants of Mauritius, the nomadic Bedouin of the Middle East, and the Indians of North America. In 1978 he was honoured with a Fellowship by the International Explorers Club.

Dr Becker has written *Sandy Tracks to the Kraals*; *The Peoples of South Africa* (three volumes); *Path of Blood: The Rise and Conquests of Mzilikazi, Founder of the Matabele of Southern Africa*; *Rule of Fear: The Life and Times of Dingane, King of the Zulu*; *Hill of Destiny: The Life and Times of Moshesh, Founder of the Basotho*; *Peoples of Southern Africa*; *Tribe to Township*; *Trails and Tribes in Southern Africa*; *Mauritius '62*; and *Inland Tribes of Southern Africa*.

He is also the author and presenter of the award-winning television series *The Tribal Identity*.

HILL
OF
DESTINY

The Life and Times of Moshesh,
Founder of the Basotho

PETER BECKER

PENGUIN BOOKS

TO GEORGE STEGMANN—*Ndabezitha!*

Penguin Books Ltd, Harmondsworth, Middlesex, England
Penguin Books, 625 Madison Avenue, New York, New York 10022, U.S.A.
Penguin Books Australia Ltd, Ringwood, Victoria, Australia
Penguin Books Canada Ltd, 2801 John Street, Markham, Ontario, Canada L3R 1B4
Penguin Books (N.Z.) Ltd, 182–190 Wairau Road, Auckland 10, New Zealand

First published by Longman Group Ltd 1969
Published in Penguin Books 1982

Maps drawn by Edward Purcell

Made and printed in Great Britain by
Rirchard Clay (The Chaucer Press) Ltd, Bungay, Suffolk
Set in Linotype Times

KGOTLA LA MOSHOESHOE
(*Moshesh's Kgotla*)

Akga mahlo, diala, Mokwena,
   Cast thy far-seeing eyes, oh Comrade
O a akgele morao, maswetso
   Back into the deep abysm of time
Nakong tsa hae Phiri ya Matlama
   During his days—the Hyena of Matlama,
Namane ya Khudu, mora Mokhachane
   Khudu's child, the son of Mokhachane
Motlolo wa Peete, sefate—seholo
   The progeny of Peete, the big genealogical
   tree,
Qheku le soto la ho fepa madimo,
   The ill-fated old man who fed the cannibals,
Le hara madimo ke bolela boRakotswane—
   And I'm referring to the cannibals among
   Rakotswane's people—
Sheba morao, o bone Basotho
   Look back and behold the Basotho
Kgotla ha Thesele wa Mokhachane!
   At the court of Moshesh of Mokhachane!

Ephraim A. S. Lesoro

In recent days Mohlomi, the seer, had been visited by the spirit of his father who predicted disaster for all peoples inhabiting the interior of South Africa. Clouds of red dust would rise in the east heralding the approach of mighty, warfaring tribes; defenceless Sotho clans would be scattered, butchered and reduced to poverty; famine would sweep across the valleys and hills, and kraals would be overrun with beasts of prey. Sotho patriarchs stripped of all possessions and driven by hunger would slaughter and devour their own children; friends would rise up against friends, brothers against brothers and sons against fathers.

Contents

Maps

ILLUSTRATIONS

1 Eugene Casalis, founder of the French Evangelical Mission Station at Thaba Bosiu

2 Evening service at the Morija Mission Station, 1834

3 A Basotho War Dance on Thaba Bosiu, in honour of Sir Andrew Smith, 1834

4 A Boer commando on patrol in the vicinity of Moshesh's domain

5 Sir Harry Smith, High Commissioner of the British Cape Colony, 1847–1852

6 Sir George Cathcart leading the British into battle against Moshesh's army in 1852

7 Josias Hoffman, first president of the Orange Free State

8 Moshesh at the age of seventy-four

9 The Khubela Pass taken by the author from the summit of Thaba Bosiu

10 Sir George Cathcart at the time of the British invasion of the Lesotho

11 Advocate Jan Hendrik Brand, president of the Free State Republic during the twilight of Moshesh's life

12 The Boer Hero, Louw Wepener

13 An artist's impression of the Khubelu Pass during the second Boer–Basotho war

14 The author identifying the graves of Basotho dignitaries on the summit of Thaba Bosiu

15 The author's guides, Tseliso and Albert Khalema, at Moshesh's grave

MAPS

ACKNOWLEDGEMENTS

Photograph No. 1 is from *The Evangel in South Africa* by Du Plessis; Nos. 2, 3, 6 and 8 are from the Charles Bell Collection in the Africana Museum in Johannesburg; No. 4 from Brewer's *Sir Harry Smith* 1854; No. 10 is from *The Illustrated London News Vol. 72*, 1852; Nos. 9 and 15 were taken by the author. The maps were drawn by Edward Purcell

PREFACE

THIS book, the biography of the great Moshesh, founder and potentate of the Basotho nation, follows naturally on my recent biographies of Mzilikazi, King of the Matabele and Dingane, King of the Zulu. These three rulers rank among the historical giants of 19th-century South Africa. Indeed, their names are legendary from the Cape to the Zambesi and beyond.

In the course of many years of research into Moshesh's life, I came into contact with hundreds of kind and knowledgeable people of all races and creeds. It is with deep sincerity that I place on record my gratitude for the cooperation and hospitality I received throughout the Lesotho, and I should like to mention especially the following Basotho dignitaries: The late Regent of the nation, Chieftainess Mantsebo Seeiso, Chiefs Letsie Theko (Thaba Bosiu), Nkuebe Peete (Matsieng), Kuini Mopeli and Kopano Selomo (Butha-Buthe), Princesses Mamotsoene Ntaote and Makwena Mohale (Matsieng) and Headmen Azoel Lehao and Tsosane Mphutlane (Thaba Bosiu). My thanks are also due to my guides, the late Clark Khetheng, Dickson Rafutho, Jacob Rehadie, Tseliso and Albert Khalema, Herbert Taka and Lechesa Matela.

Informants, and especially those who replied to my questionnaires, are far too numerous to mention by name. I shall be eternally indebted to them for their unflagging cooperation at all times. The following informants were particularly helpful and instructive: Eva Moshesh of Durban, direct descendant of Moshesh, Martha Lebotsa of the Lesotho Government Archives, S. M. and J. M. Mohale and V. R. Mokhoro (Matsieng), Gershon Lijane (Thaba Bosiu), Agnes Ramainoane, Sehloho, Ratsiu and Maria Tsoenyane (Teyateyaneng), Thabo Mesehle, Cloris Mathaba, Louis Matshaba and Eugene Tsehlana (Morija) and April Lerume and Atwell Mopeli (Witsies Hoek).

I received the most valuable hitherto unpublished information concerning Louw Wepener from Mrs. Lulu Stegmann, a descendant of this famous Boer hero. I have the

happiest recollections of rewarding and enjoyable times
spent at Thaba Bosiu, Morija, Masitise, Likhoele and other
mission stations of the Paris Evangelical Missionary
Society. I greatly appreciate the advice given me by the
various missionaries, and especially Messrs. Michel Bernard
(Morija) and Albert Brütsch (Mafeteng).

Without the unstinting help of the personnel of Archives
I visited throughout South Africa, this biography could well
have become an insurmountable task. I must mention par-
ticularly Moira Farmer, head of the Gubbins Africana
Library of the Witwatersrand University, the staff of the
Johannesburg Africana Library and Louise de Wet of the
Africana Museum Johannesburg. Information received
from Connie and James Walton (Cape Town) and Les
Roberts (Durban) proved most helpful.

A very special word of thanks is due to Fred Webster
who scrutinized my manuscripts, and to Sheila Wahl who
typed them.

Finally my deepest love to Connie, my wife, and to my
children, Harold, Peter, Nandi and Lindi. They kept silent
guard at 'kwaVulindlela' while the midnight oil was burning.

PETER BECKER
'kwaVulindlela',
Johannesburg

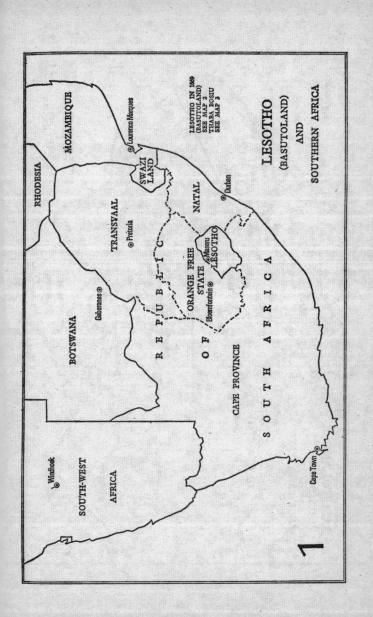

LESOTHO
(BASUTOLAND)
AND
SOUTHERN AFRICA

LESOTHO IN 1869
(BASUTOLAND)
SEE MAP 2
THABA BOSIU
SEE MAP 3

MOZAMBIQUE

RHODESIA

Lourenço Marques

SWAZI
LAND

TRANSVAAL

Pretoria

NATAL

Durban

BOTSWANA

Gaberones

R E P U B L I C

O F

ORANGE FREE
STATE

Bloemfontein

Maseru
LESOTHO

SOUTH-WEST

AFRICA

Windhoek

S O U T H   A F R I C A

CAPE PROVINCE

Cape Town

1

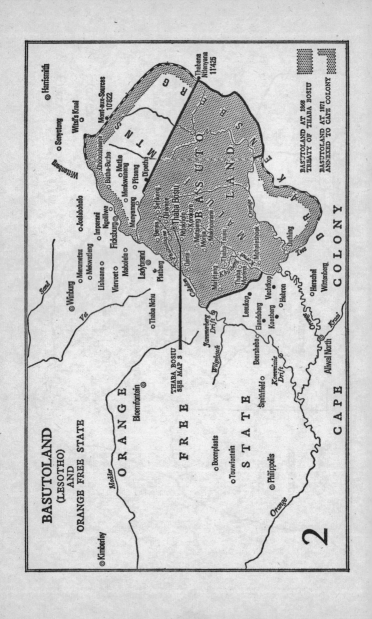

BASUTOLAND
(LESOTHO)
AND
ORANGE FREE STATE

BASUTOLAND AT 1868
TREATY OF THABA BOSIU

BASUTOLAND AT 1871
ANNEXED TO CAPE COLONY

ORANGE   FREE   STATE

CAPE   COLONY

BAS UTO LAND

DRAKENSBERG MTNS

Kimberley
Modder
Bloemfontein
Boomplaats
Touwfontein
Philippolis
Orange
Smithfield
Kommisie Drift
Beersheba
Koesberg
VechtKop
Hebron
Aliwal North
Kraai
Wittenberg
Herschel
Leeukop
Blandsberg
Wilgebosch
Jammerberg Drift
Leribe
Tsing
Orange
Tees
Kraai
Thaba Nchu
Vet
Winburg
Sevil
Lishuane
Vierveot
Maboleia
Ladybrand
Platberg
Merumetsu
Mekwatleng
Imparai
Ngolihwe
Ficksburg
Joalaboholo
Wittenberg
Witte's Kraal
Senyotong
Harrismith
Mont-aux-Sources 10822
Zhocoosneum
Butha-Butha
Metlie
Menkwaneng
Munyameng
Pitseng
Dipetsa
Berga Sethong
Quitnie
Nwatich
Moroosi's Marita
Maharaneng
Khiri
Thaba Khuba
Khiri
Mirimini
Thaba Bosiu
Krokom
Cledoa Qomi
Mphalseng
Mohaieseng
Duthing
Thabana Ntlenyana 11425

THABA BOSIU
SEE MAP 3

2

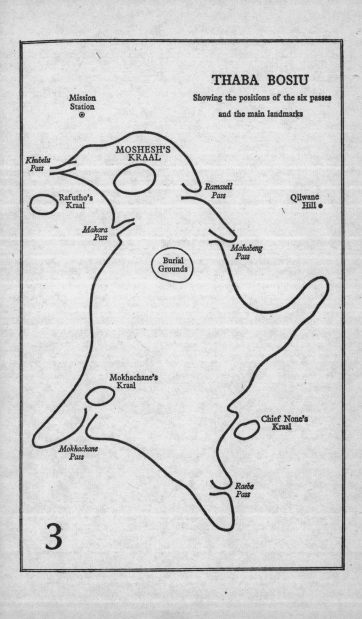

THABA BOSIU

Showing the positions of the six passes

and the main landmarks

Mission
Station

MOSHESH'S
KRAAL

*Khubelu
Pass*

*Ramaseli
Pass*

Qilwane
Hill

Rafutho's
Kraal

*Makara
Pass*

*Mahabeng
Pass*

Burial
Grounds

Mokhachane's
Kraal

Chief None's
Kraal

*Mokhachane
Pass*

*Raebe
Pass*

3

PART ONE

CHAPTER ONE

THE CALEDON VALLEY

Peoples of the Valley—Family life and ritual—Moshesh: birth and childhood—Circumcision and graduation to manhood

'THIS mountain is my mother,' said Chief Moshesh to his missionary friend, Eugene Casalis, 'and had it not been for her, you would have found my country without inhabitants.'[1] It was the year 1837, and he was referring to Thaba Bosiu, a sprawling, flat-topped hill crowned with lofty sandstone precipices—a magnificent stronghold situated to the immediate south of the Caledon river, in the heart of the Republic of South Africa. Moshesh was reflecting on the turbulent history of the Basotho tribe he had founded some fifteen years before out of a motley rabble of emaciated, war-weary warriors, starving women, children and grey heads, and bands of cannibals. But by 1837 he was middle-aged and prosperous and deeply revered by his subjects.

A contemporary of the Zulu conquerors Shaka and Dingane and of the Matabele tyrant, Mzilikazi, Moshesh was known throughout the tribal territories of South Africa and the British Cape Colony. Of humble descent, he had not always lived on Thaba Bosiu, but had fled together with a handful of followers into its impregnable heights in 1824, during the Dark Age of South African tribal history—a ghastly era of internecine warfare launched by the mighty Shaka.

In tracing Moshesh's extraordinary life history we must consider first the environment into which he was born and then the forces responsible for his rise from a humble background to the status of founder and potentate of a powerful

[1] E. Casalis, *The Basutos*, p. 78.

tribe. In about 1787 his father, a petty-chief named Mokhachane, headed the Bamokoteli clanlet, one of the several
Bantu[1] groups inhabiting the Caledon Valley in the region
of presentday Leribe. Numbering no more than three to
four thousand, the Bamokoteli were an offshoot of the
parent Bakwena or Crocodile tribe of Botswana and were
held in subjugation by the neighbouring Basekake to whom
they paid regular tribute in hides, grain and cattle.

With minor exceptions the people who inhabited the
interior of South Africa as far distant as the Limpopo river
in the north, the Orange in the south, the Kalahari desert in
the west and the Drakensberg range in the east, all pursued
a similar way of life and spoke related dialects. They
comprised mainly Sotho-speaking peoples, one of South
Africa's largest ethnic groups.

The most prominent clans of the Caledon Valley were
the Mapetla, the Mapolane and the Baphuthi, while the
Basia, the Batlokwa, Bafokeng and Makwakwa occupied
separate areas on the highveld in what is today the Harrismith district. These clans were in turn subdivided into
clanlets, each living independently of the other under the
rule of hereditary chieftains. They were respected patriarchs whose duties included presiding over courts of justice,
officiating at religious ceremonies, allocating land to newly
wedded couples, organizing cattle raids into neighbouring
territories and mustering the warriors in time of feud.
Dressed in a distinctive leopardskin mantle and leopardskin
head band decorated with plumes, a Sotho chieftain was
respected by his subjects but seldom feared. Indeed, it was
not uncommon for subjects to address him by name and
even to interrupt or contradict him in the course of conversation. His councillors, warriors and menials did not
make obeisance to him, not even on special occasions such
as the sitting of the *kgotla* or tribal court.[2]

[1] The ethnological term for the tribes of Southern Africa.
[2] By contrast Zulu and Matabele kings were both revered and
feared. For example, on approaching a gathering of subjects
they would be greeted with a tumultuous roar of 'Bayete', the
royal salute followed by further exclamations such as 'Lion',
'Bull-Elephant' or 'Great King'. Commoners adopted the
humblest attitudes in the presence of a ruler and if summoned

The Sotho-speaking clans were not a warfaring people, and yet they were forever squabbling and skirmishing over grazing rights. They were avid pastoralists who assessed the status of chiefs and commoners alike by the numbers of cattle they possessed. In fact cattle entered into almost every aspect of their way of life. Cows provided kraals with fresh and curdled milk; hides were converted into clothing, dung mixed with clay was used for plastering hut-floors, and cattle formed the *bohali* or dowry demanded by a father for his daughter's hand in marriage. In times of worship, when the people assembled to deliver prayers of repentance or thanksgiving either to Molimo, the Supreme Spirit, or to their ancestral spirits, handpicked oxen were slaughtered for sacrifice.

The Bamokoteli of the Caledon Valley were avid cattle-breeders, but although surrounded by larger and more powerful clans including the Batlokwa or Wild Cat People, they were left in comparative peace for their herds were too few to attract the attention of the more ambitious cattle-raiding chiefs.

In the 1790s Mokhachane, the clanlet's petty-chief, lived with his wife Khudu—the Tortoise, daughter of Ntsukun-yane, chief of a Bafokeng clan in a modest kraal not a stone's throw from the Tlotsi stream, a murky tributary of the Caledon river. Known as Menkwaneng, this kraal barely differed from thousands of other family settlements scattered throughout the Valley. It comprised a small circle of dome-shaped grass huts built side by side to embrace a palisaded cattlefold. Similar impoverished kraals punctuated the immediate vicinity of Menkwaneng, and during Summer months while the herdboys tended their fathers' cattle in the surrounding countryside and the women laboured in the fields of sorghum millet, pumpkin and gourd, the menfolk were to be found idly gossiping or sipping home-brewed sorghum beer in the shade of the huts or trees. During the Winter, after the crops had been reaped,

---

would crawl towards him on hands and knees. No one dared speak unless addressed first by the king; no one dared spit, sneeze or cough, for this was an offence punishable by execution. (See Peter Becker, *Path of Blood* and *Rule of Fear*.)

Mokhachane's subjects seldom ventured from their kraals, although a few were assigned to lifting cattle from the grazing grounds of nearby clans, and others to hunting antelope, wildboar, jackal, lion, leopard and other game which abounded in the Valley.

Mokhachane's people were also skilled craftsmen. In the confines of the kraals the women fashioned clay pots of varying sizes and shapes for storing grain, milk, water and beer; from reeds they wove baskets both small and large, funnel-shaped beer strainers, sleeping mats, winnowing trays and huge spherical granaries. The men carved food bowls, milk pails, spoons, stools and flutes, as well as a large variety of ornaments. They also brayed and tanned antelope and cattle hide from which they made shields, simple loin-garments, sandals, cloaks and voluminous *karosses*[1] for themselves and their families. Talented smithies extracted metal from ore for assegais, battle-axes, adzes and hunting javelins.

In about the year 1787 disaster descended upon Mokha-chane's clanlet. This was a lean year, for most of the ripen-ing sorghum had been destroyed by premature frost, and with the arrival of Winter leaden clouds had drifted in from the Drakensberg and Maluti ranges in the south, bringing scudding rain and then a heavy fall of snow. Pumpkins and gourds not yet harvested shrivelled in the icy grip of the storm that swept the Valley; cattle perished; huts laden with ice crumbled, leaving many a family to face death from exposure. When eventually biting winds drove the clouds northwards, the sun emerged, the streams came to life and the Caledon roared down its course to the Orange. In the weeks that followed, a mellow winter's sun en-veloped the Valley, drying the earth and beckoning clans-men now steeped in gloom to repair their kraals and to look to the Spring with enthusiasm. But by October no rains had fallen in the Valley and in November even the most skilful rain-makers, summoned by Mokhachane, failed to induce the heavens to open. A broiling sun bit deep into the parched earth; the fields remained untilled, the seeds un-planted and the Tlotsi stream slept. The Bamokoteli led by

[1] Rugs made of pelts.

Mokhachane sacrificed regularly to the Supreme Spirit calling 'Pula! Pula'—'Rain! Rain!' but the drought persisted.
Famine pervaded the land.

It was during this fateful year that Moshesh was born.
News of Khudu's pregnancy had reached Bamokoteli
settlements in June and the people rejoiced that Mokhachane, their petty-chief, was to be blessed with an heir. At
the height of the great drought a small party of Khudu's
female relatives arrived at Menkwaneng from beyond the
Caledon and together with a small group of Bamokoteli
midwives took charge of the confinement. An inquisitive
crowd gathered at the kraal and fixed its eyes on a spot
above the tiny doorway of Khudu's hut where a bunch of
reeds tied to the thatch signified the impending birth of
Mokhachane's child. In due course when the birth was
announced by one of the midwives, a great cheer went up
from the crowd, and Mokhachane, beaming with joy, called
upon his subjects to celebrate. Hardly had he spoken than
he was seized by his councillors and beaten gently in
accordance with custom. Good-humouredly he ran from
the scene pursued by the happy throng, and on reaching the
gates of the cattlefold, he turned suddenly to indicate the
place where large quantities of sorghum beer and piles of
boiled beef had been set out for the guests. And so, during
the remaining hours of the day and throughout the night,
the Bamokoteli danced and feasted. It is said that even old
Peete, Mokhachane's father, known to all as aloof and
timid, competed with the best of the dancers. He admitted
later that he had long awaited this great event.

Meanwhile the midwives were fussing about Khudu and
her baby, and as soon as the umbilical cord had been cut, the
afterbirth was buried outside the hut lest it should fall into
the hands of a sorcerer seeking to bewitch the petty-chief or
his heir. It was then that the child was named. They called
him Lepoqo meaning Trouble or Dispute, in commemoration of the troubled times into which he had been born. In
later years Lepoqo was to be renamed Moshoeshoe, pronounced Moshweshwe, but known mainly by his nickname
Moshesh.

Khudu was confined to her hut until Lepoqo's navel
string had shrivelled and fallen off. She was then escorted

by her attendants to a reed enclosure where she was kept in
further isolation under guard of the clanlet's senior female
dignitaries. A beast was slaughtered and its gall bladder removed, emptied over Lepoqo's body and then fastened
around his neck as a precaution against the influence of evil
spirits. Finally his head was shaved with a short-bladed
lehare or crudely fashioned razor.

At the conclusion of her prolonged period of isolation
Khudu was visited by Mokhachane who brought gifts of
charms specially prepared by witchdoctors for the baby. A
feast was held and again the Bamokoteli rejoiced, sang
praise-songs and made sacrifices to the shades of the dead.

Much of Lepoqo's early infancy was spent on his
mother's back, and during his waking hours he was entertained not only by the women but also by adolescent girls in
whose charge he was placed from time to time. First he was
breast-fed and later weaned on finely ground *lesheleshe* or
sorghum porridge. He soon became podgy and bright-eyed,
and by the age of four or five he was playing with an assortment of stones and bones which, so he told his father, represented the cattle and inmates of Menkwaneng. He and
his agemates frolicked naked about the huts, chasing after
calves, quarrelling and creating so much noise that they
provoked the adults, who were accustomed to an afternoon's nap, to reprimand or beat them.

From the day he lost his incisor teeth at the age of six or
seven, Lepoqo came under the strict supervision of his
father. He was given a short loin cloth to wear, and was
sent with the older boys to be taught how to milk the cows
and herd the calves and goats. Suddenly the cattlefold had
become a place of special importance to him, and he enjoyed learning the names given to the cows, oxen and calves
by his mentors. Lepoqo conceived a deep affection for
animals, and in later years after he had risen to the para-
mountcy of the Basuto nation and was domiciled on the
mountain fortress, Thaba Bosiu, he derived untold pleasure
in recalling the occasion during his childhood when he was
given a spotted kid-goat by his father.

'I built it a little house,' he would reminisce, smiling

broadly, 'and I chose the tenderest grass for it; but, oh! it was so beautiful! I hardly think there is another like it!'

It is said that Lepoqo and his goat were inseparable, and that whenever people passed nearby, they were invariably butted heavily in the rear. Until the age of twelve Lepoqo allowed few matters to occupy his mind more earnestly than the care he lavished on this spotted goat. Small wonder that one day when he saw it snatched up and dragged by a leopard into a stretch of reeds flanking the Tlotsi stream, he vowed in an outburst of rage mingled with tears of anguish never to rest until he had avenged the death of the companion he cherished most at Menkwaneng.

On rainy days and often at nights it was customary for Lepoqo and his friends to meet in an appointed hut where, seated side by side around a cattle-dung fire, they would listen wide-eyed to tales narrated by one of the older women of Menkwaneng. They never tired of fables featuring the cunning jackal, the deceitful hyena, the restless partridge, the blundering lion or leopard, the fleet-footed springbok, the wise tortoise, the evil puff-adder and a host of other animals, birds and reptiles. But they dreaded ghost stories, for then their minds were filled with haunting visions, and they trembled with fear.

On reaching puberty Lepoqo was placed by Mokhachane in the *thakaneng*, an isolated section of the kraal reserved for adolescent boys. Given an assegai and hunting stick, he gained the status of a cattleherd and was assigned to the duty of milking cows, securing the gates of the cattlefold after dark and reporting cases of injury or sickness found among the beasts to his father. In the mornings after driving his herd to pasture, he would join fellow cattleherds in a variety of activities: bird-nesting, collecting grasshoppers for roasting and eating, digging up edible bulbs, turning up stones in search of scorpions, snaring birds, hunting rats, hares, partridges and rock-rabbits, paddling or bathing in the Tlotsi stream, moulding toy cattle from clay, riding calves, shying stones at targets and exploring kratzes and caves in the hills. He also competed in running, sham fighting and wrestling, and although he would have admitted that he was happier now than ever before, there were times when he was bullied by older boys or chastised by his father for neglecting to keep the cattle away from the crops.

By the age of fifteen Lepoqo was counted among the leaders of the *thakaneng* despite the fact that he was neither tall nor as well-proportioned as many of the older boys. Even-tempered, self-assured, quick-minded and gifted with a ready sense of wit, his popularity was unrivalled, but his greatest admirers were the junior herdboys who found him friendly, sympathetic and unaffected. They recalled the time he had thrashed a senior boy for persistently bullying the youngest inmate of the *thakaneng*; and there was also the occasion when he was set upon and cudgelled by a group of agemates for daring to intervene in a fight which he considered unevenly matched. But it was his daring in climbing the precipitous rock-faces of hills and his skill at hunting which attracted most attention, and established his high status in the *thakaneng*. It must be assumed that Lepoqo resembled his mother in character, for Mokhachane was imbued with few real qualities of leadership and is known to have been whimsical, moody and indecisive, and also withdrawn in times of trouble.

Among the important features of Lepoqo's adolescent years was the arrival in Bamokoteli country of Makwanyane, son of a commoner named Ntseke. Makwanyane's early infancy had been spent in a kraal near Menkwaneng, but he had been sickly and frail and his father, assured by a diviner[1] that the child had been bewitched and would die unless hidden, had taken him secretly to a settlement far beyond the Tlotsi stream where he was reared. As the years passed Makwanyane became healthy and strong, and at the age of thirteen he was fetched by his father and placed in the *thakaneng* at Menkwaneng. It was there that he met

[1] Diviners diagnosed diseases and predicted events by casting selected bones and other 'magical' items. These included anklejoints of the antbear, wildboar, hyena, monkey and goat and the knuckle-joints of a lion. Also included were a vulture's beak, stones taken from a crocodile's stomach, cowries and other shells, a piece of tortoise shell, pips of certain indigenous fruits and tips of an ox-hoof.

Lopoqo who became his closest friend and lifelong companion.

At the beginning of 1803 when Lepoqo was about sixteen and Makwanyane fourteen, a meeting was held by petty-chief Mokhachane, his councillors and patriarchs of kraals, to discuss arrangements for the circumcision of the adolescent boys of the clanlet. It was decided that the *mophato* or circumcision lodge, an enclosure built of green branches, should be erected near the Tlotsi stream on the outskirts of Menkwaneng.

Having announced the names of the adolescents due for circumcision, Lepoqo's included, the men agreed to bring their sons to the *mophato* when the moon waxed full at the beginning of Autumn.

As the months passed and the appointed time drew near it became clear to the elders of the clanlet that the plans for the boys' circumcision would have to be abandoned. For until their meeting with Mokhachane three months before, rain had been plentiful and the ripening crops lush, but suddenly the rains ceased and week after week the sun burnt down on the Valley, its remorseless heat scorching the grazing lands, bleaching the fields of sorghum and destroying the crops of pumpkin and gourd. The drought persisted for almost two years, and is known to this day as *tlala sekoboto*—the great hunger. Having lost all their crops and most of their cattle the peoples of the Valley were faced with famine, and only by eating bulbs and roots dug from the veld were they able to avoid disaster.

The drought broke in October 1804 and during the remainder of the Summer showers fell regularly throughout the Valley. Now the crops yielded an abundant harvest and the cattle and goats grew fat and heavy in udder. A *mophato* was built in March 1805, and the petty-chief set aside a day for the boys to be circumcised. When the time arrived Lepoqo, his friend Makwanyane and scores of other herdboys were brought to the lodge by their fathers where they huddled together full of fear in anticipation of the ordeal awaiting them. Only one comforting thought traversed their minds: when once they were circumcised and had completed the period of initiation which followed, they would graduate to adulthood; privileged to share the com-

pany of men, privileged to take part in the activities of the
kgotla, and privileged to marry.

In the meantime a black bull had been slaughtered, dismembered and roasted, and for three days while the elders
feasted Lepoqo and his fellow initiates were confined to the
mophato. Their heads were shaved and they were given
fortifying medicines by the herbalists of the clan as a precaution against the evil influences of sorcerers. At dawn on
the fourth day they were circumcised in rapid succession by
a clansman renowned for his dexterity with an assegai
blade. Most of them wept—some screaming hysterically—
for they were given no opiate to relieve them of pain. It is
said that Lepoqo, while attempting to staunch the flow of
blood from his own wound, also tried to comfort the
younger boys, exhorting them to be brave. Eventually he
and other initiates were given a narcotic prepared from the
leshona, an indigenous bulb, which put them quickly to
sleep. Hours later when they awoke they were taken into a
hut within the *mophato* and told to rest.

During the following weeks while their wounds healed
the boys were subjected to considerable hardship. Dressed in
cloaks of tanned cattle-hide, they were taken on long,
fatiguing marches without food or water, along river beds,
through chasms, over krantzes and along steep, rocky hill-
slopes. If they complained they were flogged and reminded
that only the hardiest among them could qualify as the
future cattle-raiders and warriors of the clanlet.

Back at the *mophato* the initiates were cuffed incessantly
by specially appointed bullies, and if they overlooked even
the most trivial rules of the lodge they were thrashed.
Lepoqo endured this trying time with uncommon dignity
and soon won the admiration of the overseers of the lodge.
He was never still, and apart from attending to the many
duties demanded of him, he also found time to assist and
comfort his fellow-initiates. Small wonder that he was to be
nicknamed Tlaputla—the Busy One.

After six arduous months in the lodge the initiates were
informed by Mokhachane that a day had been fixed for
their graduation to manhood. Accordingly one morning at
the first light of dawn they were led to the Tlotsi stream
where first they washed and then daubed their bodies with a

mixture of red clay, fat and powdered medicinal herbs. Thereafter they were each given a loin-cloth and a club and sent back to the lodge to be inspected by Mokhachane and a medicine man. Meanwhile all utensils, all clothing, skin blankets, in fact everything handled by the initiates during past months, were flung into the huts and set alight. And as the entire *mophato* went up in flames the boys hurried away shielding their eyes with their hands for they knew that should they set eyes on the conflagration they would bring misfortune on their newly earned adulthood.

As the smoke swirled into the sky Menkwaneng resounded to the cheering and singing of a crowd of spectators, and later when the initiates were ushered into the cattlefold by the overseers they were applauded and presented with ornaments and clothing. At a signal from one of the dignitaries the spectators burst into song, and suddenly there was a rumbling of stomping feet as they flung themselves into a wild tribal dance.

During the following four days and four nights the Bamokoteli feasted, ignoring the initiates who remained confined to the cattlefold. The celebrations came to an end on the fifth day. Brought into the *kgotla* the initiates were pronounced worthy of manhood by Mokhachane; worthy of becoming warriors, cattle-breeders and kraal patriarchs. They were also briefly addressed by each councillor in turn, and finally at great length by old Peete, Lepoqo's grandfather.

Beaming with pride the old greybeard swaggered into the centre of the *kgotla*, and extending an arm in the direction of Lepoqo called upon the Bamokoteli to cast admiring eyes on his grandson, the heir-apparent of the clanlet. A roar of approval drowned the old man's voice, and suddenly initiates rushed forward, swarmed about Lepoqo, chanting a vow to follow and serve him. They vowed to follow him even unto death.

CHAPTER TWO

EARLY MANHOOD

*The great hunt—Journey into the Caledon Valley—
Visit to Mohlomi, the seer—Mohlomi's wise counsel—
Chief Makara faces death—Murder on the banks of
the Tlotsi—A gruesome ceremony—Lepoqo is renamed Moshweshe and later Moshesh*

IN 1805 Lepoqo, at the age of eighteen, was of medium
height, broad-shouldered, narrow-hipped and as lithe as a
leopard. His limbs although not unduly muscular were well-
shaped and solid, and he walked with a buoyant step. Pleasant of disposition he had an amiable yet essentially manly
face. A broad forehead, a flat but superbly chiselled nose;
large, alert, jet black eyes; pronounced cheek-bones; heavy
lips and a firm chin revealing the barest hint of a beard.
'Agreeable and interesting of countenance', he was every
inch a man of 'noble and dignified' deportment.

After graduation to manhood Lepoqo spent most of the
first few weeks in the *kgotla* where at first he followed discussions with avid interest. Usually he was accompanied by
a small party of comrades, former fellow-initiates, who having elected to serve an indefinite term as the petty-chief's
menials, had not returned to their parents' kraals.

In September messengers were sent by Mokhachane to all
Bamokoteli settlements with orders for the men of the
clanlet to assemble at Menkwaneng for a hunting trip into
the territory embracing the mouth of the Tlotsi stream.
Soon the petty-chief's kraal became a hive of activity.
Hundreds of hunters assembled at the *kgotla* where they sat
in groups whetting their assegais and yarning about previous hunts. They were given protective potions by the
witchdoctors, a decoction of charred herbs and springbok
fat and finally a special potion to ensure accuracy of aim
and fleetness of foot. A black, greasy medicine was rubbed
by herbalists into incisions cut into their arms and legs.

The hunters departed for the hunting grounds after three

days' wait at Menkwaneng, and on arrival they spread out along the river bank, eventually forming up in a circle several miles in circumference. At the command of the leaders of the hunt they moved slowly forward; whistling, cat-calling, chanting and beating the ground with branches, sticks or plaited oxhide thongs. Startled by the sudden hullabaloo of approaching hunters a confusion of eland, wildebeest, zebra, koodoo, springbok and other species both large and small, savage and timid bounded away towards the centre of the converging circle. Then struck with terror they scattered in all directions, some stampeding blindly to freedom through the menacing ring of hunters, some rearing and kicking wildly and others bunching helplessly together to be slaughtered beneath a deluge of assegai blades.

Lepoqo brought down an eland bull, an achievement which filled him with pride. He never forgot this his first hunt since graduating to manhood, and the eland's magnificent hide adorned his hut floor until the time of his death over sixty years later.

On his return to Menkwaneng, Lepoqo, accompanied by three of his menials, set out on a journey through the Caledon Valley hunting antelope, buffalo and zebra, and calling upon the chiefs of the Mapetla, Mapolane and Buphuthi clans. In the course of his travels Lepoqo would have noticed that the Valley was dotted with low, flat-topped and conical-shaped hills crested with sandstone cliffs, and one day while climbing the Maluti mountains in the tracks of a tawny, black-maned lion, he must have observed that the country extending to the eastern and southern horizon was knotted with chain upon chain of hazy, majestic ranges. He was afraid of venturing too far out of the Valley, so when he had caught up with the lion and had slain it, he retraced his steps down the rugged Maluti slopes and set out for home.

Lepoqo reached Menkwaneng in November and during the following weeks he went daily to the *kgotla* where in the presence of a large audience of men he would recount the experiences he had in the course of his journey into the Caledon Valley. Sometimes at nights he would visit the

herdboys in the *thakaneng* and repeat to them the more
exciting stories he had told in the *kgotla*. In this way he
captured their admiration, and became a source of extreme
pride for at least three of the inmates—his younger
brothers, Poshuli, Mohale and Mopeli. Soon his adventures
were being bandied about in kraals throughout Bamokoteli
country, and he was acclaimed as the clanlet's most daring
and courageous son.

Not far beyond the Caledon river in what is today the
Ficksburg district, lived a chief of the Bamonaheng clan,
Mohlomi by name, a wise, kindly, peace-loving old man,
and a seer, healer and rainmaker of great repute. Indeed,
his insight into the phenomena of the spirit world was
legendary in all the interior of South Africa.

During the past forty years or more Mohlomi had visited
clans inhabiting regions as far east as the Drakensberg
range and as far west as presentday Botswana. He was
known to every chief, headman and witchdoctor worthy of
mention, and in the eyes of old Peete, he was a messenger
of God, the one man Lepoqo should meet if ever he was to
become a great chief in the mould of the ancestral rulers.
Summoning Lepoqo, Peete suggested they visit Ngolilwe,
the seer's great kraal, without delay.

After two months' negotiation with Mohlomi's councillors, Peete and Lepoqo were invited to Ngolilwe. They
arrived at the great kraal one morning in February 1806.
Having been ushered into the *kgotla* they were given
curdled milk and sorghum bread, and were then taken to a
straw hut near the entrance of an immense cattlefold.
Seated outside the hut door on a straw mat they beheld the
seer. He was conversing happily with his councillors, a skin
hat pulled squarely over his iron grey hair and a leopardskin *kaross* draped over his shoulders concealing most of
his bent, lathy form. A heavy brass ring embraced his
leathery neck, and from his ears hung large earrings. A
benevolent smile traversed Mohlomi's craggy face as he
beckoned the strangers to draw near and be seated, and then
he asked them the purpose of their visit to Ngolilwe.

Old Peete replied that he had brought Lepoqo, his grandson, the heir-apparent of the Bamokoteli to Ngolilwe, be-

lieving that he would derive untold benefit from Mohlomi's
wisdom. Lepoqo, he explained, had only recently qualified
for manhood, but was blessed with qualities of leadership
which he, Peete, so sadly lacked.

According to presentday tribal chroniclers Mohlomi
turned his black deep-set eyes on Lepoqo, eyes which
revealed the faintest expression of surprise. It was seldom,
said the seer, that men fresh from the circumcision lodge
troubled to consult him, for invariably they shunned the
company of old men, regarding them as incapable of im-
parting worthwhile advice. In the course of many years of
journeying from clan to clan he, Mohlomi, had striven to
dissuade the younger generation from the age-old custom
of cattle-raiding and skirmishing; they should rather seek
peaceful coexistence with peoples sharing their borders.
Peace bred happiness, while strife bred tribulation. There
were far too many hot-headed men who squandered their
time sharpening assegai blades when their days should be
devoted to threshing corn.

In the many years of his chieftaincy, Mohlomi continued,
his own people, the Bamonaheng had suffered few attacks
from neighbouring clans. This was partly the result of a
policy he had pursued since early manhood; to enter into
marriage with at least one daughter of each of the belligerent chiefs living on either side of the Caledon. In this
way he had created bonds of friendship with the people he
feared most. He commended this practice to Lepoqo.

Mohlomi lamented the high frequency of drunkenness he
had encountered among all men, irrespective of age. He
could think of chiefs who in days gone by had been virile,
upstanding young men, but having succumbed eventually
to the destructive influence of sorghum beer, had grown
addled and weak-limbed and were plagued constantly by
hallucinations. Lepoqo would do well to exclude this worth-
less habit from his way of life, for then with the support of
the spirit world he could rise to become the most influential
chieftain of the Caledon Valley.

Peete and Lepoqo spent several days at Ngolilwe, but
details of their subsequent discussions with Mohlomi are
obscure. It is known, however, that on the morning of their
departure, while sitting with the old seer in the *kgotla* for

the last time, Lepoqo was heard to ask what potions he
should take in order to gain wisdom and power. Acquisi-
tions such as these, Mohlomi told him, were dependent not
on potions but on clarity of mind, goodness of heart and
service to one's fellow-man. The seer advised Lepoqo
always to keep close to old Peete, to cherish his friendship,
and to protect him from harm, for this old man was endowed with latent psychic gifts, and could serve to keep
those whom he loved in touch with the most illustrious
spirits of the clanlet. Old Peete had many years still to live,
but when the time came for his departure from earth to a
higher plane, Lepoqo must take charge of the corpse, for he
alone was capable of performing the burial rites necessary
for assuring the disembodied spirit safe conduct to the
domain of the ancestors. Mohlomi confessed that, like
Peete, he had a strong affection for Lepoqo, and beckoning
the young man to his side he gave him an ox, a spear, a
shield and finally one of his pendant earrings which he said
possessed talismanic powers. The seer then bade his guests
farewell and returned to his hut.

In contrast to the excitement he had enjoyed in recent
months Lepoqo was to find the next two years uneventful
and dull. Apart from the occasional hunts in which he
played a leading part, few activities captured his interest,
and he became restless and plagued by an insatiable urge for
adventure. He scorned the sedentary habits of his fellow-
clansmen and even avoided the sittings of the *kgotla*. By
1808 he had become so weary of the humdrum routine of
kraal life that he decided to undertake another journey into
the Caledon Valley. In fact, he eventually reached Botswana and came into contact with such great tribes as the
Bangwaketsi, the Bakwena and the Bamangwato. On his
return to Menkwaneng he became involved in an incident
that was to set the stage for his rise to power over his
father's clanlet.

Not many miles from Bamokoteli territory lived the
Bafokeng or Mist People under the rule of Chief Makara,
an astute cattle-raider, herbalist and rain-maker of considerable repute. Middle-aged and genial, Makara was re-

garded with respect not only by his own subjects, but also by strangers who had sought his advice on supernormal matters, or had received healing for their ailments. But Makara was also an avaricious and unscrupulous stock thief, and was feared and despised by some of his neighbours, including Moshesh's people, the Bamokoteli.

In 1808 Makara turned his covetous eyes on the herds of some of the more prosperous clans of the Valley. He had been planning to attack the Bamonaheng when suddenly his people were attacked at night by an unidentified force of warriors and they were put to flight. Most of the Bafokeng scrambled into the hills surrounding Butha-Buthe, but Makara himself, accompanied by a party of councillors, warriors and herdsmen driving a herd of cattle, reached Menkwaneng where they begged Mokhachane, Lepoqo's father, for protection.

Fearing that by harbouring the fugitive chief he might antagonize the other chiefs of the Valley, Mokhachane refused, and he had Makara and his followers bound and held in the cattlefold under guard. When news of Makara's capture reached Bamokoteli kraals, the men of the clanlet came flocking to the *kgotla* at Menkwaneng. Extolling Mokhachane they demanded the execution of the captive chief, and the distribution of his herd among the kraal patriarchs. It was then that Lepoqo strode into the centre of the *kgotla* brandishing a stick, and calling for silence addressed the throng.

The Bamokoteli, he said, were not to be hasty in deciding the fate of Makara, for he was a chief of no ordinary stature. He was a herbalist, rain-maker and warrior whose skills could be exploited to the ultimate benefit of the clanlet. Makara should be set free and his cattle restored to him on condition he settled among the Bamokoteli as a vassal of Chief Mokhachane. He should be helped to retrieve his scattered clan and bring it safely into the Tlotsi district. Makara was not to be harmed.

Lepoqo's proposal was accepted with a roar of approval, and Makara and his men were fetched from the cattlefold and given beer and food. Turning to Lepoqo the chief praised and thanked him, and later, drawing him aside beyond earshot of the people of Menkwaneng he said: 'My

child ... your power will grow, and you will become a
great chief.'

As history was to reveal, Lepoqo did become a great
chief, the most influential in central South Africa, and even
in his old age whenever he harked back on his turbulent rise
to power he derived untold pleasure in quoting the pro-
phetic words spoken by Chief Makara at that momentous
meeting of the *kgotla*.

In the weeks following Makara's release he and Lepoqo
used to meet frequently after dark beside the open hearth in
the *kgotla* at Menkwaneng. Joined later by Makwanyane,
Lepoqo's closest friend, they would reminisce, gossip, bandy
yarns and bemoan the lowly status of the Bamokoteli when
compared with most of the other clans of the Valley. They
pledged one day to destroy the Basekake to whom the
clanlet was forced to pay tribute in cattle, grain and hides.
Once Makara's people had been brought into the Tlotsi district no clan in the Valley, not even the Basekake, would
match the Bamokoteli in battle.

Early one morning while strolling along the banks of the
Tlotsi, the three men came suddenly upon five Basekake
warriors whom they drove into a bed of reeds and then
cudgelled to death. They dumped the corpses into a pit,
covered them with stones and sand, and slunk away
through the reeds, resolving never to breathe a word about
the incident to anyone else.

The murder of the warriors, Lepoqo was to confess in
later years, tormented him, and for many months he lay
awake at nights praying to the spirits of the clanlet for
forgiveness. But no sooner had he been granted peace of
mind than he was involved in yet another unhappy incident
—this time a gruesome ceremony—and for many more
months he was to be subjeced to mental anguish. Apparently some of the Mist People had decided to desert their
chief, Makara, and had run off with some of his cattle.
Makwanyane, heading a Bamokoteli force, was sent in
pursuit of the renegades and locating them at sunset in a
thicket, pounced on them, killing four, including Khama
their leader, and wounding several others, before they could
escape into the surrounding darkness. Before returning to

Menkwaneng, Makwanyane had Khama's head and arms removed from the corpse and wrapped in cowhide, and as soon as the stolen cattle had been collected he returned with his party of warriors to Menkwaneng, taking the gruesome parcel with him.

Among the first to welcome Makwanyane home was Lepoqo. They rejoiced together, went down to the Tlotsi stream together where the victorious warriors were being ritually cleansed by Mobe the witchdoctor, and they returned together to Menkwaneng. It was then that Lepoqo saw a noisy gathering of children and youths at the cattle-fold, and to his horror he discovered they were viewing the head and arms of the ill-fated Khama which had been pinned to the cattlefold gates. Swinging round at the lowing and snorting of beasts, he saw a great herd being driven towards the kraal. At a command from Mokhachane the cattle were driven towards the cattlefold, and for more than an hour they moved round and round in a huge circle beneath the hideous trophies attached to the gates. The men present, chanting loudly, called on the cattle to take notice of the cold, lifeless eyes and lifeless hands of Khama the thief, and fervently urged them to flee in future from all clansmen except their masters the Bamokoteli.

Lepoqo watched the ceremony in awe, and he quaked at the thought of the vengeance Khama's spirit might wreak upon the clanlet. He therefore went in search of Mobe the witchdoctor and finding him among the rejoicing crowd, ordered him to prepare in haste whatever ritual he considered necessary to protect the Bamokoteli from evil supernatural influences. Mobe sent Lepoqo immediately to select a black bull from the swirling stream of cattle, and sent a spectator to fetch Chief Mokhachane. By this time the parade of cattle had ceased, and as the beasts were being returned to the fields, word was passed around that all the menfolk were to assemble in the cattlefold.

Having arrived with a black bull in the centre of the throng, Lepoqo stood back as Mobe the witchdoctor thrust an assegai deep into the beast's heart and sent it bellowing and convulsing to the dung-bedecked floor of the cattlefold. Ntseke, Makwanyane's father, aided by menials, then fell to skinning and dismembering the bull, while Mobe sliced off

the tip of its tongue, dug out its eyes and cut pieces of
tendon from its legs. All these items together with herbs
taken from a medicine horn, he dropped into a small
earthen pot which he placed in the flames of a newly lit
fire.

Meanwhile Ntseke and his helpers had filled a large
earthen pot with strips of meat sliced from the carcass and
this they also placed on the fire. Watching in silence the
spectators saw Mobe remove a portion of the bull's pleura,
dip it into the first pot and drop it into the second with
extended fingers. They sang a mournful song as Mobe,
beckoning Makwanyane and his band of fighting men,
daubed their bodies with a mixture of spring water and half
the bile squeezed from the bull's gall-bladder. After completing this part of the proceedings Mobe rubbed the remaining bile into incisions he had cut into the men's ankle,
knee, elbow and wrist joints. Removing the smaller of the
pots from the flames, he ground its charred contents into a
powder which he mixed with fat and pressed into an empty
cow-horn. This medicine, Mobe declared, would render the
Bamokoteli immune from supernatural interference. Cheering these words the spectators, headed by Mobe, streamed
into the *kgotla* to take part in a beer-drink and later to sing
and dance.

During the following week when all the excitement had
died down at Menkwaneng, Lepoqo and Makwanyane
met in the cattlefold to discuss ways and means of freeing
the clanlet from the yoke of Basekake oppression. Makwanyane suggested stirring the people into revolt, but
Lepoqo refused to encourage bloodshed, for in his mind he
could hear the admonishing voice of old Mohlomi, the seer,
whose advice he had once earnestly welcomed but had
failed to follow. Lepoqo wanted to live in peace both with
his kinsmen and his enemies.

In the following months the two drifted apart and on the
few occasions when they met they invariably quarrelled.
For example, Makwanyane captured a cattle-thief in 1809,
and persuaded the men of the *kgotla* to have him put to
death. When Lepoqo heard of this he was upset, and beseeched his father to pardon the prisoner and set him free.

He was ridiculed by the warriors, berated by Makwanyane and accused of disloyalty by some of the elders. However, eventually he won the support of the *kgotla*, but to his great disappointment Makwanyane stormed out of the *kgotla* in a huff, followed by a group of guffawing companions. He had lost Makwanyane's friendship.

Shunned by his old friend, Lepoqo found life at Menkwaneng uninspiring and frustrating, and often he wished the could become as great a warrior as Makwanyane. One evening after a secret meeting with Mobe the witchdoctor, he decided to leave his father's kraal for a while and prove his worth as a warrior in some distant territory. When the inmates of Menkwaneng were asleep he hastened to a hut occupied by menials and invited them to accompany him on a cattle-raid into Mapolane territory, a few days' journey to the west.

The chief of the Mapolane, Moeletsi by name, was said to own as many herds as the Bamokoteli and Basekake clans together, and many of his cattleposts were manned only by herdboys and were situated several hours' march from the capital kraal. One such cattlepost was concealed in a valley beside the Kilibileng river, and according to Lepoqo he could rob it without undue risk provided he had a strong enough force to support him. All the menials in the hut and many more besides agreed to join him, so at daybreak he led them over the Tlotsi stream and headed for the Malutis.

During the following week Lepoqo and his men travelled only at nights, taking a circuitous route to the Mekhalaleng river, which they followed westwards as far as its confluence with the Khilibileng. They reached the outskirts of the Mapolane cattlepost one moonlit night and slipping through the gates fell on the unsuspecting herdsmen whom they gagged and bound with strips of goatskin. The raiders made off with about five hundred cattle, taking the herdboys with them to prevent their alerting the Mapolane kraals in the district.

At daybreak they reached the Mekhalaleng river and veering eastwards drove the herd through the stretch of hilly country they had traversed the day before. Although they had agreed to hide the cattle by day and travel after dark, Lepoqo pressed on until dusk before calling the first

halt. It was almost midnight when they moved on, just as
the moon was rising, and next morning at dawn they drove
the cattle into a densely wooded chasm and flung themselves on to the ground to sleep. Henceforth they travelled
only under cover of darkness.

One morning a little after sunrise the Bamokoteli, catching sight of the raiders approaching in the distance with the
cattle, ran out to meet them and escort them into Menkwaneng. Two weeks before when told of Lepoqo's sudden
departure his father had cursed him and vowed to punish
him on his return. The raiding party, he had told the men
of the *kgotla*, was bound to be decimated, and in any case
Chief Moeletsi having once been provoked by the intruders
would earmark the Bamokoteli clanlet for reprisal. But now
Mokhachane like the rest of his people hurried across the
veld to welcome Lepoqo home.

'Lepoqo has swept off Moeletsi's cattle,' he could hear his
subjects chanting, 'Lepoqo has shaved Moeletsi's beard.'

After welcoming his son back to Menkwaneng, the petty-
chief announced that a feast would be held in his honour. It
was then, according to tribal chroniclers, that one of the
inmates of the kraal, a club-footed menial renowned for his
buffoonery, hobbled into the centre of the *kgotla*. To the
delight of the throng he demonstrated with characteristic
gestures how Lepoqo had shaved the illustrious Mapolane
chief. 'Shwe! Shwe!', he hissed, imitating the scraping
sound of the razor. Lepoqo stepped forward and with
hands held high he silenced the crowd.

'Ke Moshweshwe!' he cried, 'I am Moshweshwe,' and
the people applauded, realizing that the time had come for
Lepoqo to forsake his childhood name for one commemor-
ating his first real heroic deed.

'Wena Moshweshwe'—'you are Moshweshwe!' they
chanted, and from that moment the heir-apparent was
known by no other name. It was only in years to come
when he had risen to fame that he became better known not
only throughout Southern Africa, but also in countries
beyond the seas, by a simpler version—Moshesh.

CHAPTER THREE

PROPHECY OF DOOM

*Moshesh marries and builds his own kraal—Birth of
Mohato—Moshesh revisits Mohlomi, the seer—
Mohlomi's deathbed prophecy—Moshesh leads the
clanlet into revolt against the Basekake overlords—He
and his father quarrel—He establishes a new settlement
at Butha-Buthe*

DURING the Winter of 1810, after the crops had been harvested, Moshesh decided to marry and build a kraal of his
own. Five years before, his father had suggested he should
seek the hand of Mamabela, daughter of Chief Seephephe
whose clan, an offshoot of the Bafokeng or Mist People,
inhabited the narrow strip of country flanked by the Futane
and Caledon rivers. Moshesh had refused, saying he would
not be bound by family ties, but now at the age of twenty-
three a change had come over him; he craved the company
of a wife, and he asked his father to help him choose one.

Mokhachane's thoughts returned to Mamabela. She was
the only daughter of Chief Seephephe's senior wife and was
a little younger than Moshesh. She was said to be a good
woman; in fact, both old Peete and other elders of the clanlet considered her the ideal person for bearing Moshesh's
heir.

When it was agreed that Mokhachane should enter into
negotiation with Chief Seephephe, the petty-chief set out
for Bafokeng territory and returned in due course with
news that the betrothal had been arranged. Mokhachane
undertook to provide the required *bohali* or dowry cattle
and authorized Moshesh to have them delivered to the
Bafokeng chief.

Moshesh was not to meet his future bride until after the
delivery of the cattle. He gave Mamabela a necklace, earrings, an assortment of trinkets and a magnificent jackalskin *kaross*. Their first meeting and, indeed, those to follow
were always brief and always attended by a chaperone. But

Moshesh had few opportunities for visiting Mamabela, as
he spent most of his time building a kraal not far from
Menkwaneng.

On an appointed day Mamabela, adorned in her finery
and accompanied by her parents, a retinue of childhood
friends and a procession of wellwishers, set out for Bamokoteli territory, and arriving at Menkwaneng at sunset was
escorted to some huts provided by Mokhachane. On the
following morning Mamabela and her followers formed up
in the courtyard where they were met by a large party of
Bamokoteli headed by Moshesh.

Suddenly they all broke into a song and started dancing,
the one party striving to outshine the other. At noon
wooden platters of cooked beef and pots of beer were
brought into the courtyard and the merrymakers feasted.
The celebrations lasted until late afternoon when the bride's
father, calling for silence, ritually offered tokens of food in
honour of the ancestral spirits. Then, wishing the bride and
groom a long life of prosperity, he appealed to Moshesh to
treat his daughter kindly, unless, of course, she became in-
subordinate, insolent or frigid and deserved to be chastised.
Should he find her objectionable or unfaithful, or should she
be barren, Moshesh was to send her home and retrieve his
dowry cattle. However, the chief was confident Mamabela
would serve her husband well, and he asked to be kept
informed of her behaviour as well as her health.

After Seephephe had spoken, the bride and groom were
daubed with the gall of an ox, and entrails smeared with
medicines were hung round Mamabela's neck. The couple
accompanied by their closest friends then entered a hut
where they spent the night feasting, but at sunrise Mamabela took leave of Menkwaneng and returned to her father's
kraal.

Moshesh did not see Mamabela during the following
month. He built her a hut in his new kraal while she, on the
other hand, assisted by handmaidens, made garments and
collected household utensils. Mamabela's return to Menkwaneng was followed by further ceremony, and she spent
the first few nights not with her husband but with Khudu,
her mother-in-law. At last, placing a pot of beer in her

hut—a sign that she was ready for marital relations—she finally joined Moshesh.

The Spring rains fell early in 1810, Moshesh was to recall in later life, and the crops of sorghum grew lush. He possessed a fine herd of milch cows and oxen, and his goats, although decimated by some mysterious disease, were nevertheless admired by his friends. Moshesh in 1810 was a contented young man. Mamabela, his wife, was industrious, mindful of his comforts, and always eager to please him. He had rewon Makwanyane's friendship, and the two of them spent many leisurely hours together recalling experiences they had shared in the past and discussing affairs of the clanlet.

The domination of the Bamokoteli by the Basekake occupied much of the two men's thoughts, for since Moshesh's successful raid on the Mapolane clan the Basekake had demanded additional tribute and had threatened to raze Menkwaneng to the ground and butcher its people should the petty-chief fail to comply. These threats weighed heavily on the minds of Moshesh and Makwanyane especially as they realized that the petty-chief Mokhachane, had become resigned to a life of subservience. Unless they themselves stirred the Bamokoteli into revolt, the clanlet would be doomed permanently to bondage. They decided, however, that the time for revolt had not yet arrived. If they were to succeed in crushing the parasitic Basekake they would have to be patient for a short while longer.

A son was born to Moshesh and his wife in the Winter of 1811. They named him Mohato, and according to custom Mamabela was renamed Mamohato—Mother of Mohato. At the time of this happy event old Mohlomi the seer happened to arrive in the Butha-Buthe district twenty miles north-east of Menkwaneng. He had just returned from another of his journeys to the clans of the Caledon Valley and, homeward bound, had called on a friend named Matekane. Reflecting upon his first meeting with the illustrious greybeard Moshesh decided to visit him, so collecting a sleeping-mat, a *kaross* and weapons he took leave of his wife and baby and set out for Butha-Buthe.

It is regrettable that so little is known of this, Moshesh's second meeting with Mohlomi, for in years to come, during the course of his long and eventful career, he often harked back on that most momentous occasion declaring that of all men he had ever known there was none whose memory he cherished more ardently than that of the aged seer.

On his arrival at Butha-Buthe Moshesh was ushered into Matekane's kraal and in the cattlefold he found Mohlomi surrounded by hundreds of clansmen most of whom, like himself, were strangers from outlying districts. He could see a marked change in the seer's appearance: the iron-grey hair had turned milky-white; the eyes, formerly large and mobile, were now puffy and impassive. Mohlomi's voice, however, had retained much of its youthful timbre and continued to command the undivided attention of his listeners.

After a short while Mohlomi left the cattlefold, entered Matekane's hut and lay down on a sleeping-mat to rest. He sent for Moshesh whom he berated for the cattle raids he had conducted into the domain of the influential Mapolane chief Moeletsi. Nevertheless he did say he was pleased the operation had been concluded without bloodshed or harm to the chief and his family. Mohlomi looked weary, thought Moshesh, yet he continued to dominate the conversation for fully an hour, recounting mainly his recent journey through the Valley. Reaching for a skin-bag the seer proudly extracted a multicoloured pocket-handkerchief given him by a clansman who in turn had procured it from an itinerant Portuguese trader. Presenting it to Moshesh he said there were white-skinned people living in the south of the Maluti mountains, and he advised him to solicit their friendship and to start trading with them.

The conversation turned to Moshesh's future. Mohlomi confessed that he envied the heir-apparent for his youth and virility. The sun was setting on his own life, and soon his soul would be whisked away from its earthly environment in order to commence a new life in death. He predicted that a long tortuous road lay ahead for Moshesh, but the day was fast approaching when he would rule over Bamokoteli in place of his father, Mokhachane. Moshesh was to pray to his spirits to endow him both with wisdom and a keen sense of justice; for then one day he would be

revered by his subjects, and he would rise to become the
most powerful and prosperous chief in the Valley. The
happiest rulers, the seer continued, were those who knew
the idiosyncrasies of their subjects, understood their whims,
recognized their attributes, overlooked their shortcomings
and gave encouragement to their aspirations. And if a ruler
was to enjoy immunity from revolt and assassination he
would have to see constantly to the needs and comforts of
his subjects as a whole and to the aged, to cripples, widows
and orphans in particular. Ultimately Moshesh would succeed or fail as a chief according to the way in which he
conducted the affairs of the *kgotla*.

Moshesh did not stay long with Mohlomi, for the old
man was frail and needed rest. He would visit the seer again
in his kraal Ngolilwe and feast on his wisdom. He saw in
Mohlomi a father of all men and the spirits' most gifted
spokesman.

Three years were to pass before the next meeting between
Mohlomi and Moshesh, and during this time the old man
slid gradually into his dotage and was confined mainly to
his hut. Legs and arms twisted with arthritic pain, his
groins lame from the onslaught of diseased kidneys, he
endured the dragging daylight hours and haunting nights
with stoic fortitude. Moshesh on the other hand had been
blessed with good fortune. His herds and flocks had multiplied; his granaries were full to overflowing, and his popularity had increased beyond his wildest dreams. Furthermore, in 1813 Mamohato, his wife, had borne him a second
son whom he named Molapo, and his heir Mohato, now a
bright, healthy toddler, was a constant source of pride and
amusement to him.

In 1815 news reached Moshesh that Mohlomi was critically ill and on the brink of death, so he set out immediately
for Bamonaheng territory. Apparently two weeks before, to
the consternation of his relatives and councillors, the old
seer had arranged to be taken to some friends living south
of the Caledon river. On the morning of his departure, after
travelling only a few miles, he had collapsed and had been
brought back to Ngolilwe, astride a pack-ox, in a state of

semi-delirium. On arrival at Mohlomi's kraal Moshesh was
told that the seer was asleep, but the moment he reached the
old man's side and beheld his face, he knew he was looking
upon a mask of death. He found a dozen or more dignitaries bunched around the stricken seer, some sobbing and
others wailing. Soon a witchdoctor arrived and sprinkled
the patient and the mourners with protective medicines.

For several hours Mohlomi slept, his chest heaving visibly and his eyes half-shut staring glassily into the thatch
above. In the evening he awoke, raised his weary, wasted
body onto an elbow and with quivering lips announced that
he was about to enter the realm of the spirits, and wanted
everyone present to bear witness to his parting words.
Moshesh and the other mourners pressed closer about him,
and then Mohlomi caught sight of one of his wives who
had just entered the hut, weeping loudly.

'Maliepollo, my wife,' he croaked, 'the spirits have
spoken to me, and I am about to die.'

The woman wailed mournfully, but silenced by her dying
husband, Maliepollo paused and dried her tears. Death,
continued the seer, was not to be mourned but rather to be
celebrated, for it signified the release of a tormented soul
from its eroded, pain-ridden encasement. He, Mohlomi,
welcomed death, for the relief it promised; but there was
another reason: In recent days he had been visited by the
spirit of his father who had predicted disaster for all
peoples inhabiting the interior of South Africa. Clouds of
red dust would rise in the east heralding the approach of
mighty, warfaring tribes; defenceless Sotho clans would be
scattered, butchered and reduced to poverty; famine would
sweep across the valleys and hills, and kraals would be overrun with beasts of prey. Sotho patriarchs stripped of all
possessions and driven by hunger would slaughter and
devour their own children; friends would rise up against
friends, brothers against brothers and sons against fathers.

'My friends,' Mohlomi continued, 'I had wanted to move
my subjects out of the way of this war ... and take up
my abode on the plateau of Qeme, but sickness has prevented me.'

He urged everyone present always to be vigilant and to flee at the first sign of the red dust cloud over the eastern horizon.

'I greet you all,' he whispered, 'for I must depart to where my fathers rest.' And so he died.

A tremulous wail rose from the hut, and with a heavy heart Moshesh, elbowing his way through the weeping dignitaries, slipped through the narrow hut-entrance and set out for home.

News of Mohlomi's passing spread swiftly across the Caledon Valley, and although in some parts his deathbed prophecy caused concern, by far the majority of tribesmen dismissed it as no more significant than a dying man's hallucinations. Moshesh had been troubled at first fearing the clans were doomed to destruction, but when a year had passed and there was no sign of the 'red dust clouds', he also rejected the seer's prophecy as the product of an addled mind.

But in 1816, unbeknown to the peoples of central South Africa, the clouds of dust had already risen in the east beyond the Drakensberg. Shaka the tyrant had usurped the Zulu throne, and was destined soon to become the most fearsome conqueror in all Southern Africa. Indeed, as a result of his bloody rule not only would the east coast peoples be plunged into a maëlstrom of carnage, but also those living to the west of the Drakensberg.

At about this time a severe drought struck central South Africa destroying crops and herds throughout the Valley. Among the clans who suffered most were the Bamokoteli who, it will be recalled, paid tribute in grain and cattle to their overlords the Basekake. Reduced to poverty by the drought, the Bamokoteli could not meet their commitments and were therefore threatened with annihilation. Mokhachane conferred with his councillors, but they could not find a way out of the dilemma. Moshesh and his friend Makwanyane, proposed that the Bamokoteli should rise in revolt, but they were overruled by the older men and advised to help find the tribute due to their masters rather than stir up strife and bring about the clanlet's destruction. At all costs the Basekake were to be appeased, not provoked.

During the following days Moshesh and Makwanyane visited kraals along the Tlotsi stream and exhorted the younger men of the clanlet to sharpen their assegais and war-axes and stand by for battle. On a given day the cream of Bamokoteli manhood converged on Moshesh's kraals, but when night fell, just as they were about to set out for Basekake territory, a messenger arrived with orders for Moshesh to muster a force and accompany his overlords on a cattle raid against the Mist People. Next morning, having spent the night among the Bamokoteli, the messenger was summoned to Moshesh's hut where he found the heir-apparent writhing in agony on the floor, his body wrapped in a heavy *kaross*. Makwanyane who was present sat bewildered beside his stricken friend. Moshesh, he told the messenger, had taken ill during the night, and according to Mobe the witchdoctor he had been poisoned by an unknown enemy. He was therefore far too ill to join the Basekake raid, and his fighting force, renowned for the part it had played in shaving the mighty Moeletsi's beard, refused to be controlled by anyone else. Should Moshesh recover within the next day or two he would hasten to the assistance of the Basekake.

The messenger left for home and he was barely out of sight when Moshesh who had been neither ill nor in agony, flung aside his *kaross* and sent Makwanyane to summon the councillors and warriors for urgent discussion. When they had all assembled in the *kgotla* he suggested that the Bamokoteli should undertake the cattle raid into the territory of the Mist People independent of the Basekake. Why should the booty cattle fall into the hands of the oppressors, he asked, and in any case the time had come for the Bamokoteli to rise in revolt against the accursed Basekake.

Moshesh's proposal was received with loud applause and not an hour later the Bamokoteli led by himself and Makwanyane were heading for Bafokeng territory. They attacked the unsuspecting Mist People one morning at dawn, driving them from their kraals and capturing some six hundred head of cattle. Returning home soon afterwards Moshesh and his raiders were intercepted by a party of Basekake, and after a brisk struggle they abandoned the booty cattle and fled into a coppice close by. A little later they emerged from their hiding place and caught sight of the Basekake on the distant horizon. Their overlords were hurrying home to report their clash with Moshesh's force to their chief.

At sunrise on the following morning the Bamokoteli, headed by their two dauntless young leaders, set off in the tracks of the victors and after a full day's march reached a circle of granite-topped kopjes in the centre of which they beheld a large Basekake settlement and beyond it the booty cattle. Taking shelter towards evening in a growth of reeds flanking a stream nearby they waited, and when night fell Moshesh, Makwanyane and a small following crept into the slopes of the nearest kopje and looked down into the settlement below them. The Basekake were feasting and dancing within a ring of fires, and by the tone of their voices Moshesh concluded that many of them were already befuddled with sorghum beer. As midnight approached and the merrymakers retired one by one to their huts, Moshesh and his party hurried back to the stream, and summoning the rest of the force returned to the outskirts of the kraal.

The Bamokoteli waited until the fires were deserted, then slipping into the settlement snatched up burning wood and set the huts alight. The settlement roared into flame and the Basekake came tumbling through the tiny hut doors screaming, cursing and hurling threats at their unseen assailants. Some perished in the flames, some died beneath the onslaught of assegais and battle-axes, and others came staggering into the open, their bodies singed and blistered. Meanwhile the panic-stricken booty cattle came charging past the blazing settlement. In the morning when the fighting was over they were rounded up by herdsmen and driven to Menkwaneng.

Moshesh and his raiders spent almost a week in Basekake territory firing outlying kraals by night and hiding by day, and having captured some twenty thousand cattle they returned triumphantly to Menkwaneng. Indeed, the gallant Bamokoteli had plucked the Basekake roosters' tail feathers, and as time revealed they had freed the clanlet forever from bondage. For, from then on, the Basekake ceased to demand tribute from petty-chief Mokhachane, and in due course they would seek an alliance with his son, Moshesh.

The victorious raiding party, Moshesh told the missionary Casalis, twenty years later, was given a tumultuous welcome on its return to Menkwaneng. As it entered the *kgotla* a praise-singer dressed in skins, feathers and a large assortment of clay-bead ornaments called for silence and pacing to and fro before the warriors, recounted first the exploits of ancestral heroes and then Moshesh's exploits in Basekake territory. Poetic words of praise poured from his talented lips and each time he mentioned Moshesh's name, the crowd would roar 'Pula! Pula!—Rain! Rain!'

It had been a joyous occasion, Moshesh recollected, but it had also marked the beginning of a strained relationship between himself and his father. Mokhachane had refused to take part in the proceedings claiming that as Moshesh had embarked on the cattle-raid without the *kgotla*'s permission, he had incurred not only his father's wrath but also the wrath of the spirits. Mokhachane had grown suspicious of Moshesh, fearing that if he gained too much power he might aspire to usurping the leadership of the clanlet. Never had his subjects acclaimed him as they had acclaimed his son.

When the excitement died down at Menkwaneng, Moshesh pondered the changes that had come over his father. Mokhachane, he told himself, had never really been a friendly person, but he had become increasingly sullen and cantankerous in recent times as a result of incessant beer-drinking and *dagga*-smoking. Mokhachane was invariably befuddled and often indisposed, so he could hardly be expected to be happy.

As the months passed the relationship between Moshesh and his father deteriorated further, and in 1818, as a direct result of this squabble, the clanlet split into two factions—a small, conservative yet influential core of elders supporting the petty-chief and a larger section comprising mainly the younger set favouring Moshesh. Rumours spread that the heir-apparent was conspiring to drive his father from Bamokoteli territory, and despite a fervent assurance by Moshesh to the contrary, the situation worsened. For without his knowing it, the less responsible element among his supporters had started questioning Mokhachane's ability to rule, and were suggesting he should stand down in favour of his more enterprising son. Tension mounted.

In 1819, his patience exhausted, Moshesh decided to leave his father and move into the Butha-Buthe district where he had been given land by his father-in-law, Chief Seephephe. During the Winter he selected a kraal site at the northern foot of Butha-Buthe hill, some five miles from the Caledon river and he sent parties of women to cut thatching grass and reeds and men to chop pliable poles. By August the hut sites had been marked out and building started. Poles planted in circles were bent inwards and fastened to form low, dome-shaped frames, and flexible sticks entwined with the poles were bound at the joints by nimble fingers. Then came the thatching, and by October not only had most of the huts been completed, but a start had been made to the cattlefolds, and patches of veld had been cleared and tilled for planting. The big move eventually took place in January 1820.

Nothing could dampen Moshesh's confidence now, and on occasions when he recalled Mohlomi the seer's prophecy he brushed it aside, refusing to believe that the Caledon Valley could ever be consumed by the flames of war, or its inhabitants reduced to starvation and hounded by cannibals. Life had become a wonderful experience, and he would allow nothing to alter it.

CHAPTER FOUR

THE WILD CAT PEOPLE

*Qhobosheane, Moshesh's new kraal—Zulu upsurge—
The 'red dust clouds' gather—*Difaqane *tragedy—Dis-
aster stalks the Wild Cat People—Assault on Butha-
Buthe hill—Zulu–Batlokwa collison*

MOSHESH named his kraal Qhobosheane. Situated on a
slight rise and encircled by a dense hedge of thorn branches,
it consisted of no more than three or four huts, and a large
pallisaded cattlefold. Before bringing his wife and sons to
Butha-Buthe Moshesh had immunized the kraal against evil
influences. He planted medicines and charms at the entrances of the huts, beside the granaries and in the cattlefold. He envisaged Qhobosheane as the most peaceful spot
in the entire Valley.

Although it had been his intention to devote the first few
months to establishing his people at Butha-Buthe, Moshesh
was obliged to make periodic trips to Menkwaneng either in
order to attend an important sitting of the *kgotla* or to
inspect the sorghum he had planted near his former kraal.
In June having harvested his crops and brought them by
pack-oxen to Qhobosheane, his visits to Menkwaneng became less frequent, and he saw his parents only when summoned by Mokhachane. He was happier at Qhobosheane
than he had ever been before, and he gave thanks regularly
to the spirits for the abundance of good fortune they had
bestowed upon him. In December he and his followers celebrated the ripening of their first crops at Butha-Buthe as
well as the birth of his third son, Masupha.

One morning in 1821 Makwanyane arrived at Qhobosheane with two strangers he had captured near the Caledon river. They were tall, heavy-limbed warriors from beyond the Drakensberg, and they bore huge oval oxhide
shelds and long-bladed stabbing spears. Questioned by
Moshesh, the strangers said they had deserted from the

Zulu army after learning that the mighty Shaka, King of the Zulu, had ordered their execution for cowardice. Life under Shaka's rule was perilous, for since his usurpation of the Zulu throne five years before he had built an invincible army and had pursued a ruthless career of slaughter. The defenceless east coast clans had crumbled beneath the onslaught of his regiments, and their once peaceful settlements had been surrounded, looted and razed to the ground. The Zulu had captured their maidens and hustled them off to become Shaka's concubines. They slew the greybeards and drafted all able-bodied men and youths into the Zulu army. Chiefs, headmen and kraal patriarchs who dared criticize the tyrant were disembowelled or even impaled. By 1820 the Zulu had conquered all territories extending from the Tugela river in the south to the Pongolo in the north, and from the Nyati or Buffalo river in the west to the Indian Ocean in the east. Many thousands of refugees had fled into the forests and mountain slopes, and thousands more, led by their chiefs, were fleeing north-westwards, aiming to cross the Drakensberg and establish new settlements in the interior of South Africa, out of reach of the Zulu.

Asked by Moshesh if the Zulu were likely to penetrate regions as far west as the Caledon Valley, the strangers replied that regiments were already on the march in pursuit of renegade chiefs. They could soon be expected to reach the territories of the Sotho-speaking clans. Moshesh's thoughts flashed back to old Mohlomi's prophecy, so summoning his messengers he sent them to Menkwaneng and the kraals of neighbouring clans with a warning for the chiefs to keep their subjects on the alert for the Zulu. Some of his followers suggested fleeing into the Malutis, and they might have done so had Moshesh not sent scouts to look out for the invaders along the banks of the Caledon.

Weeks passed. Sentinels posted on the summit of Butha-Buthe hill watched in vain for an approaching army, and soon the Zulu captives were accused of lying. Even the stories of Shaka's tyranny was considered a figment of the imagination by most Bamokoteli. Moshesh on the other hand, remained deeply concerned, for the more he questioned the captives the more vividly could he see in his

mind's eye 'clouds of red dust' rising over the eastern horizon. If the Bamokoteli were to survive, he told his people,
precautions as suggested by Mohlomi the seer would have
to be taken.

Accordingly Moshesh sent a party of men to line the four
passes leading to the top of Butha-Buthe hill with mounds
of boulders, and a second party to carry grain and gourds
into selected caverns and fissures. Finally he decreed that
should the Zulu invade the Valley, the Bamokoteli must flee
together with their stock into the heights of the hill.

The first puffs of red dust appeared over the Harrismith
district in 1822 when the Hlubi, a fugitive Zulu-speaking
clan led by its chief Mpangazitha, arrived in the territory of
the Batlokwa or Wild Cat People, a large clan ruled by a
woman named Mantatisi. Six months before, the Hlubi,
then occupying a strip of territory flanked by the Nyati and
Tugela rivers had been attacked by Chief Matiwane who, in
turn, together with his clan, the amaNgwane, had been put
to flight by the Zulu army. Mpangazitha, fearing both Matiwane and Shaka, had fled into the slopes of the Drakensberg, eventually crossing into the western foothills beyond.
The Hlubi dared not pause in any place for long for fear of
falling into the hands of Matiwane. They streamed into
what is today the Orange Free State, reaching a vast,
shallow valley through which the Wilge river flows tardily
towards the upper Vaal.

Mpangazitha fell fiercely upon the first of the Wild Cat
kraals, firing huts, massacring the terror-stricken inmates,
stripping fields of ripening crops and looting cattlefolds.
Taken unawares the Batlokwa, headed by their queen,
Mantatisi, fled with household goods and provisions, and
driving tens of thousands of cattle and goats before them
they streamed into neighbouring Basia territory. After a
brief rest the Wild Cat People moved westwards, where they
joined battle with the Bafokeng or Mist People through
whose territory they had hoped to pass. Meanwhile Mpangazitha, Chief of the Hlubi, had attacked and dispersed the
Basia, and hot on his heels, having recently entered the
Harrismith district was his dreaded foe—Matiwane.

The movements of these three chiefs created a fashion in inter-tribal warfare that was to become unique in Sotho history—a ghastly series of massacres which produced no tangible results and reduced the peace-loving peoples ... of central South Africa ... to a state of abject misery.

Known as *difaqane*, these wars began when Mantatisi drove the Mist People from their country and then moved on to the west either to destroy other clans or to disperse them. In this way, a congestion involving hundreds of thousands of people developed. Sotho groups both large and small turned westwards each trespassing on the domains of another. Powerful armies annihilated their weaker neighbours, confiscated their possessions and moved on, knowing full well that if they loitered they too would be attacked by wave upon wave of people advancing from the east. *Difaqane* hurled the Sotho people into a maëlstrom of destruction, until eventually an estimated twenty-eight distinct clans disappeared, leaving not a trace of their former existence.[1]

Accompanied by her son, Sikonyela, a short, slender eighteen-year-old youth, Mantatisi led about forty thousand Wild Cat People over the Caledon river and advanced on Qhobosheane, Moshesh's settlement. Arriving at the kraal she found it deserted for Moshesh, determined not to become involved in the ravages of *difaqane*, had fled together with his people and herds onto the summit of Butha-Buthe hill. He watched from the heights of the sprawling hill as the Wild Cat People surged past Qhobosheane. He had heard from fugitive Bafokeng warriors, he reflected, that Mantatisi, head of the invincible Wild Cat army, was possessed by an evil spirit. Some people claimed that her warriors drank from her huge, pendulous breasts and others that she had only one eye, a large luminous object situated in the middle of her forehead. Mantatisi's warriors, he noticed, were dressed uniformly in black lion-skins, black mantles and capes and black feather headdresses. Daubed black from head to toe with a mixture of soot and fat, they were equipped with large oval shields, heavy clubs and javelins and a curious metal-bladed, sickle-shaped weapon

[1] Becker, *Path of Blood*, p. 52.

resembling a scimitar. No clan in the Valley could match
the might of the Wild Cat army, least of all Moshesh's
people.

Although Moshesh had fortified Butha-Buthe hill in anticipation of a crisis such as this, and although confident that
the stores of grain could outlast the lengthiest siege, he
realized that provided the Wild Cat People persevered long
enough, nothing could prevent their reaching the summit of
the hill. Not even the boulders his people intended rolling
upon them would stop their advance. And while he pondered the fate of his subjects, Moshesh watched the Batlokwa set fire to Khapong, Makwanyane's kraal, and then
rest for the night about a mile from Butha-Buthe hill. When
darkness fell he and his people looked down on a myriad of
fires and the silhouettes of Mantatisi's feasting warriors.
The assault on the hill, they told themselves, would be
launched on the morrow.

When day broke Bamokoteli watchers on the hill caught
sight of the Batlokwa advancing on Butha-Buthe, so the
women and children were hustled into the caverns and the
men rushed to their posts behind the boulder-mounds lining
the passes. The Wild Cat People reached the foot of the hill
within half an hour but then suddenly swerved away into
the sorghum fields and started harvesting the ripened crops.
Apparently Mantatisi had decided to collect provisions for
the long trek ahead rather than waste time and effort dislodging a handful of refugees from the hill. She dared not
risk delaying the departure of her people from Butha-Buthe
lest they be overtaken by the invaders from Zululand.

The Balokwa laboured all day in the fields, and at sunset
as they were returning to camp, heavily laden with baskets
of grain, the warriors in the rear were attacked by a party of
Bamokoteli led by Moshesh and Makwanyane. Taken unawares the stragglers bolted, abandoning the grain and yelling for help. They were greeted with roars of derisive
laughter as they came loping into camp, and they were
berated by Mantatisi and the elders of the clan. A woman,
Maliele by name, seeking to ridicule them, ran out into the
veld, joined ranks with Moshesh's force and grabbing hold
of a warrior called Thobei shouted for the cowards to come
to her aid. A section of the Batlokwa came running out of

camp, engaged the Bamokoteli in battle and killed forty of them, including chief Makara's son, before the rest could escape and flee up the northern slopes of Butha-Buthe hill. In the course of their flight Moshesh's warriors stumbled over many hundreds of Batlokwa pots, smashing them and treading the fragments into the earth. In commemoration of their lucky escape from annihilation they thus named the encounter with Mantatisi's army Ntoa-ea-Lipitsane—the Battle of the Pots.

The Wild Cat People withdrew from Butha-Buthe Hill on the following day and embarked on an orgy of devastation unparalleled in Sotho history. During the next few weeks

clan after clan perished beneath Mantatisi's advance. Thousands of people, on learning of her approach, fled into the highlands, to regions few other than the dwarf-like Bushmen had ever considered fit for habitation. Waves of refugees rolled forward like animals before a band of hunters. Sotho groups that for many generations lived side by side in comparative harmony became bitter enemies. A general scramble for cattle took place. Battles broke out. Bands of brigands zigzagged across the Caledon Valley in search of unharvested fields to strip and granaries to raid. And ever on the eastern horizon, stalking the refugees, was Mantatisi's Wild Cat hordes, and the two Zulu conquerors from across the Drakensberg.

The course Mantatisi followed ran parallel with the Caledon river. Unknown to her, Mpangazitha's Hlubi were proceeding in the same direction, but to the immediate north, and it was only when she reached Peka, not many miles from where Maseru, the capital of the Lesotho is situation today, that she came upon this, her most dreaded enemy. A struggle for the supremacy of the Caledon Valley followed between Mantatisi and Mpangazitha. The Wild Cat People fared badly. In fact, had it not been for Mantatisi's ingenuity their marauding adventure might have ceased then and there.

Undaunted by their setback at the hands of the Hlubi, the Wild Cat People struck out northwards through the Orange Free State, attacking and subjugating clans, rounding up cattle, pillaging and leaving only desolation

in their wake. They seemed to have adhered to no planned route, for soon they were retracing their steps and
were entering the plains between the Caledon and Orange
rivers. They decimated all the clans they came upon ...
[but] on finding the Orange in flood the Wild Cat People
turned back to the Caledon, crossed it and returned to the
Orange Free State where some months earlier they had
butchered the Sotho inhabitants. They then moved off to
the north-west towards the Lesotho.

Meanwhile Moshesh had decided to abandon Qhobosheane and remain on Butha-Buthe hill with his followers.
He was afraid that the Batlokwa might suddenly return or
that some other clan caught up recently in the turmoil of
difaqane might arrive and rob the Bamokoteli of their cattle
and grain. As soon as the Batlokwa were out of sight and
were reported heading swiftly westwards, he sped away to
Menkwaneng, collected his parents, his grandfather and
other relatives, and returned with them to Butha-Buthe. He
then sent warriors to fetch the remainder of Mokhachane's
subjects, and when once the clanlet was reunited on the hill,
he became its new leader in the place of his father. From
then on Moshesh's influence grew rapidly.

While the newcomers built makeshift huts on the hill for
their families, the rest of the clanlet added boulders to the
mounds already lining the passes. The Bamokoteli remained on the summit throughout 1823. On rare occasions
they would venture into country below, either to search for
stray cattle or to hunt, but they never left the passes un-
manned and sentinels scanned the horizons from morning
till night.

One evening towards the end of the year a party of
difaqane fugitives arrived on the hill-top with news that
Mantatisi's Wild Cat People were approaching. The Bamokoteli took up their arms, hurried to their positions along
the passes and waited. Fully a week passed before the Wild
Cat People reached Butha-Buthe for they were weary, footsore and hungry, and no more than a shadow of the
formidable force they once had been.

In recent months fate had frowned upon the Wild Cat

People, and from the time they had crossed the Caledon river bound for Botswana in the west, misfortune had strode beside them. Caught up in the chaos of *difaqane* they found central South Africa swarming with starving refugees and innumerable parties of bandits. Wherever they went they found settlements abandoned, fields untilled and un-planted, and

> apart from roots, bulbs and berries, there was little food to be found in the veld, certainly not enough to feed so large a horde as that of Mantatisi.... Many of the Wild Cat People started dropping out along the route. Women and children, and especially the aged and ailing became stragglers who invariably died of exhaustion, exposure or hunger or were devoured by beasts of prey that always followed at a distance.

In central Botswana Mantatisi's army was lured into ambuscades, and hundreds of warriors perished beneath the onslaught of barbed javelins hurled by the Bangwaketsi of Chief Makaba. Veering southwards into the territory of the Batlhaping or Fish People, the Batlokwa were attacked and driven eastwards by a force mustered by Robert Moffat, a young missionary stationed at Kuruman. Thereafter, for about four months the Batlokwa hung about Mafeking 'lick-ing their wounds, foraging in the neighbourhood and con-ducting half-hearted raids into the villages of the Barolong tribe'. Then moving on into the Orange Free State plains, they were intercepted by the fearsome Matiwane and driven into the Caledon Valley. For more than a week they struggled eastwards until eventually they reached Butha-Buthe hill where they encamped on the very site they had chosen eighteen months before.

After resting a few days Sikonyela, who meanwhile had assumed command of the army in place of his mother, decided to attack Moshesh's stronghold and clear it of grain and cattle. The Wild Cat People began climbing the four passes early one morning, but before they were halfway up they were put to flight by Moshesh's men who rolled wave upon wave of colliding, crashing boulders upon them. Three times they retraced their steps up the passes, and three

times they were flung back to the bottom of the hill. In due
course Sikonyela abandoned the operation, and learning
that his scouts had come upon Bamokoteli sorghum and
pumpkin fields in a valley to the south, he sent a party of
warriors to reap and bring the harvest into camp.

One evening at dusk envoys from Moshesh arrived at the
Batlokwa camp, and asked to be taken either to Sikonyela
or his mother. Brought before Sikonyela they said they had
come on behalf of their master to plead for mercy. They
had brought the Batlokwa oxen for slaughter as a token of
Moshesh's friendship. Moshesh, said the envoys, begged
that grain and pumpkins stolen recently by the Batlokwa be
returned to his people, for otherwise they would perish
from hunger. Furthermore, as the springs on the hill-top
were drying up, he asked if his water carriers could be given
safe conduct by the Wild Cat People to one of the streams
in the valley. It is said that Sikonyela scoffed at the envoys,
and suggested they bring Moshesh himself to fetch the
sorghum and pumpkins and also to draw water from the
streams.

On their return to the hill-top the envoys conferred with
Moshesh. Sikonyela, they said, was an arrogant upstart,
and was unlikely to leave Butha-Buthe until Moshesh and
his people either surrendered or perished.

As the days passed into weeks and the Wild Cat People
remained in the area, Moshesh began to despair and he
sacrificed, made offerings and prayed to the spirits for help.
One morning a wizened old woman was brought to him by
Makwanyane and Ratsiu. She was a *difaqane* refugee, she
said, formerly a member of the dispersed Bafokeng clan,
and as Moshesh had given her sanctuary she had decided to
help him rid Butha-Buthe of the Wild Cat People. She was
an instrument of the spirits, a diviner and prophet whose
supernormal powers had been unrivalled in Bafokeng territory. If Moshesh would allow a warrior to accompany her
to the foot of the hill, she would resurrect the *kokoi*, a
terrifying serpent, and with its help put the Wild Cat People
to flight.

Moshesh did not believe the woman at first, but persuaded by Makwanyane and Ratsiu he sent her down the

hill next morning accompanied by a warrior named Rahoho. She carried in her arms a serpent-like object made of goatskin, and in full view of Sikonyela and his people she started daubing it with medicines, calling upon the spirit of the *kokoi* to possess it and destroy the Batlokwa. But the *kokoi* refused to be resurrected, and, seeing this, Sikonyela and his warriors charged, captured the old woman, trampled the goatskin into the ground and beat Rahoho to death.

'*Kokoi, Kokoi*, the savage beast ... the snake,' they chanted, '*Kokoi! Kokoi! Kokoi!*'

The Wild Cat People jeered and guffawed, and mockingly imitated the movements of a snake with their arms. Not even the real *kokoi* could have put them to flight, far less the ridiculous goatskin brought by the idiotic old woman. In the meantime Moshesh's warriors had ventured halfway down the hill and started rolling boulders onto their foe, 'but no damage was done, the Batlokwa simply striking the boulders with their sticks with cries of derision'. The Batlokwa made merry until sunset when suddenly they stoned the old Bafokeng woman to death and returned to camp.

A day or two after this unhappy incident Moshesh was visited by a clansman named Motingwe who claimed he could lead the Bamokoteli to freedom. Apparently Motingwe had left his father's kraal on the Tlotsi stream some years before, and had settled sixty miles to the south-west near Qilwane, a conical-shaped hill. Told about his people's dilemma he had set out for Butha-Buthe determined to persuade Moshesh to flee with his clanlet by night and lead it on to a flat-topped hill adjoining Qilwane. The summit of this hill, Motingwe explained, was vast in area—flat as a hut floor, crowned with lush grasslands, watered with fast-flowing springs and embraced by a gigantic chain of precipices. Overlooking the Phuthiastana or Little Caledon river, it lay in the heart of a fertile, sparsely populated territory teeming with game. It could be climbed by way of several passes walled either with towering rocks or earth embankments, and it was considered impregnable by all who knew it. Motingwe offered to lead the Bamokoteli to the hill, but Moshesh refused, saying he would prefer to inspect it himself before coming to a decision. Later, realizing he dared not leave his people while the Wild Cat People remained in the vicinity, Moshesh sent Mohale, his brother, to look over the hill with Motingwe, and assess its potential as a stronghold.

At about the time of Motingwe's visit to Butha-Buthe news reached Moshesh that a Zulu regiment led by a renegade *induna* called Sepetsha had arrived on the right bank of the Caledon. These strangers, he was told, had planned to attack Butha-Buthe hill, but learning of the presence of the Wild Cat People had decided to wait and watch developments. One evening Moshesh sent messengers to the Zulu camp with gifts of grain and pumpkin for Sepetsha. Moshesh, they told the *induna*, would have invited the Zulu to take shelter on Butha-Buthe hill and share his depleted stores of grain, but he had been prevented from doing so as the approaches to the hill had been cut off by the Batlokwa under the command of the youthful Sikonyela. The Wild Cat People, the messengers continued, although no longer a powerful force were laden with stores of sorghum, gourd and pumpkin and their herds swarmed like locusts in the surrounding valleys. Should Sepetsha's regiment attack by night, not only would it put the war-scarred Batlokwa to flight, but it would take possession of an abundance of booty. Sepetsha could count on Moshesh as an ally.

On a moonlit night about three weeks later, the Zulu fell upon Sikonyela's camp and butchered the sleeping Wild Cat People. Panic swept the base of Butha-Buthe hill as tens of thousands of Batlokwa fled into the darkness, and in the morning when they were reported heading swiftly eastwards, the Zulu fell to looting the deserted camp, and later to rounding up a herd found grazing on the western slopes of the hill.

Moshesh looked down from the crest of his stronghold onto Sepetsha's regiment below, but he would not venture down the hill lest he be captured and put to death. He had intended sending Sepetsha an ox or two during the afternoon, but then scanning the eastern horizon he had caught sight of Sikonyela's army advancing in great haste towards

Butha-Buthe hill. The Wild Cat People had remustered and were returning to the attack, he told himself; he would keep the beasts and slaughter them for his own people when the battle about to be fought between the Batlokwa and the Zulu was over.

Indeed, it was not long before Sikonyela's army arrived, and taking the Zulu unawares drove them helter-skelter first into the slopes of a hillock nearby and then eastwards along the banks of the Caledon. In the late afternoon the Wild Cat People having abandoned the chase returned to Butha-Buthe hill and reoccupied their camp. During the following day they buried their dead, collected what few items of loot had been left behind by the Zulu and then moved off in a northerly direction bound for a secret rendezvous where their womenfolk and children awaited them. They were never to return to Butha-Buthe.

Moshesh and his people rejoiced, and little did they know that at that happy moment Mohale and Motingwe were striding home from the flat-topped hill they had gone to inspect in the west. Momentous events lay ahead for Moshesh and his clanlet. They were on the brink of a great upheaval, one fraught with untold dangers and heartache.

CHAPTER FIVE

EXODUS

Moshesh leads the Bamokoteli westwards—Old Peete is captured and devoured by cannibals—Thaba Bosiu, the Hill at Night—The Bamokoteli build kraals on the hilltop—They attack and disperse Chief None's clan

ON arrival at Butha-Buthe Mohale and Motingwe were taken to Moshesh whom they found in discussion with Mokhachane, old Peete and an uncle named Libe. Told to report about the flat-topped hill they had visited, Mohale said it was an ideal place of refuge, a great natural fortress nestling in the heart of an immense valley. He was convinced that if the Bamokoteli should occupy its summit they would be beyond reach of the most powerful foe—even Shaka's Zulu. There was, however, one drawback: the surrounding country was overrun by cannibals said to be as cunning as jackals and as voracious as vultures. They would have to be driven from their lairs and exterminated, for otherwise some of the Bamokoteli were bound to end their lives, sooner or later, in a cannibal's cooking-pot.

As a result of the *difaqane* wars, Mohale explained, thousands of starving clansmen had been driven to devouring enemy corpses and later those of fallen comrades and relatives. Later, having acquired a taste for human flesh, they had formed themselves into hunting bands, setting off daily in search of victims.

Moshesh was determined to move the Bamokoteli to the flat-topped hill in spite of the cannibals, but he was challenged by his father and some of the elders. The granaries, they cried, were almost empty, and the cows' udders were dry and shrivelled; if the clanlet undertook so long and hazardous a journey many of its women and children would perish. In any case, they could see no point in starting life afresh on a desolate flat-topped hill, especially one known to be haunted not only by cannibals, but also by lions, leopards and hyenas. Mokhachane forbade his son to undertake so foolish a venture.

In reply Moshesh explained that if the Bamokoteli remained at Butha-Buthe they would perish in any case, firstly because the hill was not impregnable and secondly because Matiwane, one of the renegade conquerors from Zululand had been reported lurking in the vicinity of the Caledon and might attack at any moment. But Moshesh was adamant. If no one agreed to accompany him to the flat-topped hill, he would go on his own.

The disagreement between Mokhachane and his son caused the Bamokoteli to choose sides, the more elderly people supporting the petty-chief and the young set, Moshesh. Eventually the majority voted in favour of trekking to the west, and looked to the heir-apparent to lead them. From that day on Mokhachane's influence dwindled fast and he refused to voice an opinion even on the most trivial matter.

During most of June 1824, a fierce east wind pummelled Butha-Buthe hill, compelling the Bamokoteli to postpone their departure. But when it dropped suddenly in July, and the winter air became mellow-warm, Moshesh ordered the clanlet to gather its belongings, descend the eastern pass and proceed to a spot near the old Qhobosheane kraal. There it would be met by an escort headed by Makwanyane.

First the women and children streamed into the valley below, then the men, and finally the cattle and goats driven by herdboys. When they were all assembled at the appointed place the journey began. In the van of the procession strode the warriors, their heads plumed and bodies draped in skins; next came the women carrying infants, sleeping-mats, baskets and small utensils; and lastly the elderly folk, cripples, children and dignitaries among whom were Mokhachane, old Peete, Ratsiu, Libe and others. One half of the youths helped the herdboys control the stock, the others watched over a herd of pack-oxen stacked high with impedimenta.

The first day's travel brought the Bamokoteli to the Mate valley where they settled for the night near Menkwaneng. Next morning at daybreak, with Moshesh and Makwanyane leading the procession, they crossed the Tlotsi stream, swung southwards and headed for the Malutis. Soon they reached a string of foothills, and as slowly they filed along a narrow game-track, the procession first began stretching and then it disintegrated. The Bamokoteli reached Pitseng by nightfall, and they slept on a hillslope, little disturbed by the cacophony of animal sounds that filled the surroundings.

Leaving Pitseng the procession crept westwards along a stony, rain-rutted pass used by Bushmen hunters which threaded its way through a mass of rocks and boulders, tumbledown thornbush and mile upon mile of matted undergrowth. To the left the Malutis undulated across the skyline; to the right sandstone cliffs stood side by side like mammoth sentinels, and always in front were chasms which seemed to plunge into the very bowels of the earth. The travellers trudged through bleak, inhospitable country patrolled by vultures, scavenged by hyenas and governed by lions. It was the one part Moshesh would have avoided had circumstances been different.

After about three hours' travel on the fourth day Moshesh discovered that some of the older folk were finding the journey too arduous, and were dropping out along the way, so he had them fetched by warriors. Indeed, the pass had become so treacherous that by sunset, when a halt was called, the clanlet had covered little more than three miles that day. Most of the people were footsore, many complained of aching legs and backs, all were so weary that they rolled up in their *karosses* and slept the moment they had eaten the evening meal.

On the following day the Bamokoteli moved five miles farther along the pass and they suffered two casualties. An old man stumbled and fell to his death below the pass, and a woman collapsed and died. The sixth day brought them safely to Dipetha, but on the seventh disaster struck as they descended into the Menyameng valley and plodded along the base of the Maluti range. For apparently old Peete, Moshesh's sister Mamila, two young women Mamakhobalo and Maneko whom he had recently married, as well as a dozen or more of the stragglers were cut off from the main party by cannibals and dragged away in a north-westerly direction. The cannibals also carried off eleven babies which they had snatched from the arms or the backs of their terrified mothers. News of the tragedy grieved Moshesh, and he sent a party of warriors under Rachokochane, his most cunning scout, to track the cannibals down and recapture the ill-fated victims. The loss of old Peete caused him special concern, for it will be recalled that Mohlomi the seer had declared Moshesh solely responsible for his protection and burial. Should old Peete be devoured by cannibals, he, Moshesh, would have to face the wrath of the spirits.

Rachokochane and his men located, attacked and dispersed the cannibals in the region of Sefikeng; they managed to recapture Moshesh's wives and sister but could find no trace of either his grandfather or the eleven infants. The old man, they were to learn later, had been put to death by Rakotswane, leader of the cannibals, and on the same day his corpse had been dismembered and eaten. Rachokochane and his men were shown a blood-stained rock on a hill where they found not only old Peete's garments but also those of the babies.

In the meantime Moshesh and the clanlet had been pressing on towards the flat-topped hill, and during the afternoon of the ninth day they caught sight of the tall, rocky pinnacle of Qilwane hill. Then the flat-topped hill hove into sight, and they marvelled at its steep slopes and the unending procession of sandstone cliffs that lined the summit.[1] A beautiful aura seemed to embrace the entire hill, charging the weary travellers with renewed excitement.

As they drew nearer they came upon a community of Bamantsane clansmen whose chief, None, was a distant relative of Moshesh, and after a brief exchange of greetings they turned westwards skirting fields of unharvested sorghum. On arrival at the western limb of the hill, about an hour before sunset, they started the laborious climb to the summit along a craggy pass. It was well after dark before the last of them reached the top of the stronghold, so they called it Thaba Bosiu, the Hill at Night.

Rachokochane arrived on the hill-top two days later, accompanied by the women he had retrieved from the can-

---

[1] The hill is roughly a mile in length, half a mile wide and three to four hundred feet high. The height of the precipices varies from forty to fifty feet.

nibals. Told of old Peete's fate Moshesh is said to have wept
and made sacrifices to the spritis for fear they would wreak
vengeance on him and his family. Another thought plagued
his mind: as Peete's corpse had not been laid to rest in
accordance with Mohlomi the seer's wishes, his spirit was
likely to be earthbound. It would be Moshesh's duty to release it from bondage and direct it to the shades of the
ancestors where it belonged.

During the months following the arrival of the Bamokoteli on the hill-top, Thaba Bosiu became a hive of activity.
While Moshesh, Mokhachane and the elders inspected the
summit for kraal sites, the women set off under guard to cut
thatching grass and reeds in the vicinity of the Phuthiastana
river. The spot eventually selected for Moshesh's own kraal
was situated not far from the top of the north-western or
Khubelu pass, and in line with the Ramaseli pass on the
opposite slopes. His father chose a site on the south-western
limb of the hill, where it was flanked on two sides by precipices, and overlooked another pass named Mokhachane's
pass. For some time to come the Bamokoteli were to live in
makeshift huts, in caves and under stone ledges, and while
the two main kraals were being built by handpicked craftsmen, Moshesh with the help of his brothers and Makwanyane organized the remaining men and all the youths into
fortifying the Khubelu, Ramaseli and Mokhachane passes.
They carried boulders from the hill-slopes—some flat and
jagged, others round and smooth—which they packed in
mounds along the cliffs lining the passes. When the task
was completed they fortified the three other passes, the
Mahabeng, the Raebe and Makara, in similar fashion.

Of all the problems commanding Moshesh's attention in
the first few months at Thaba Bosiu none caused him
greater concern than the food shortage. At first he had been
reluctant to permit his people to hunt or go in search of
edible berries, roots and insects in the valleys below, but
later he consented on condition they kept away from Chief
None's clan, and kept a close lookout for cannibals. One
day a party of men went down the Ramaseli pass to hunt,
but no sooner had they reached the foot of the hill than
they decided to raid the nearest of None's kraals. Driving

the inhabitants into the veld, they pillaged the granaries, snatched up sheaves of unthreshed sorghum, stacked in piles beside the huts and headed for home. Meanwhile None mustered his fighting men, and sent them after the raiders, but by the time they reached the bottom of Khubelu pass, the Bamokoteli were halfway up the hill and out of range of their assegais.

When news of the incident reached Moshesh he cursed and berated the marauders, accusing them of flouting his authority. It had been his aim to preserve Chief None's friendship, he told them, but now the Bamantsane would look upon the Bamokoteli as enemies. Later having called all the men of the clanlet together he warned them again to keep away from None's kraals and fields. Selecting three oxen from his own herd he had them delivered with an assurance that he, Moshesh, deeply regretted the intrusion of his subjects and would prohibit them from hunting along the eastern slopes of Thaba Bosiu, the Hill at Night.

Delivering the oxen at None's kraal the messengers found the chief in an ugly mood. At first he refused to accept the beasts claiming they were too few to compensate the losses suffered by his subjects. In due course he changed his mind, but when the messengers left he warned them that unless Moshesh sent him five more oxen he, None, would order his warriors to destroy the Bamokoteli.

Since their arrival in the area the Bamokoteli had pastured their cattle on the summit of Thaba Bosiu, but fearing the water supply might prove inadequate, they took part of the herd to the Phuthiastana river each day under guard of warriors. One morning as the cattle swarmed along the river side Chief None and his men arrived, cut off about three hundred from the main herd and drove them rapidly homewards. Suddenly they were sighted and intercepted by a Bamokoteli force which chanced to be returning from collecting firewood in a thicket close by. They were also attacked in the rear by cattleguards, and in the fight that followed None was taken prisoner, three of his warriors slain and the rest driven pell-mell across the river into the wooded folds of the hills beyond. The Bamokoteli gave chase for a short while, then turning about, returned to the summit of Thaba Bosiu, taking Chief None with them.

Moshesh received the captive chief with kindness, and released him three days later on receipt of a ransom of seventeen cattle. Bidding None farewell he suggested that past differences should be forgotten and that henceforth they strive to cultivate a happier relationship between their clans.

In October the Bamokoteli planted their first crops in the valley below the eastern slopes of Thaba Bosiu, about three miles from Qilwane hill where None's lands were situated. Moshesh, who by this time had become recognized as chief of the clanlet, visited the valley daily to inspect the vast expanses of sprouting sorghum. Sometimes he would amble over to Qilwane and pass an hour or two in conversation with None and the councillors of the Bamantsane clan. During recent months None had come to look upon Moshesh as a friend, and had even spent a night with him on Thaba Bosiu. Towards the end of 1824 their association came to an abrupt end, and they again became bitter enemies.

The trouble started as a result of the sudden death on the hill-top of Seephephe, father of Mamohato, Moshesh's senior wife. The old man had joined Moshesh eight months before and had taken part in the exodus from Butha-Buthe to the Hill at Night. On the evening of Chief None's visit, Seephephe had eaten a heavy meal of sorghum bread, and had suddenly collapsed and died in full view of a large gathering of dignitaries. Next day after None had left, Moshesh was visited by Poshuli, his brother, who said he knew the cause of the old man's death. He had evidence to prove that the bread he had eaten had been bewitched by None under Moshesh's very eyes. Why had Moshesh agreed to his release in exchange for cattle, demanded Poshuli, and why did he not have the scoundrel killed? None was known to be plotting the destruction of the Bamokoteli, if not by force of arms then by means of witchcraft. He should be captured and slain without delay.

Moshesh interjected. He did not believe that None was responsible for Seephephe's death, and in any case he would not have him killed lest the spirits take offence and punish not only himself but also the clanlet. No, Poshuli should cast such evil thoughts from his mind, and look upon None not as an enemy but a friend.

One day at dawn Poshuli stole down the hill at the head of a column of warriors, and set fire to several of None's kraals. The chief, his family and subjects fled northwards past Qilwane hill, crossed the Phuthiastana river and scattered into the hills beyond.

The hubbub created by the fleeing Bamantsane roused Moshesh and the rest of his people on Thaba Bosiu from their slumbers and they hurried to the eastern edge of the hill-top. Seeing the horde of fugitives in flight, their huts in flames and their cattle storming hither and thither through the smoke they scampered down the Raebe pass, fanned out into the valley and looted the deserted kraals. By nightfall they had brought all the grain and most of the cattle onto the hill-top.

Moshesh derived little pleasure from the dispersal of None's people, and fearing that they might be decimated by Poshuli's force he sent a party of warriors under Makwanyane with orders to put a stop to the fighting and return to the hill-top. He was angry with Poshuli, resented his high-handed manner and intended clipping his wings. He would have him brought before the *kgotla* and punished.[1]

A week passed before Poshuli accompanied by Makwanyane and their fighting men returned to Thaba Bosiu, but by this time Moshesh's anger had passed, and although urged to do so by the elders he refused to punish his brother. Poshuli, on the other hand, told that Moshesh had been annoyed, poked fun at him, much to the amusement of the victorious warriors. Small wonder that in years to come when he embarked on a career of brigandage Poshuli exploited Moshesh's mildness of character, often involving him in embarrassing and complicated political situations.

No two brothers could have been less alike than Moshesh, the recently emergent chief of the Bamokoteli and the furtive, unprincipled and recalcitrant Poshuli.

[1] After a short spell of wandering None and his people settled at Korokoro.

CHAPTER SIX

ALLIANCE WITH SHAKA

Moshesh incorporates two bands of cannibals in his clan—Matiwane, the conqueror, establishes kraals north of the Caledon—Moshesh seeks Matiwane's friendship, but becomes his enemy instead—He enters into an alliance with the king of the Zulu

OF the many problems that faced Moshesh and his people on Thaba Bosiu, the most serious was the shortage of food, for the harvest was not due until June 1825. The grain pillaged from the Bamantsane, although a great help, was inadequate for the needs of the clanlet, and the womenfolk were obliged to go down daily into the surrounding valleys and gather edible berries, roots, leaves and insects. Bands of hunters were sent regularly to track game along the river banks, and youths to set snares and traps in the plains beyond Qilwane Hill. Fortunately there was enough water for household needs, for there were eight fast-flowing springs on the hill-top, and another five in the cliffs along the southern slopes.

The first half of 1825 passed without incident, but in July, at the height of the reaping, Moshesh and his people caught sight of a horde of Makholokwane clansmen, victims of the *difaqane* wars, trudging across the veld towards the east. About a week later the strangers were reported by scouts to have settled on the western slope of a hill near Leribe. Fearing they might tamper with the Bamokoteli herds and crops, Mohale, Moshesh's brother, heading a party of fighting men attacked them early one morning and drove them across the Caledon river.

Three months later another horde appeared in the Leribe area and took shelter in some caves on Mautse hill. They were found to be cannibals, and barely a week after their arrival they captured some Bamokoteli women and children cutting reeds on the south bank of the Phuthiastana stream. 'Notwithstanding the children's cries, and the wailing of the

women, they were slaughtered' and eaten by the cannibals
'without pity or remorse'.

Some of the cannibals were dressed in skirts, aprons and
loincloths made of human skin, and they stank of putrified
flesh.

On enquiry Moshesh discovered that these hideous creatures were the same Makholokwane whom Mohale had
attacked and scattered three months before. They had been
driven by privation to this depraved way of life, and were
said to have become as elusive and vicious as a pack of
rabid jackals. Moshesh's heart filled with remorse for the
part his people had played in the Makholokwanes' unhappy
fate. In the presence of his father, his brothers and the
dignitaries of Thaba Bosiu, he prayed to the spirits for forgiveness, vowing that he would never again attack cannibals
in the Caledon Valley. One day he would attempt to
rehabilitate them and incorporate them as members of the
Bamokoteli clanlet.

Towards the end of the year a rabble of emaciated, hun-
ger-crazed *difaqane* refugees—they were remnants of the
once flourishing Basia clan—reached Thaba Bosiu and
pleaded with Moshesh for food, shelter and protection. He
received them kindly, assuring them that provided they fell
in with the way of life of his people they were welcome to
remain with him as permanent members of the clanlet.
Shortly afterwards the remnants of the Marabe clan arrived
on the hill-top. Until recently they had been domiciled on
and around Joalaboholo or Big Beer hill, roughly between
Thaba Bosiu and the Caledon river, but had been driven out
and decimated by the Wild Cat People. Aware of the security Moshesh's people enjoyed on Thaba Bosiu, they too had
come to the stronghold with a plea for protection. Like the
Basia they were given sanctuary on the hill-top and became
loyal and devoted subjects.

Strangers continued to arrive throughout the summer, including a second band of cannibals under their chief, Motle-
joa. Thaba Bosiu soon became overcrowded and Moshesh
was beset with several problems he had not anticipated. He
discovered among other things that his own Bamokoteli re-

sented the presence of so many strangers on the hill, and
were squabbling and even fighting with them. So in spite of
further cannibals that roamed the valleys below and the
reports he had received that Matiwane, the conqueror from
Zululand, had been spotted near the Caledon, Moshesh decided to relieve the congestion on Thaba Bosiu by establishing two kraals at its base.

Apparently at the time Matiwane's people were erecting
kraals and laying out fields for cultivation in the vast territory stretching from the Caledon to the vicinity of what is
today the town of Bethlehem. A protagonist in the drama
of *difaqane*, the conqueror had emerged triumphant over
all his adversaries, including the renegade Hlubi chief,
Mpangazitha, whom he had slain in battle some months
before. Moshesh's apparent indifference towards the encroachment of Matiwane's powerful army on Bamokoteli
territory baffled the people of Thaba Bosiu, and some of the
newcomers deserted, crossed the Caledon and joined the
conqueror's army. It was only after several months that
Moshesh took fright and decided to seek the formidable
intruder's friendship. He sent scouts to locate Matiwane,
and envoys to present him with grain and skins.

Moshesh's envoys were intercepted beyond the Caledon
by Matiwane's warriors, but explaining the purpose of their
visit they were conducted to Senyotong, the conqueror's
newly erected kraal. Brought before Matiwane, they were
questioned about the strength of Moshesh's army and the
size of his herds, and asked to describe the fortifications
built by the Bamokoteli on Thaba Bosiu. The conqueror
treated them with lavish hospitality, and when the time
came for their departure home he assured them that the
Bamokoteli would be left in peace provided they remained
south of the Caledon and Moshesh continued to send grain
and cattle as tribute to the *Inkosi Yamakhosi*—Matiwane,
king of kings.

About a month after the envoys' return to Thaba Bosiu
a little herdboy was descending the Khubelu pass with his
charges early one morning when his attention was arrested
by the bellowing and snorting of a herd of cattle not far
from the new kraal of Rafutho, the smithy. Recognizing

some of the beasts as belonging to his father, the boy decided to fetch them. But when his eyes fell upon the corpse of a warrior in the midst of the cattle, he turned about, retraced his steps up the pass, and reaching Moshesh's kraal blurted out the news for all to hear. A party of men, among whom were Moshesh and the envoys who had visited Matiwane, accompanied the boy down the hill. The envoys identified the dead warrior as Madilika, one of Matiwane's half-brothers whom they had befriended during their stay at Senyotong.

On close inspection of the corpse, Moshesh discovered that Madilika had died from an assegai wound, and by the condition of the blood in which he lay he concluded that the killing had taken place not long after dark on the previous evening. He had the body wrapped in an oxhide and carried up the hill. 'Keep absolute silence about this,' he warned his companions. It was important that news of the killing be prevented from filtering back to the conqueror, Matiwane.

On its arrival at Moshesh's kraal, Madilika's corpse was taken into the cattlefold where the private parts and pieces of flesh were sliced from it by Mobe, the medicine man. These he mixed with roots, herbs, fats and bits of blood-stained grass and soil collected at the scene of Madilika's death, and before long he had prepared a potent decoction which he presented to Moshesh. The chief is said to have been jubilant, and he predicted that if Matiwane attacked Thaba Bosiu, he would be destroyed not by the Bamokoteli army, but by Mobe's medicine.

Meanwhile, back at Senyotong, Madilika's disappearance had been causing Matwane concern. A few days before, he had trapped Madilika in the company of one of his concubines and had ordered his execution. But Madilika had fled, and crossing the Caledon river had headed for Thaba Bosiu hoping he would be given protection by Moshesh, whose envoys he had befriended recently at Senyotong. One evening just after dark Madilika had been overtaken by one of Matiwane's executioners in the vicinity of the Hill at Night. A fight took place and he was stabbed in his side. Fleeing again Madilika had managed to stagger to the foot of the Khubelu pass where he collapsed and died some ten hours before the discovery of his corpse by the herdboy.

On the executioner's return to Senyotong he reported to Matiwane that the fugitive, although gravely wounded, had escaped, so the conqueror sent scouts to search for him and bring him back for execution. The scouts received news of Madilika's death and the removal of his body long before they reached Thaba Bosiu. After reporting back to Matiwane they were sent again to the Bamokoteli stronghold, but this time they spoke to Moshesh in person, demanding not only Madilika's corpse, but the medicine prepared by Mobe. Moshesh denied all knowledge of the slain warrior, and suggested that he might have been caught by cannibals or beasts of prey.

Moshesh was to admit in later years that in spite of the medicine prepared for him by Mobe, he feared Matiwane more than any other *difaqane* conqueror. Perhaps what really troubled him was a thought planted in his mind by an elder. According to the old man Matiwane's witchdoctors had the power to nullify Mobe's decoctions and expose the Bamokoteli to destruction by the amaNgwane army. The conqueror must be appeased, Moshesh told the *kgotla*, and in addition he must be persuaded to accept the Bamokoteli as his vassals.

Moshesh sent a large load of tribute to Matiwane comprising jackalskin *karosses*, cowtail fly switches and baskets of grain and snuff. But the conqueror refused to accept the gifts, fearing they had been doctored with destructive medicines. He ordered Moshesh's envoys to return to their master and tell him his gifts were not wanted at Senyotong. They were also to say that the conqueror considered Moshesh an enemy of the amaNgwane, who were planning not only to annihilate the hill-dwelling Bamokoteli, but also to kill Moshesh himself and convert his corpse into war medicines.

When he learned of the rebuff his envoys had been given at Senyotong, Moshesh sent Makwanyane, together with a dozen or more senior men of the clanlet, to remonstrate with Matiwane and dissuade him from attacking Thaba Bosiu. This time he sent the conqueror thirty head of cattle which Matiwane accepted with a warning that although he considered the beasts fair compensation for Madilika's corpse, he remained as determined as before to destroy both Moshesh and the Bamokoteli.

In January 1826 as he waited feverishly for the ama-Ngwane to attack, Moshesh devised a scheme for saving his people from Matiwane's vengeance. He would become Shaka's vassal—Shaka, King of the Zulu, mightiest of all conquerors and Matiwane's bitterest and most feared enemy. At that time Shaka was living at Gibixhegu, Take Out the Old Man, a great military kraal built some years before on a ridge overlooking the Umhlatuze valley, seventeen miles from presentday Eshowe. Largest of the King's kraals, Gibixhegu comprised no less than 1,400 beehive-shaped huts built side by side to form a circle fully three miles in circumference. The kraal was encompassed by a dense hedge of menacing thornbush branches and manned by many thousands of warriors. It was in the central section of Gibixhegu, the vast arena where Shaka reviewed his regiments, that he first heard of Moshesh. He had been watching a war dance, performed in his honour by his Izicwe regiment, when an *induna* reported the arrival of a party of strangers from beyond the Drakensberg. Told that the strangers had brought him several bundles of gifts, he had them escorted into the cattlefold and then repaired there himself followed by a retinue of plumed and skin-bedecked *indunas*.

First to be presented to the King was Poho, leader of the group, who related how he and his companions had set out from Thaba Bosiu three weeks before bearing ostrich, crane and *sakabuli* (Long-tailed Widow Bird) plumes, lion and leopard skins and elephant tusks for delivery to the mighty Shaka. All these gifts had been sent by Moshesh himself, as a token of his desire to serve the Zulu conqueror as a vassal chief. The Bamokoteli, although situated far east of the Drakensberg range, would bring regular tribute of feathers, skins and tusks, or, for that matter, whatever other items Shaka required.

It is said that Shaka listened with profound interest, and after he had examined the gifts, he paraded to and fro before the visitors loudly extolling Moshesh's farsightedness. Poho and his companions, he said, were to return to their

chief and tell him that the King of the Zulu had accepted
the gifts and would henceforth recognize him as a vassal.

'Say to Moshesh,' he continued, 'that when he sees my
armies he must collect all his flocks and herds at the foot of
his mountain, and my people will pass them by.' He would
expect delivery of the tribute at each full moon, for in this
way he would have proof of Moshesh's loyalty. Shaka then
had fifty oxen fetched from a nearby cattlefold, and presenting them to Poho said they were for Moshesh. At the next
full moon when the Bamokoteli envoys returned to Gibixhegu with the tribute they would be given not fifty head of
cattle for the chief but a hundred at least.

Matiwane learnt of the alliance between the Bamokoteli
and the Zulu about a week later, for Moshesh, overjoyed at
the outcome of his envoys' visit to Gibixhegu, had spread
the news northwards as far as the Vaal river and westwards
throughout the Caledon Valley, the Northern Cape and
Botswana. Matiwane, he assured his people, would not dare
attack Thaba Bosiu now!

CHAPTER SEVEN

A GREAT VICTORY

Moshesh's warriors collect tribute for Shaka—His envoys are intercepted and robbed by Matiwane's men—Shaka sends emissaries to Thaba Bosiu—A Zulu army invades Matiwane's territory—Moshesh is accused of duplicity—He encourages cannibals to settle at Thaba Bosiu—Matiwane's force attacks Thaba Bosiu

No sooner had Poho returned from Zululand, than Moshesh sent the army to fetch plumes and pelts from surrounding areas. The warriors were told that if game was scarce this side of the Orange they were to sneak across the river and continue the hunt in the Cape Colony. At all costs, however, they were to avoid clashing with white men.

While the army was away in the south, Poho and his party set out again for Zululand bearing the second consignment of tribute for Shaka. As the months passed other parties of envoys followed in Poho's tracks, always reaching Gibixhegu when the moon waxed full. One day in June Poho and his followers were intercepted by an amaNgwane regiment and robbed of Shaka's tribute. Most of them fled to Thaba Bosiu, but a small party led by Poho continued the journey to Zululand and reported the incident to the King.

Shaka is said to have flown into a rage, and on being told that the robbers were Matiwane's subjects he vowed to have the territory between the Caledon and Vaal rivers cleared of amaNgwane vermin as he put it. Still in a rage, he also ordered Poho to return to Thaba Bosiu and report his disappointment to Moshesh. He, the *Ingonyama yamaZulu*, Lion of the Zulu, would not be kept waiting for the tribute, and he looked to Moshesh to honour their agreement.

Informed of Shaka's wrath Moshesh sent messengers to locate the hunters and order them to return with whatever items they had collected for delivery to Zululand. Soon another load of tribute was under way to the east, but again the envoys and their bearers were attacked and robbed by Matiwane's warriors, and in a skirmish which followed five of them were stabbed to death.

Moshesh sent eight of his dignitaries under guard to Gibixhegu with orders to impress upon the King the need for crushing the amaNgwane. They were received by Shaka in the central arena of the military kraal, and although at first he promised to send a division against Matiwane, he decided later to wait a while. For he was suspicious of Moshesh, believing he had no intention of delivering the agreed tribute and had exploited Matiwane's notoriety in order to solicit the protection of the Zulu. He, Shaka, King of the Zulu, would first send emissaries to investigate.

The Zulu emissaries reached Thaba Bosiu one evening in June and were escorted into the *kgotla* where they were welcomed by Moshesh, Mokhachane, scores of dignitaries and several hundred cheering warriors. At a feast held in the kraal they were entertained to a display of dancing by Bamokoteli men and maidens, but they were disinterested, preferring to help themselves to food and especially sorghum beer. Their phenomenal capacity for beer, Moshesh recalled in later years, amazed and annoyed him, for he was a total abstainer and disapproved of intemperance such as this.

On the following morning Moshesh, his councillors and the Zulu emissaries met for discussion in the *kgotla*, and when the question of the tribute arose the chief called upon his bearers and warriors to recount the attacks made upon them by Matiwane's people. He also sent for a party of hunters ambushed recently by the amaNgwane near Leribe, and asked them to show the visitors the wounds they had received in their bid to escape. Had these hunters not managed eventually to repulse the attackers, said Moshesh, they would have been slain and robbed of the tribute they had collected for Shaka.

The emissaries praised the hunters for their bravery and loyalty to the King of the Zulu, and promised to have Matiwane destroyed before Spring. Three days later they returned to Gibixhegu.

At the end of August a Zulu army crossed the Drakensberg, hurried westwards over the Highveld plains and burst into the Caledon Valley. Thousands of Sotho-speaking clansmen, many of whom had only recently extricated themselves from the grips of *difaqane*, fled northwards, arriving in due course at Senyotong, Matiwane's kraal, where they pleaded for protection. Learning of the army's arrival, Matiwane collected all his people and headed westwards along the right bank of the Caledon. They crossed the river in the region of presentday Wepener and went into hiding among a jumble of hills between Thabana Morena and Mafeteng. Meanwhile the Zulu had advanced on Senyotong and other amaNgwane kraals, but finding them deserted, recrossed the Caledon into the Valley and bivouacked in the vicinity of Qeme. There they met a party of Bamokoteli scouts sent by Moshesh to direct them to Matiwane's hideout.

After a short rest the Zulu moved on, spending the first night at Masite, the second at Thabana Morena, and the third at Likhoele. They attacked Matiwane's people on the following morning, and during the late afternoon, although superior in numbers, the amaNgwane buckled beneath the unrelenting onslaught of Shaka's perfectly disciplined warriors. When night fell, Matiwane collected his scattered followers and fled towards the Caledon, reaching it just before sunrise next morning. By midday the amaNgwane had gone into hiding not a stone's throw from the future settlement of Beersheba.

The Zulu arrived two days later and engaging the amaNgwane in battle put them to flight and captured their cattle. When night fell they encamped on the north bank of the Caledon, and on the following morning recrossed the river and set out for Zululand. Matiwane assured by his scouts that the enemy was now on its way home, gathered his people and returned to Senyotong.

No sooner had Matiwane resettled in his kraal, than he learned of the rôle played by Moshesh in the Zulu attack on the amaNgwane. Moshesh, he was told, had betrayed him, had led the Zulu to his hideout and had urged them to take all his cattle as compensation for the tribute stolen by the amaNgwane from the Bamokoteli envoys. Matiwane vowed to avenge the wrong Moshesh had done him; but he no

longer wanted Moshesh's corpse for medicines. He would
have it cast instead to the hyenas.

Informed in September of Matiwane's wrath, Moshesh
waited for the amaNgwane to attack, but when the rains
came in October and there was no sign of the enemy, he
gave orders for the fields to be tilled and the crops to be
planted. And while the Bamokoteli toiled he and his councillors met in the *kgotla* to discuss the threat. They concluded that unless steps were taken to increase the size of
the army, the clanlet would be doomed to destruction. Some
of the younger councillors proposed that envoys be sent in
every direction to look for *difaqane* refugees and persuade
them to settle around Thaba Bosiu. They were opposed by
the elders who claimed that if Thaba Bosiu were turned into
a haven for homeless strangers, Moshesh would be confronted by an unruly hotchpotch whose loyalty would
always be suspect. Many thousands of *difaqane* victims,
they argued, had turned to cannibalism, and if Moshesh
incorporated them in the clanlet, he would be dealing with
awesome creatures akin to beasts of prey—shrewd, savage
and beyond taming. The cannibals had been a constant
threat to the Valley folk, and they deserved to be annihilated, not protected.

In reply Moshesh said he would never permit the slaughter of cannibals, for although he too abhorred their heinous
activities, he believed they could be rehabilitated without
undue difficulty. He proposed that envoys be sent under
escort to locate all cannibal bands in the area and assure
them they would be given cattle, goats and seed provided
they settled near Thaba Bosiu and recognized Moshesh as
their chief. They were also to be promised land for tilling
and grazing for their stock, and should they ever be molested or attacked, they could count on him for protection.

The elders protested but they were silenced by Moshesh,
as he continued to address the *kgotla*. He was weary, he
barked angrily, of the rantings of dignitaries whose insight
into the clanlet's affairs was confined to the gossip they
heard around the beerpots. Had the elders given deep
thought to the dangers confronting the Bamokoteli since
the arrival of the conqueror, Matiwane? Had they con-

sidered the attitude of the spirits to cannibals? He, Moshesh, had been advised by the spirit of Mohlomi, the seer,
to have compassion on cannibals, for they carried within
their bowels the remains of departed souls. Cannibals were
living sepulchres, and had to be protected in much the same
way as ancestral graves were protected from desecration.
This was a delicate matter, he warned the elders, and he
advised them to pray Mohlomi's forgiveness lest they had
offended him.

During the following months Moshesh's envoys visited
cannibal bands throughout the Valley and in areas as remote as presentday Winburg in the north and Queenstown
in the south. Some they located in blood-bespattered caves,
some in chasms strewn with skulls and bones and others on
hill-tops. And although always regarded with suspicion, the
envoys managed to win the confidence of many who could
see in Moshesh's offer 'an unhoped-for means of restora-
tion to their former position'. While vast numbers of cannibals refused to be lured from their lairs and hunting
grounds the great majority of them praised Moshesh for his
attitude to their way of life. No other chief had ever sought
to help them; they had been regarded everywhere as vermin
deserving of extermination.[1]

As the months passed Moshesh's reputation as a benefactor grew and a steady stream of strangers flowed towards
Thaba Bosiu. By June 1827 the population on the hill-top
alone had risen to an estimated three thousand, and in the
valley close by the number of kraals had increased from two
to seven. Moshesh's army, too, had grown, and was abund-
antly supplied with battle-axes, clubs and shields manufac-
tured by Rafutho, the smithy, and his band of craftsmen.
Granaries bulged to overflowing. Cattle and goats were
plentiful. Small wonder Moshesh boasted that he feared
neither Matiwane nor any other *difaqane* conqueror. Not
even Shaka's invincible army would succeed in dislodging
him from his mighty fortress—Thaba Bosiu.

One morning in July as he emerged from his hut, Moshesh's attention was arrested by shouting warriors, a num-

[1] According to French missionary Arbousset, the territory
flanked by the Orange and the Vaal was inhabited by some
7,000 cannibals.

ber of whom came running towards him from the northern
edge of Thaba Bosiu. Matiwane's army was advancing on
Thaba Bosiu! It had been detected by scouts not many miles
north of the Caledon. Straight away Moshesh sent messengers to his subjects in the valley with orders for them to
abandon their kraals and come onto the hill together with
their stock and grain. There was chaos on Thaba Bosiu as
the Bamokoteli began 'rushing about in wild confusion', but
when directed by the warriors to the cattlefold where Moshesh awaited them, they quickly regained their composure.

Moshesh exhorted his people to be brave, assuring them
that Matiwane's army would fail to penetrate the defences
of Thaba Bosiu. Should it attempt to climb the passes, it
would be beaten back by a bombardment of boulders.

Scouts arrived while Moshesh was speaking and reported
that part of the invading army had almost reached the
Phuthiastana river, so the chief sent three of his medicine
men, Makume, Phea and Motoboli to plant destructive
medicines in the fords. At noon news reached Thaba Bosiu
that four divisions of amaNgwane had effected a crossing in
the west, and joined by two more divisions coming from
Qeme, they were advancing swiftly on Moshesh's stronghold.

During the late afternoon, Matiwane's army hove in view
and halted about half a mile north of the Khubelu pass
where it bivouacked. Towards sunset one of the divisions
moved off in a southerly direction and pitched camp at the
foot of the Mokhachane pass.

On the following morning, just before daybreak, the
amaNgwane mustered near Rafutho's kraal, and started
moving up the Khubelu pass as the first rays of the rising
sun crept into the Valley. Halfway up they paused a short
while to study the fortifications above them, and then continued, step by step, until they entered the shadow of a tall,
bush-clad precipice.

According to Msebenzi, a tribal chronicler,[1] the heavens
suddenly exploded, emptying a deluge of boulders upon
them, crushing the vanguard. The Bamokoteli who were
'light and active ... came down to finish off the
wounded ... They then rolled down the second rampart or

[1] See N. J. Van Warmelo.

boulder mound and further reduced the amaNgwane's strength, for the stones struck them in the chest and stomach.' Again Moshesh's men 'came down, and they clubbed the remaining amaNgwane to death'. Matiwane's warriors turned and fled down the pass. Some stumbled and were trampled to death, some were rocketed by bouncing boulders into the lower slopes and others were felled by assegais hurled from the cliff-tops. Bruised and footsore the ama-Ngwane scrambled to the foot of the hill, where they were regrouped by their *indunas* into regimental formation. At the command of the *indunas* the amaNgwane withdrew to their main encampment near Rafutho's kraal. Throughout the remaining hours of the day and well into the night they nursed their wounds, chanted war songs and whetted their stabbing spears.

The amaNgwane returned to the attack on the following morning. This time they proceeded along an unfortified pass on the eastern slopes of Thaba Bosiu. They believed they would wipe out the Bamokoteli to a man before the sun set again over the Valley. Meanwhile the Bamokoteli army led by Moshesh, and officered by his brothers, Poshuli and Makhabane, and his friend Makwanyane and chief Makara, had descended the Khubelu pass and creeping up on the enemy force attacked it in the rear. Fighting fiercely the amaNgwane started retreating northwards, and although for a while they managed to rally and check the Bamokoteli advance, they were attacked so fiercely on the right flank by Moshesh's own column that they fled across the Phuthiastana river and headed for Senyotong.

Moshesh pursued the enemy as far as the Caledon river. Fearing that Matiwane might muster his entire army and cut off the Bamokoteli from their stronghold, he led his men quickly back to Thaba Bosiu.

Victory celebrations were held on the hill-top, where the jubilant chief presented his victorious warriors with gifts of cattle. The dispersal of the amaNgwane had been Moshesh's most gratifying achievement since the Bamokoteli's occupation of the Hill at Night.

CHAPTER EIGHT

MOSHESH APPEASES OLD PEETE'S SPIRIT

One of Moshesh's wives is killed by a lion—Matiwane's clan dispersed by the Matabele—Moshesh goes cattle-raiding with Moorosi—He learns of Shaka's assassination—Moshesh captures the cannibals who devoured old Peete—Mohato is renamed Letsie—The Wild Cat People loot Thaba Bosiu

WHILE the Bamokoteli were celebrating their victory over Matiwane's force, tragedy struck Moshesh's kraal—one of his younger wives was caught by a lion and mauled to death. In the years that the wars of the *difaqane* raged in central South Africa, most species of game had been greatly reduced in number by hordes of starving fugitives, but beasts of prey, especially lions, had multiplied. Many had become intrepid man-eaters.

Whereas the people on the hill-top were never really in danger of attack by these fearsome beasts, those inhabiting kraals in the valley lived constantly on tenterhooks. A herd-boy had been carried off not a week before Matiwane's assault on Thaba Bosiu, and another had been devoured near the Phuthiastana river three months before. Then one night at the height of the victory celebrations came the attack on Moshesh's wife. The most astounding aspect of the tragedy was that she had encountered the beast not far from Moshesh's kraal, at the top of the Ramaseli pass. Her terrifying screams accompanied by the deafening roar of the lion sent the people of Thaba Bosiu running panic-stricken in every direction.

It was almost midnight, 'and very dark when the lion leaped upon her', said Moshesh, recalling the incident in later years. He together with 'a number of his men, in accordance with their custom when an adversary of this kind was to be attacked, armed themselves as for battle, and advanced in close order. The lion, finding itself hard pressed, dropped his victim, turned around, and uttering a frightful roar threw himself upon the band, who immediately took to flight. A moment after, the cries of the woman recommenced; the animal had once more seized her in his jaws and was making off with her. There was a rally, a fresh attack, a fresh rout, renewed cries from the poor victim, who, after a moment of respite, felt herself once more in that terrible grip. This scene was repeated six or eight times ... the woman's cries becoming fainter and fainter.' Eventually Moshesh and his gallant party, eluded by the lion in the darkness abandoned the pursuit, and with heavy hearts returned to the kraal. As expected the beast had vanished by the break of dawn. All that the sorrowing chief could find of his ill-fated wife were some items of clothing and 'a few half-crunched bones'.

From that day on huge fires were kept burning from dusk to daybreak every night, at the top of the six passes. And although the surrounding slopes often resounded to the roar of lions, never again did one of them venture onto the summit of the Hill at Night.

Moshesh had no further contact with Matiwane during the Summer of 1827, and Bamokoteli envoys bearing tribute to Zululand for Shaka passed unmolested through the Harrismith district. From time to time deserters from Senyotong arrived at Thaba Bosiu—they were invariably Sotho-speaking clansmen who had joined the amaNgwane rather than perish in the turmoil of *difaqane*—and they reported that Matiwane was weary of waging war, seldom venturing beyond the gates of his kraal. Plagued by the setbacks he had suffered in recent months, he had become edgy and morose and had quarrelled with his *indunas* and councillors. Matiwane had ordered the execution of two greybeards who dared disturb him from his afternoon sleep.

In February 1828 greater misfortune befell Matiwane's clan—it was attacked and put to flight by the Matabele, a powerful, hostile tribe inhabiting a vast territory from the Magaliesberg range in the north to the Limpopo river. Threading a way through the Qeme district the amaNgwane crossed the Orange river into the Colony and headed in full flight for Zululand. When news of Matiwane's departure reached Thaba Bosiu the Bamokoteli rejoiced, and

Moshesh predicted that peace would return to the Caledon
Valley.

There was little activity at Thaba Bosiu until June when
the reaping began, and in July after the last of the harvest
had been brought into the kraals, Moshesh and his councillors considered that whereas grain was now plentiful the
number of cattle owned by the clan was inadequate for the
needs of the growing population. It was decided that Moshesh, aided by a newcomer named Moorosi, should lead a
raiding party into tribal territories south of the Orange.

Of the many men destined to play a rôle in Moshesh's
life drama, perhaps the most complex in character was this
very Moorosi, a marauder of considerable notoriety. He
had once been a powerful chief, but his clan, an offshoot of
the Baphuthi or Duiker People, had been drawn into the
swirl of *difaqane* and robbed of its possessions. Reduced to
abject poverty in 1828, Moorosi had climbed the Khubelu
pass, and pledged allegiance to Moshesh in return for food,
shelter and protection. Moshesh had taken an immediate
liking to him, being impressed by his 'open, candid way of
speaking', as well as his 'perfect self-possession, quickness
and good address in conversation', and had welcomed him
to Thaba Bosiu.

Moshesh was fascinated by Moorosi's descriptions of the
multitudinous herds owned by the Xhosa tribes, and of the
amenities enjoyed by white men beyond the Orange.

Incessant bad weather in July and August compelled
Moshesh to postpone the cattle raid they had planned into
the Cape Colony. But at the first sign of Spring in September, he set out at the head of a thousand Bamokoteli,
supported by some five hundred Baphuthi under the wily
Moorosi. He was also accompanied by two hundred youths
bearing rations for the raiders, about twenty herdsmen
driving slaughter-oxen before them and a group of menials
who were in charge of pack-oxen loaded with sleeping
mats, *karosses* and cooking utensils.

The raiders proceeded south-westwards through the
Mafeteng, Zastron and Herschel districts, and threading a
trail along the Stormberg range, in the vicinity of Dord-

recht, stole into that part of Xhosa territory inhabited by the Thembu, or Tamboekies as they were often called.[1]

Learning of the approach of the raiders, Tawana, the local chief, assuming they were Zulu sent by Shaka to devastate Xhosa territory, went into hiding with his peoples in some bush-clad hills overlooking the Great Fish river. Moshesh and his raiders looted Tawana's deserted kraals, and finding the hill-slopes and valleys teeming with cattle, goats and sheep rounded them up. Soon a stream of captured animals started moving northwards under escort, bound for Thaba Bosiu.

The raid lasted five days, and on the sixth Moshesh led his men back to Thaba Bosiu. The customary thanksgiving sacrifices were conducted on the hill-top, followed by feasting and dancing. Finally all the captured Tamboekie cattle were fumigated against the influence of evil spirits. Warriors bearing lighted branches, slowly encircled the beasts and then, bursting into song they capered round and round until eventually the herd was concealed by a cloud of smoke. After the cattle had been pronounced purified by the witch-doctors, they were distributed among the dignitaries of the clan; thirty oxen and twenty heifers being kept apart for delivery to Shaka.

Moshesh sent the fifty beasts to Gibixhegu in the charge of Poho and a party of envoys and menials, but they were destined never to reach Zululand. For, on arrival at the foot of the Drakensberg, news reached Poho that Shaka was

[1] In generations past the Thembu had crushed hordes of diminutive Bushmen and Hottentots inhabiting that part of the Cape Colony, and had taken their women as booty. Gradually a race of half-castes emerged from within the Thembu clan. These people differed considerably from other Xhosa peoples: they were shorter, their skins were bronze-coloured and their cheekbones prominent. Although they retained a way of life similar to that of the Xhosa, many of their customs remained typically Bushman. Perhaps the most noteworthy of these was the practice of amputating the first knuckle-joint of the little finger. The Boers of the Colony named them 'the little Thembu'—that is, Tamboetjes or Tamboekies (see Dr. Peter Becker, *The Star Research Bureau, Johannesburg,* 3 June 1965).

dead! The King had been assassinated by his half-brothers, Dingane and Mhlangana, and a servant named Mbopha.

When Moshesh heard the news he was deeply troubled. He realized that as a friend of Shaka he was likely to be regarded by the assassins as an enemy, and could no longer count on the Zulu for protection. The chief brooded, sacrificed to the spirits and called upon Peete, his most illustrious ancestor, for guidance. It was then that he harked back on the advice given him many years before by Mohlomi, the seer. After old Peete's death he, Moshesh, was to take charge of the corpse and bury it according to traditional rites. Should he fail to do so, he would bring misfortune both on himself and his family.

Since the death of his grandfather at the hands of the cannibals, Moshesh had often pondered Mohlomi's warning, but had been unable to decide what he should do. Now suddenly it struck him that if cannibals were to be regarded as living sepulchres, he could perform the appropriate rites, as decreed by Mohlomi, over the stomachs of those who had devoured old Peete. Accordingly he sent a party of warriors under Makwanyane to Sefikeng with orders to capture Chief Rakotswane and his cannibal band, and bring them to Thaba Bosiu.

Makwanyane was away at Sefikeng for several days, and when he returned with the cannibals he was met by an angry mob who demanded they be put to death. Moshesh intervened. Calling his people to order, he said he would have no bloodshed on Thaba Bosiu, far less the slaughter of the very people through whose bowels the remains of old Pette had passed. He explained to the cannibals his reason for having had them brought to Thaba Bosiu, and promised to return them safely to Sefikeng provided they cooperated with him.

After leading the cannibals into the cattlefold, Moshesh ordered them to lie down, side by side in rows, and scooping up some moist, warm *mosoang*[1] rubbed it over their naked bellies. Then he and Mobe, the medicine man, took turns in praying, calling upon God, the Molimo, to bless Peete's spirit and imbue it with power to communicate with the people of Thaba Bosiu in time of trouble. At the end of the

[1] Intestinal manure of an ox slaughtered for sacrifice.

ceremony Moshesh invited the cannibals to join the Bamo-koteli in a feast of thanksgiving, and later, presenting Rakotswane with a gift of cattle, had him and his followers escorted back to Sefikeng.

The *difaqane* holocaust burnt itself out during that Summer, and an eerie serenity pervaded the Valley. After the harvest of 1829, during July, Moshesh decreed that all eligible youths of the tribe should be circumcised, for this had not been done since the occupation of Thaba Bosiu. A *mophato* was therefore built on the hill-top, and scores of boys, including the chief's own son, Mohato, were subjected to the long ordeal of initiation. And in the Spring when the lodge was closed and the initiates returned to their kraals as fully-fledged men, Moshesh commemorated the occasion by renaming his son Letsie.

At about that time Moshesh was seen constantly in the company of Moorosi, the marauder, for he was planning a second cattle raid into the Cape Colony. In actual fact, Moshesh had developed an insatiable greed for cattle, and was determined that the forthcoming raid should be even more lucrative than the first. Moorosi persuaded him to invite the Wild Cat People now settled not a day's march from Thaba Bosiu, to join the expedition. He sent Poho to Joalaboholo—the Great Beer, capital kraal of the Wild Cat People, to confer with Sikonyela. But the chief declined Moshesh's invitation, offering instead to keep watch over Thaba Bosiu should Moshesh himself lead the raid into Xhosa territory.

Accompanied by a combined force of Bamokoteli and Baphuthi, Moshesh set out for the Colony in September. Before his departure he had placed his uncle, Ratsiu, in charge of the clan's affairs, and had appointed his son, Letsie, to keep watch over the cattle and goats. Unknown to either Ratsiu or Letsie, Moshesh and his force had hardly reached the foot of the hill, when a young man, Moka-kailane by name, slipped down the Raebe pass, and headed for Wild Cat territory.

About a year before, Mokakailane had arrived at Thaba Bosiu to plead with Moshesh for sanctuary. Chief Sikon-

yela, he told Moshesh, had caught him having intercourse
with a harem woman, and had sought to kill him. Moka-
kailane had therefore fled from Wild Cat country and had
come to Thaba Bosiu where he soon won Moshesh's favour.
He was to have accompanied the raiding force to the Cape
Colony, but feigning illness had been allowed to remain behind. His flight from Thaba Bosiu, coinciding with Moshesh's departure was unnoticed. Reaching Joalaboholo, he
found Sikonyela in the *kgotla*.

When Mokakailane told him that Moshesh's cattle had
'been left in the care of women', Sikonyela called his warriors together and set out for Thaba Bosiu. After crossing
the Caledon, Sikonyela sent messengers to Ratsiu informing
him that the Wild Cat People were coming to keep watch
over Thaba Bosiu during Moshesh's absence. Ratsiu was to
have beasts slaughtered and beer brewed for the warriors.
He was also to have accommodation prepared for them on
the hill-top.

On arrival at Thaba Bosiu the Wild Cat army bivouacked
near Rafutho's kraal. Summoned by Ratsiu next morning at
dawn, Sikonyela led a section of his force up the Khubelu
pass. He was met on the summit by a large group of irate
old men who cursed him, spat on him and demanded that
he remove himself and his verminous followers from Moshesh's stronghold. Suddenly the old men fell upon him with
sticks and assegais, and seeing him fall to the ground, pelted
the warriors with stones. One old greybeard called Rathaba,
advancing with battle-axe in hand, was struck down and
killed by a Wild Cat warrior, and in a moment the rest of
the old men turned and fled.

Ignoring Ratsiu, Letsie and other dignitaries of Thaba
Bosiu, Sikonyela strode with his men to Moshesh's cattlefold, and throwing the gates wide open sent all the beasts
found inside down the Khubelu pass. The chief and his
followers then looted Moshesh's kraal, and finding some
women bunched together in a hut—among them were two
of Moshesh's wives, Mamohato and Masekhonyana—took
them prisoner. Next the intruders headed for old Mokhachane's settlement which they also looted, and they were
about to set it alight when they were taken unawares by a
party of Bamokoteli, comprising mainly retired warriors

and recently circumcised youths, led by Moshesh's son, Letsie. A skirmish took place and the Bamokoteli were put to flight. Withdrawing from Mokhachane's kraal the Wild Cat People returned to Moshesh's *kgotla* where they feasted, made merry and chanted tribal hymns in thanksgiving to the spirits.

In the meantime two of Moshesh's veteran warriors, Ratsosane and Pelea, had been mustering all able-bodied men, irrespective of age, both on the hill and in the valley, and had formed them into a fighting force. When night fell they surrounded the *kgotla* and crept towards the Wild Cat People, many of whom were brain-soaked in sorghum beer and had fallen into a heavy, befuddled sleep. They could see Sikonyela beneath the *kgotla* tree, seated in Moshesh's chair. He was among the first to catch sight of them, and jumping to his feet, called his men to arms. The Bamokoteli charged, but were driven back and pursued into the darkness, having slain no more than a dozen of the sleepers. Next morning at first light of dawn, the Wild Cat People withdrew wearily from Moshesh's kraal, but were attacked so fiercely by inhabitants of the hill, that they abandoned much of the booty and all the women they had captured and hurried down the Khubelu pass. Two days later they broke camp, and retraced their steps to Wild Cat territory.

News of Sikonyela's duplicity reached Moshesh in the Cape Colony about a week later, so he called off the cattle raid and returned with his own force to Thaba Bosiu. Moorosi's Baphuthi were to follow some days later with a drove of cattle, goats and sheep pillaged from the Xhosa. Arriving home Moshesh was slated by Mokhachane, Ratsiu, the councillors and elders, for they blamed him for Sikonyela's raid on Thaba Bosiu. Why had he been so stupid, they asked, to invite a jackal to tend his lambs? Had Sikonyela and his followers not fallen victim to sorghum beer, and had the heroes Ratsosane and Pelea not come to the rescue of those left behind on the hill, much innocent blood would have been spilt on Thaba Bosiu. The stronghold would have fallen into Batlokwa hands. Ratsiu insisted that in future either Moorosi or Poshuli should lead the cattle raids into neighbouring territories, and that Moshesh should remain on the hill, and attend to the affairs of his subjects. Moshesh was the ruler and father of the clan, and as such he dared not expose his people to danger.

The day after his return home Moshesh sent Poho to Joalaboholo, the Great Beer, with four oxen for Sikonyela. Presenting the beasts to the chief, the envoy explained they were a token of friendship from the Bamokoteli. Moshesh, he continued, expected that in return Sikonyela would explain why the kraals on the hill-top had been looted; why Rathaba, the old man, had been killed and why Bamokoteli women and cattle had been captured. It is said that Sikonyela 'bent his head in shame',[1] and uttered not a word in defence of himself or his subjects. But in a sudden change of mood, he said he wanted neither Moshesh's oxen nor his friendship, and he advised Poho to return home and warn his master to keep well out of the way of the Wild Cat People.

Next time he would come uninvited to the Hill at Night. It was not four oxen he wanted. He wanted all Moshesh's cattle, all his maidens, all his grain and, in fact, all Thaba Bosiu.

[1] According to informant Azariel Sekese.

CHAPTER NINE

NEW DANGERS

Moshesh sees a horse for the first time, and has riding lessons—Letele leaves Thaba Bosiu and joins the brigand, Hendrik Hendriks—Moshesh's army annihilates the marauding Koranna—It decimates Piet Witvoet's banditti—Moshesh meets the Griqua, Adam Krotz, and promises to send a missionary—The Matabele storm Thaba Bosiu

BY the summer of 1829 an estimated five thousand people, drawn from a dozen or more distinct Sotho-speaking clans, were living on or in the immediate vicinity of Thaba Bosiu under Moshesh. Because of the heterogenous nature of Moshesh's growing clan, most of the people, and especially the newcomers, began referring to themselves as Basotho, or Sotho People, and to Moshesh's domain as the Lesotho. Gradually the clan name, Bamokoteli fell into disuse. During that year Moshesh's cattle, goats and sheep multiplied rapidly, for almost daily, herds lifted from Xhosa territory by Moorosi's marauders were delivered to Thaba Bosiu. One of these stolen herds included a chestnut mare, the first horse Moshesh had ever seen.

Presenting the animal to Moshesh, Lipholo, one of Moorosi's dignitaries, explained it had been taken from a white man near Dordrecht. Lipholo had come to teach the Basotho chief to ride it. Moshesh is said to have mounted with little difficulty, but he could only maintain his balance with the aid of staves used like walking sticks, as the horse ambled about the kraal. In due course he was able to discard the staves and make use of a bridle comprising a wooden bit and reins plaited from reeds. He was soon an accomplished rider.

Among the many newcomers to Thaba Bosiu, some were dignitaries such as Chief Letele, son of the illustrious seer, Mohlomi. Towards the end of the year another of Mohlomi's sons, Mojakisane, arrived in the area together with a

large section of the Bamonaheng clan. Moshesh, assuming
they had come to join him sent them cattle and goats for
slaughter as well as grain and milk. Later he sent them
seven hundred cattle on condition they were returned if the
Bamonaheng should decide not to settle at Thaba Bosiu.
Mojakisane accepted the gift with intense gratitude, assuring Moshesh that he and his followers would remain permanently in the Lesotho as part of his clan.

Moshesh's generosity was condemned by the elders of
Thaba Bosiu and two of his brothers, Poshuli and Makhabane, demanded that the cattle be taken away from Mojakisane. When Moshesh refused, they slipped into the valley
one night at the head of a powerful force and locating the
Bamonaheng, rounded up most of the seven hundred beasts
and drove them back onto the hill.

On the following day Poshuli and Makhabane were summoned to the *kgotla* where they were reprimanded by Moshesh and the councillors. Poshuli insisted that as a son of
Mokhachane he was entitled to overrule any policy he considered detrimental to the clan. In any case, he refused to be
domineered by Moshesh. The chief was so annoyed that, to
everyone's surprise, he threatened his brother with death.
Letele, son of Mohlomi, the seer, demanded Poshuli's immediate execution, but again to the surprise of the councillors, Moshesh rebuked him. Thaba Bosiu, he cried, was a
place of peace, not a hyena's lair. Poshuli would be fined no
more than four oxen, as befitted his transgression. If Letele
insisted on having him killed, he would be advised to move
with his people to the domain of the tyrant, Mzilikazi, King
of the Matabele. There he was more likely to quench his
thirst for blood.

After Poshuli had been punished and the *kgotla* had
adjourned, Letele left in a huff, called his people together
and led them down the Khubelu pass. Finding the Bamonaheng clan, about a week later, in the vicinity of Thabana
Morena, he tried to persuade its chief, Mojakisane to join
him in plotting Moshesh's overthrow. Snubbed by the chief
Letele moved on, linking up eventually with a brigand
named Hendrik Hendriks, leader of several bands of half-
breed cut-throats known as the Koranna. Hendriks, whose
notoriety was unrivalled both north and south of the

Orange, lived with his turbulent rabble in the hills overlooking the lower reaches of the Caledon river.

Yellow-skinned, flat-faced, frizzy-haired and diminutive in stature, the Koranna had once inhabited parts of the Cape Colony, but falling foul of colonial justice, had migrated northwards driving a multitude of cattle, sheep, goats and horses before them. Most of these animals had been stolen either from Boer farmers or Xhosa chiefs. They spoke Dutch and dressed in European fashion, and having settled beyond the Orange frequented the Colony's northern frontiers where they traded stock for contraband arms and ammunition. The Koranna had eventually split into bands of *banditti*, and during the *difaqane* wars had haunted the plains of South Africa, ruthlessly butchering and robbing defenceless Sotho-speaking clans. In 1830, not long after Letele left Thaba Bosiu, Moshesh was to come face to face with the Koranna. This would be his first encounter with a foe mounted on horses and armed with weapons of smoke and thunder.

When Letele met Hendriks, the brigands were living in a grimy village of reed-huts, situated on the top of Elandsberg, a hill 'where rising rocks, step by step, were like the successive ramparts of an enormous ... impregnable mountain fortress'. Told by Letele about Moshesh's enormous herds and fields of grain, Hendriks decided to invade the Lesotho. He vowed he would exterminate the inhabitants of Thaba Bosiu in much the same way as the boys of his village exterminated field mice trapped in a granary.

Hendriks and his band of ruffians set out for Thaba Bosiu one morning, and reaching Qeme hill about two days later pitched camp on its northern slopes. That night they seated themselves round a huge fire, roasting goat meat and gulping sorghum beer. A handful of guards kept watch over the horses driven earlier into a shallow, eroded hollow close by. Others were posted among the saddles, muskets and accoutrements stacked in rows beneath a cluster of thorntrees.

By midnight the Koranna were tipsy and although some lay sprawled out beside the fire, fast asleep, by far the majority continued to drink, blissfully unaware that they were being encircled by a large Basotho force under com-

mand of the indomitable warrior Makwanyane. A week
before Moshesh had been warned by a fugitive from Elandsberg about the impending attack. It was therefore no coin-
cidence that the Basotho should have arrived at Hendriks's
bivouac under cover of darkness. Indeed, they had slunk
into the area on the previous day, and had gone into hiding
about a mile from Qeme hill.

The Basotho pounced on the unsuspecting Koranna just
after midnight killing most of them with assegais and battle-
axes before they could reach for their guns or even rise to
their feet. Not a shot was fired in the course of the skirmish
which followed, and before long the brigands were wiped
out; all, that is, except Hendrik Hendriks himself and a
servant named Rolf Dikoor. These two men managed to
crawl unnoticed into the darkness and into the hollow
where the horses were kept.

Grabbing two mounts, Hendriks and Dikoor fled into the
night. The Basotho, dragging the corpses away from the
fire, sat down to feast. When dawn broke they stripped the
fallen Koranna of clothing, gathered up saddles, firearms,
karosses and utensils, rounded up the horses and returned
triumphantly to Thaba Bosiu.

Panic swept all Koranna settlements, Hendriks was condemned by the mourning widows, parents and friends of the
ill-fated band, and brigands everywhere accused him of neg-
ligence. Many threatened to kill him. The Griqua, a race of
half-breeds akin to the Koranna ridiculed him. No one
could accept the fact that seasoned *banditti*, mounted and
armed with muzzleloaders, could have been massacred by
clansmen bearing only assegais, battle-axes and sticks. Most
brigand leaders vowed to pluck the vulture, Moshesh, from
his hill-top perch. One hothead, a ruthless, *dagga*-ridden
Koranna named Pii, demanded immediate action, suggesting
that Thaba Bosiu be laid waste by a combined force of
Koranna and Griqua. Realizing, in due course, that no one
outside his own band was prepared to support him, he
called his commando together and set off north-westwards,
bound for Thaba Bosiu.

Pii reached the Lesotho one evening at dusk and pitched
camp in the valley not a mile from the Mokhachane pass.

Next morning at dawn, while his followers were saddling their horses, they were attacked by a powerful Basotho force led by Makwanyane. Most of them managed to mount and gallop away to safety, but several remained behind and were slain. When the sun rose the jubilant Basotho ransacked Pii's camp in search of loot. Jokingly they wished the yellow-skinned raiders would attack more often. How else was Moshesh to get horses and firearms for his army?

At the beginning of 1831 a commando of Koranna brigands, under Piet Witvoet, attacked Chief Moorosi's Baphuthi dispersing them and taking many of their cattle. Three days later the Baphuthi remustered, and locating the brigands on the banks of the Tele river, put them to flight. Moorosi and his men rounded up the stolen cattle and no less than a hundred abandoned horses. They also carried off a pile of firearms which they found concealed beneath a large *kaross*.

A fortnight later Piet Witvoet and his followers slunk into the Lesotho, and reaching a hill named Ntlokholo, west of Thaba Bosiu, climbed its rugged slopes to a sprawling cave where almost three hundred of Moshesh's choicest cattle were sheltered. After plucking off the herdsmen and driving the cattle into the valley below, the Koranna found themselves encircled by a Basotho force under Mopeli. Moshesh's brother. A blast of slug sent the Basotho reeling backwards. The Koranna charged, carved a bloody path through Mopeli's startled horde, and drove it up the hillside amidst the terrifying thunder of gun-fire. Soon Ntlokholo streamed with blood, and its slopes were strewn with corpses.

Suddenly the Koranna ceased fire, and collecting Moshesh's herd now scattered over the veld, moved westwards. Mopeli, nursing a shattered hand—one of his fingers had been shot away by a Koranna slug—called out to his followers to go into hiding. Not until an hour later when Piet Witvoet's band had disappeared in the haze of the western horizon did the Basotho venture down the hill. They returned crestfallen to Thaba Bosiu.

News of the devastation wrought by the Koranna on

Mopeli's force filled Moshesh with apprehension, for now
on the screen of his mind he could see hordes of yellow-
skinned horsemen storming the passes of Thaba Bosiu. He
could see their muzzleloaders spewing smoke and fire into
the ranks of the defenders of the hill. Thaba Bosiu, he told
his councillors, was no longer impregnable, and as long as
the Basotho were considered enemies by the Koranna, they
were doomed to destruction.

One day Moshesh sent envoys to visit the various
Koranna bands in their lairs, and to impress on their chiefs
his desire to pay them tribute in return for their friendship.
But the envoys never reached their destination. They were
captured and slain by Koranna brigands, in the vicinity of
Elandsberg. Moshesh tried repeatedly to solicit the Korannas' friendship, but as each attempt ended in failure, he
realized that in order to meet them on equal terms his
warriors would have to be armed with muzzleloaders and
mounted on horses.

It was at about this time that one of the army commanders reported that he knew of a friendly Griqua named
Adam Krotz, who could be persuaded to visit Thaba Bosiu,
and instruct the Basotho both in horsemanship and in the
use of firearms. Krotz, he said, had been seen hunting in the
neighbourhood, and he offered to fetch him. Moshesh was
delighted, and the commander set out for the Valley.

Adam Krotz was a cattle-breeder, hunter and casual
trader by profession, and lived in the vicinity of Philippolis,
a mission station situated immediately north of the Orange,
and superintended by a German named Kolbe. Considerably
darker in complexion and heavier in build than most of the
Griqua, he was a genial man, a devout Christian and an
elder of Kolbe's church. He was recognized both by his
kinsmen and the Colonial Boers as an astute hunter and
outstanding marksman. But he was essentially a peace-loving man, and branded all brigands, and especially Hendrik
Hendriks and Piet Witvoet as disciples of the devil. He believed they were destined to be destroyed by an army
inspired by God, and he predicted that their souls would
one day roast in the furnace of Hell. Krotz had often gone
to the rescue of defenceless clansmen against the Koranna
banditti. Little wonder that when visited by the Basotho

commander and told Moshesh wanted his advice, he called off his hunting and hastened to Thaba Bosiu.

Moshesh conceived an immediate liking for Adam Krotz. Calling to mind Hendriks and Witvoet he asked if the Griqua were as cunning and brutal as the Koranna, for they appeared to be identical people. Krotz said the Griqua were generally a law-abiding people, but he admitted that he knew of many who had joined forces with renegade Koranna, and had embarked on a career of brigandage. Known in the south as Bergenaars or Mountain Dwellers 'because they generally concealed themselves in the mountains with their booty', these ruffians spread terror not only among Sotho-speaking peoples of the Caledon Valley, but also among their own kinsmen, the peace-loving Griqua of Philippolis. He himself had never been molested by the Bergenaars or marauding Koranna and he attributed his good fortune to the protective hand of Almighty God.

'Without doubt it is because you have guns,' cried Moshesh, 'could you not get me some?'

'No,' replied Krotz, 'there is something better than that. We [the Griqua of Philippolis] have among us servants of God, who teach us to live well and fear evil. The Korannas fear them and trouble us no more. That is what you need, Moshesh, and not guns.'

These servants of God, Krotz explained, had come from a far-off land where the sun seldom shone. Their skins were not hard and dark like the people of the Valley, but as delicate and light as the nipples of a ewe goat in kid. They were 'friends of peace, disposed to do all in their power to aid' those who were downtrodden or 'in distress'. They were gentle, kindly folk who delighted in explaining the workings of the wondrous things they possessed. As a result of their influence the once destitute Griqua had become prosperous and enjoyed a great variety of amenities previously unknown among peoples of the interior. Krotz recommended the Moshesh should find similar people to settle among his subjects at Thaba Bosiu.

'Do you know any ... who would be disposed to come?' queried the chief, and when Krotz replied that missionaries sometimes visited Kolbe at Philippolis, Moshesh begged him

to persuade the first he encountered to visit him at Thaba
Bosiu.

'I will give them the best possible welcome,' he assured
the Griqua, 'I will do everything they advise me to do.'

Krotz spent a day and a night on the hill-top, and when
he took leave of Moshesh he was given a hundred head of
cattle with which to 'procure at least one missionary'.
Should he need two or even three hundred head, Moshesh
assured him, these would be sent without a moment's delay
to Philippolis.

In March Matabele scouts were spotted near the Phuthiastana river, and the Lesotho seethed with rumours of an
impending invasion by the tyrant, Mzilikazi. Three years
before, when he learned of Mzilikazi's victory over the
amaNgwane, Moshesh had rejoiced, but as time passed and
the Matabele became a threat to his own people, his jubi-
lance turned to anxiety. Indeed, by the Autumn of 1831
Mzilikazi had overrun and occupied most of the territory
stretching from the Vaal to the Limpopo. Moshesh knew
that in due course the tyrant's attention would be turned to
the peoples of the Caledon Valley.

Founder and supreme chief of the Matabele tribe, Mzilikazi was a conqueror in the pattern of Shaka, King of the
Zulu. In 1818 he had been a petty chieftain of the insignificant Northern Khumalo clanlet of Zululand, and fearing
extermination by Shaka's conquering army, had joined the
tyrant, taking some three hundred followers with him. By
1822 Mzilikazi had risen to the rank of a regimental commander in Shaka's army, and his gallantry in battle had
won him a host of privileges and the King's admiration and
friendship. In the following year he fled from Zululand
taking his followers with him, and he crossed the Drakensberg into what is today the Ermelo district.

Carving a path of blood northwards through the territories of several Sotho-speaking clans, Mzilikazi reached
the banks of the upper Olifants river. There in 1824 he built
an immense military kraal which he named ekuPumuleni,
the Place of Rest. In the following year he spread havoc
throughout the north-eastern Transvaal, subjugating Bapedi
clans, filling his regimental barracks with captive warriors

and his harems with captive maidens. In the Spring, he devastated the entire north-western Transvaal, and then suddenly he abandoned the Place of Rest, and moved his people westwards into the Magaliesberg area. Now he established a chain of military settlements extending from what is today the suburb of Pretoria north to the Limpopo river.

During the following six years Mzilikazi's power grew even more rapidly than before. His army, comprising mainly captives officered by Khumalo *indunas*, patrolled most of the Transvaal, part of the Free State and a belt of Rhodesian territory along the Limpopo. His scouts began reconnoitring the Caledon Valley as early as February 1831; those detected by Moshesh's people in March had eventually returned to their bloodthirsty master and reported having located Thaba Bosiu, stronghold of a prosperous people called the Basotho.

A Matabele army sent by Mzilikazi to destroy the Basotho and capture their stock, crossed the Caledon in April. It was sighted by Moshesh and his subjects one morning after sunrise—a noisy horde bearing huge, oval oxhide shields, stabbing spears and clubs and attired in distinctive, plumed headdresses, kilts of wild cat and monkey tails and light fur capes. 'Moshesh watched the regiments as they bivouacked on the banks of the Little Caledon or Phuthiastana river, as they bathed in the shallow waters, as they whetted their assegais and as they lined up towards sunset to take part in a prolonged series of war dances.'

When the shadows of night moved into the Valley, the Matabele lit fires forming a girdle of flickering flames in the centre of the bivouac. Meanwhile the Basotho Valley-folk had been streaming onto the hill-top, and while the warriors rested, some in the barracks and others behind the boulder-mounds lining and cresting the passes, Moshesh, together with his brothers, his sons, Makwanyane and other dignitaries gazed down on the enemy silhouetted against the glow of the fires.

The Matabele broke camp at dawn, and moved to an appointed place near Rafutho's kraal. At sunrise, after forming up in regiments, they started climbing the Khubelu

pass. The Basotho manning the boulder-mounds kept out of
sight. Their ears filled with the eerie drone of enemy voices
and the shuffle of feet in the passes below. Thirty minutes
later the Matabele reached the upper section of the hill
where suddenly the Khubelu enters a lofty weather-scarred
fissure draped in hanging shrubs, creepers and ferns.

Now for the first time, Moshesh's warriors revealed
themselves, as, from the vertical heights, they sent a
cascade of javelins plunging into the Matabele lines. The
boulders came next, a clanging mass of rolling basalt that
crushed the van of the invaders and sent survivors tumbling panic-stricken down the pass. The great majority of
the Matabele warriors managed to extricate themselves
and scamper down the lower slopes into the nearby
Valley.

The Matabele regimental commanders were frantic
with rage. They cursed and gesticulated, snatched the war
plumes from the heads of their men and trod them into
the dust. Cowardice would not be tolerated, they shouted,
and nothing must prevent their taking Moshesh's mountain and destroying the stone-rollers.[1]

The regiments regrouped. Again they moved up the
Khubelu pass.

'This second attempt to reach the summit of Thaba Bosiu
was insanely daring, but doomed to failure. The moment
the boulders started roaring down the pass, the Matabele
commanders called a retreat', and led their regiments away
from the hill to the spot where they had bivouacked the
night before. They decided to abandon the assault on Moshesh's stronghold, convinced it was impregnable, and that
by persevering longer they would expose the army to mass-
acre.

The Matabele spent the rest of the day and all night on
the banks of the Phuthiastana river. They had hoped the
Basotho would venture down the hill and attack them, but
they were obliged to listen, hour upon hour, to the irritating
strains of victory songs coming from the hill-top. Next
morning the bivouac was visited by a Basotho envoy bring-

[1] Becker, *Path of Blood,* p. 137.

ing greetings and a gift of cattle from Moshesh. The chief, said the stranger, wished to be counted among the allies and friends of the mighty Mzilikazi, and as a token of goodwill had sent some slaughter cattle in case the army became hungry during its long march back to the Magaliesberg. Moshesh expected nothing in return, except an assurance that he and his people would be left in peace.

According to pioneer missionary writers and tribal chroniclers, Mzilikazi, on learning of the repulse of his army and of Moshesh's friendly gesture, decided to exclude the Lesotho from his forthcoming marauding expeditions. He realized Thaba Bosiu was impregnable, and could see no point in risking a second attack on the stronghold.

PART TWO

CHAPTER TEN

FRENCHMEN AT THABA BOSIU

Moshesh sends more cattle to Adam Krotz—First contacts with white men—Casalis, Arbousset and Gosselin leave France, bound for Africa—They are taken by Krotz to Thaba Bosiu

THE Winter of 1831 marked the beginning of an era of peace in the Lesotho. The harvest, although smaller than in previous years, was adequate for the needs of the Basotho, and the countryside teemed with their stock. New settlements sprang up in the valley, especially in the vicinity of Qilwane hill. Recent dangers had moulded the multiplicity of factions ruled by Moshesh into a small but resolute tribe. Strangers continued to arrive on the hill and offer allegiance in return for food, shelter and protection.

Although invariably his mind was occupied with the affairs of the tribe, there were times when Moshesh could think of nothing but the missionary Krotz had promised to bring him. So far the arrangement with the Griqua had been fraught with difficulties. The one hundred cattle he had given him had been stolen near Philippolis by Danster, a Koranna outlaw. He had sent twenty more, but these had fallen into the hands of the Bushmen. Finally despite opposition from his father and the councillors, he had sent an additional thirty, but not only were these stolen again by Bushmen, but the herdboys were found slain, their bodies riddled with arrow wounds. Krotz, the councillors assured him, was no more trustworthy than Hendriks, Witbooi, Danster or any of the half-caste brigands. Moshesh brooded. If Krotz were to deceive him, he would find some other way of luring white men to Thaba Bosiu.

Moshesh was destined to meet white men far sooner than he had expected, but they were Colonial Boers, and not mis-

sionaries as he had hoped. Told in June that Boer horsemen
had been spotted north of the Caledon, he mounted his
chestnut mare and accompanied by sixteen warriors set off
to meet them. He located the white men roughly midway
between presentday Ladybrand and Platberg, in a dreary
valley where 'delayed, tumble-down kraals', and skeletons
of *difaqane* victims 'lay scattered in all directions'.[1]

It is a pity that no written record was made of the discussions that followed between Moshesh and the hunters.
Apparently he described to them the hardships suffered by
his people at the hands of the Koranna and other brigand
bands, and begged them to help him drive them across the
Orange, whence they had come. But the Boers refused,
explaining that they were prohibited by the laws of the
Colony from entering into squabbles with non-white
peoples. The Cape was British territory, and was ruled by
King William of England. They would be severely punished
if they sided with the Basotho in battle.

Moshesh and the Boers are said also to have discussed
hunting, barter, cattle-breeding and the misery suffered by
peoples of the interior in the time of *difaqane*. When the
time came for parting, Moshesh said he hoped that the trail
between the Colony and Thaba Bosiu would be kept open
for further visits by white men. Given a woollen cap and a
jacket by the hunters, he bade them a hearty farewell, and
mounting his mare, moved slowly out of camp followed by
his retinue.

Summer arrived and passed without word from Adam
Krotz, and Moshesh began to believe he would never have
missionaries at Thaba Bosiu. Towards the end of 1832 came
the news he had long awaited. Two parties of strangers
each headed by a white man were approaching the Lesotho.

Seidensticker, a German adventurer, was the first to
reach Thaba Bosiu. Dressed immaculately in riding
breeches, spurred boots, an ornamented jacket and hunting
cap, he delighted Moshesh with a description of the way of
life pursued by white men both at the Cape and abroad.
Most interesting, according to Moshesh, was a demonstra-
tion he gave in pistol shooting. But the German did not

[1] Testimony of H. J. Cronje: Theal, *BR* ii.

remain long on the hill-top, and taking leave of the chief, presented him not with a firearm, as Moshesh had hoped, but with the hunting cap he was wearing. Seidensticker also undertook to use what little influence he had at Philippolis, to find a missionary for the Basotho.

The second white man, Martin by name, arrived on foot soon after the German's departure, for his horse had been killed by lions. Nothing worthy of note is known of his meeting with Moshesh, except that he presented the chief with what must have seemed to the Basotho an extraordinary gift—an umbrella. After leaving Thaba Bosiu, both Martin and Seidensticker vanished, and were never heard of again. Although in Colonial circles they were generally thought to have been slain by hostile tribesmen, some citizens of Cape Town believed they had been murdered by Moshesh.

For a moment we must leave Moshesh and Thaba Bosiu, and picture a small English brig, gliding silently southwards through the Straits of Dover, on a misty morning in November 1832. Among the few passengers aboard were two youthful French missionaries of the Paris Evangelical Missionary Society—twenty-two-year-old Eugene Casalis and his former classmate, Thomas Arbousset. They were accompanied by a tall, brawny carpenter named Constant Gosselin.

Three months before, Casalis and Arbousset had been attending classes at the Mission House in Paris, a training centre for aspirant missionaries. Told they would be sent to join the French missionaries, Lemue, Rolland and Pellissier in South Africa, they began studying Dutch, the language of the Boers, as well as the habits and beliefs of the Hottentot and Bantu peoples. In October they had been ordained as ministers, and bidding their families farewell had hastened to England where they boarded the *Test* at Gravesend.

Casalis and Arbousset reached Cape Town in February 1833, and were taken to the home of the world-renowned negrophile, the controversial Dr. John Philip, superintendent of the London Missionary Society in South Africa. Middle-aged, tall and corpulent, Phillip welcomed the Frenchmen to the Cape, and lost no time in describing the

races of the country to them, as well as the hardships they
would have to endure as future teachers of God.

In the two weeks they stayed with Philip, Casalis and
Arbousset explored the historical sights of Cape Town, and
they took special interest in its non-white racial groups—
the Negro slaves, jet-black, flat-nosed and frizzy-haired; the
pallid, long-vested Malays and the yellow-skinned Hottentots 'grotesquely clad in sheepskins' and 'breeches of dirty
leather, stiffened by rain and sun'. Contact with 'these poor
wretches' filled them with happy anticipation for the career
awaiting them in the far interior. Not even the entreaties of
their friendly host could persuade them to remain longer
than a fortnight in Cape Town.

Boarding an east bound vessel Casalis, Arbousset and the
carpenter, Gosselin, reached Port Elizabeth six days later.
Thence they set out by ox-wagon for Philippolis. After a
long, arduous journey through the semi-desert regions of
the Great Karroo, they reached their destination, the
station of the German missionary, Kolbe.

'Without knowing it,' wrote Casalis in his diary, 'we had
reached the place and the hour where God was about to
reveal the field of labour He had destined for us.' For no
sooner had Casalis, Arbousset and Gosselin reached Philippolis, than they were introduced to the Griqua, Adam
Krotz, who in turn suggested they should settle at Thaba
Bosiu, stronghold of Chief Moshesh, founder of the Basotho tribe. Told of the promise Krotz had made to find
missionaries for the chief, the Frenchmen asked to be taken
to Thaba Bosiu.

Early one morning, about two months later Adam Kortz
arrived at Kolbe's mission station, and told the Frenchmen
to prepare for the journey northwards. Loading a wagon
with food, clothes, bedding, tools, tents and other essentials,
and leaving another packed with goods in Kolbe's care, the
missionaries joined Krotz's party and the journey started.
During the following two weeks they travelled through
what they considered enchanting country—unending expanses of grassland teaming with lion, antelope and zebra.
At the end of the third week they reached Thaba Nchu, the
Black Hill, on whose summit was situated the capital village

of Moseme, chief of one of the Barolong clans.

Moseme, a vassal of Chief Moshesh, 'a fine-looking man some fifty years of age' came down from the hill to welcome Krotz and the missionaries, and he sent messengers to Thaba Bosiu with news of their arrival. After a short rest at Thaba Nchu the travellers moved on, and two days later they were delighted to behold a small party of Basotho horsemen galloping towards them. Heading the group were Moshesh's sons, Letsie and Molapo, their naked torsos glistening in the midday sun, and the leopardskin cloaks, strapped around their necks, floating behind them on the wind.

The meeting between the missionaries and the Basotho was cordial but brief. Moshesh, said Letsie, was anxiously awaiting their arrival at Thaba Bosiu.

The 28th of June 1833 was regarded by Moshesh in later life as the most momentous day in the early history of the Basotho tribe. For this was the day he met Eugene Casalis, the young Frenchman destined to become his friend, confidant and mentor. Riding ahead of the rest of the party Casalis, Krotz and a handful of Griqua reached Thaba Bosiu in the morning, and led to the summit by Letsie, they were hailed by hundreds of cheering tribesmen, some beating drums and others firing muzzleloaders. Suddenly they were caught up in the surge of the throng, and whisked away along the path leading to Moshesh's kraal.

On arrival at the huts Casalis beheld row upon row of semi-naked dancers led by a squat, gorilla-like figure grotesquely attired in an enormous headdress of ostrich plumes and a voluminous skin-mantle. This was Rasebela, a praise singer said to be possessed by an idiot. As he rushed towards the strangers, stick in hand, and growling and snarling like an angry dog, the crowd moved backwards, and forming a huge semicircle, gathered around a lone figure seated close by on a woven mat.

'There is Moshesh,' cried Adam Krotz.

The chief eyed his visitors with 'a look that was at once majestic and benevolent. ... His profile, his well-developed forehead, the fullness and regularity of his features, his eyes, a little weary, as it seemed, but full of intelligence and softness, made a deep impression' on the missionary. Casalis felt 'at once' that he 'had to do with a superior man, trained to think, to command others, and above all himself. He appeared about forty-five years of age. The upper part of his body, entirely naked, was perfectly modelled, sufficiently fleshy, but without obesity.'

Casalis 'admired the graceful lines of the shoulders and the fineness of his hand. He, Moshesh, had allowed to fall carelessly round him, from his middle, a large mantle of panther leopard skins as lissom as the finest cloth, and the folds of which covered his knees and feet. For the sole ornament he had bound round his forehead a string of glass beads, to which was fastened a tuft of feathers, which floated behind the neck. He wore on his arm a bracelet of ivory—an emblem of power—and some copper rings on his wrists.'

'Welcome white man!' the chief exclaimed as Casalis drew near, and taking Krotz by the hand thanked him for keeping his promise. Moshesh returned to his woven mat and the missionary sat down beside him.

Viewing the picturesque confusion of warriors, elders and menials about him Eugene Casalis chuckled delightedly. He and his companions, he told himself, would be eternally indebted to Almighty God, by whose grace they had found their niche in Africa—Thaba Bosiu, stronghold of the great Moshesh, founder and chief of the Basotho tribe.

Through the medium of an interpreter Moshesh enquired repeatedly after Casalis's health, and asked him to recount the highlights of the journey he and his friends had just completed. In due course he dominated the conversation with topics of a trivial nature, and rising suddenly beckoned the Frenchman and Krotz to follow him. Immediately Rasebela, the praise-singer, leapt high into the air, yelping like a dog in pain. Plunging into the dust, at Moshesh's feet, he leapt again into the air, flung himself into a frenzied dance, and 'vociferating with incredible volubility certain rhythmic words' called upon the spirits to preserve his chief from harm. By this time Moshesh, Casalis and Krotz had left him far behind, and were strolling leisurely through the kraal, so to the amusement of the spectators Rasebela, imitating the movements of a monkey, went capering after them.

Casalis's first impressions of Moshesh's kraal are worthy of note. He described it as 'a mass of low huts, around which people circulated by narrow lanes encumbered with children and dogs'. The cattlefold, far larger than others he had seen during his journey 'was divided into enclosures, whose stone walls, perfectly circular, showed a certain talent in construction'. He recognized the *kgotla* at a glance, and then his eyes fell on the great hut of Moshesh's senior wife, Mamohato. It was 'a little higher than most and more spacious than the others', and was situated in the centre of a palisaded courtyard.

Moshesh led his guests towards Mamohato's home, and reaching the gates of the enclosure proudly drew Casalis's attention to a group of 'thirty to forty' of his 'inferior wives' who had gathered to greet him. Entering the courtyard Casalis found Mamohato stoking a fire beside the entrance of her hut. She told them to be seated on mats spread out on the cowdung floor, and sent two elderly female servants to fetch them some sorghum bread. Casalis found the large, spherical loaves difficult to handle, but he ate with relish, pausing occasionally to thank Mamohato for her kind hospitality.

'Mamohato was a tall and strong woman already of some ripe age,' Casalis reflected, 'but not wanting in attractions. Her physiognomy expressed goodness; the expression with which she looked at me seemed to say that she found me very young, and that she was happy to mother me a little.' It pleased him to see that she and her husband were devoted to each other. While they were chatting they frequently exchanged smiles, and they fingered the chubby little hands of their infant son, Ntalime, who sat between them.

Barely twenty minutes after entering Mamohato's enclosure, Casalis was told that his colleagues, Arbousset and Gosslin, had arrived with the wagons at the bottom of the Khubelu pass. Reluctantly he bade Mamohato farewell, promising to visit her again, and taking leave of Moshesh threaded his way through the kraal, followed the footpath to the Khubelu pass, and slipped down the hill.

About two hours later, having pitched camp and un-
loaded the wagons, Casalis and Arbousset were visited by
Moshesh, Makwanyane, Ratsiu and several other dignitaries.
Welcoming Arbousset and Gosselin, the chief inspected
their fascinating possessions, declaring that they filled his
heart with envy. He remained at the camp for almost an
hour, and when he left, he promised to come back on the
morrow.

Towards sunset the missionaries were visited by menials
bearing food from Moshesh for the entire camp, including
Krotz's escort. They were touched by the chief's generosity
and thoughtfulness. Moshesh, genial and gentle ruler of the
Basotho, was a child of God.

During the night black, leaden clouds rose in the east and
drifted over Thaba Bosiu. A chilly wind sprang up, and was
followed first by gentle rain and then by sleet. Snow started
falling an hour before daybreak, and continued throughout
the next two days and nights. On the morning of the third
day when the missionaries awoke, they found the snow-clad
countryside glistening in the slanting rays of a brilliant sun.
Thaba Bosiu, blanketed in white, stood out majestically
against the azure of a cloudless sky.

At about noon Casalis and Arbousset caught sight of
Moshesh at the top of the Khubelu pass. A little later his
messengers arrived with more food for them. Moshesh,
Makwanyane and Ratsiu came down the hill next day and
shared a meal with the Frenchmen in Casalis's tent.

'The repast consisted of hashed mutton, with pumpkin,
and several bowls of coffee, Casalis recalled in later years.
He had forgotten to bring plates from the Cape, and had
dished Moshesh's food onto a saucepan lid. 'What a way
of treating the poor black race even when represented by
one of the most distinguished of its chiefs,' he added.
Moshesh ate with relish, but when given some coffee, he
was put off by its murky colour and refused to drink it.
Then venturing a sip, he found 'the beverage repulsive', but
after 'some handfuls of raw sugar' had been added by
Casalis, he gulped it down. With a smack of his lips he
'inquired very particularly as to the source of this priceless

sand, the taste of which, he declared, was better than that of the most delicious honey'.

When the meal was over, Krotz reminded Moshesh of their first meeting on Thaba Bosiu.

'Here,' he said, 'are the men whom I promised you; it is for them to explain to you their plans and to arrange matters with you.'

Moshesh was grinning happily now. The white men, he said, had brought relief to his overburdened heart and he hoped they had come to live permanently with him and his subjects.

Casalis spoke up. He and his colleagues, he assured the chief, would be happy to settle in the Lesotho. Moshesh had been wise in seeking the companionship of missionaries, and provided the Basotho placed themselves in the hands of Almighty God, they would be rewarded not only with eternal peace, but also with 'a new order of belief and of manners which would secure tranquillity, order and abundance'.

'My heart is white with joy,' replied Moshesh, 'your words are great and good. It is enough for me to see your clothing, your arms, and the rolling houses wagons in which you travel, to understand how much intelligence and strength you have. You see our desolation. This country was full of inhabitants. Wars have devastated it. Multitudes have perished; others are refugees in foreign lands. I remain almost alone on this rock [Thaba Bosiu]. I have been told you can help us. You promise to do it. That is enough. It is all I want to know. We will do all you wish. The country is at your disposal. We can go through it together, and you shall choose the place which will best suit you.'

At that moment Moshesh's eyes filled with tears, and his voice became throaty. The Frenchmen were truly messengers of God. They had been sent to lead the Basotho out of the darkness of ignorance into a new world of enlightenment.

CHAPTER ELEVEN

MORIJA

Moshesh helps the Frenchmen choose a site for a mission station—Morija is founded—Casalis returns to Philippolis and is intercepted by Danster, the brigand—He delivers a sermon at Thaba Bosiu and is challenged by Moshesh's councillors—Moshesh is not impressed by the Ten Commandments—Wesleyan missionaries settle near Moshesh's domain—Sir Andrew Smith's expedition visits the Lesotho

DURING the first week in July 1833, after the snow had thawed, the Frenchmen broke camp, and loading their wagons set out accompanied by Moshesh, Makwanyane and a body of warriors in search of a site for a mission station. Travelling south-eastwards along a narrow, rutted cattle track, they lumbered across grassy plains and shallow treeless valleys. Reaching a chain of low, flat-topped hills they bumped through *dongas* and dried-up ravines, some of whose shaded depths were still dusted with snow. The countryside, moist and fresh after the thaw, basked in a mellow Winter's sun. Moshesh was jubilant. Mounted on his chestnut mare he could be seen talking now with Casalis, now with Arbousset and now with Adam Krotz. On a few occasions when game roused by the warriors appeared near the wagons, he galloped away, and flinging his hunting-spear 'with astonishing precision and power' brought down some excellent specimens which he then had collected and dismembered.

On 9 July the wagons followed by the horsemen and footmen entered the Makhoarane district, and creeping through a narrow, wooded valley swarming with game, came to the base of a low range of rocky hills. Casalis called a halt. The missionaries, he cried, had no need to travel farther, for surely this was the most beautiful spot in all Moshesh's domain. Here they would settle and toil, and if necessary, die in the cause of Christianity. This place would be called Morija, the Lord Provides.

After helping to unload the wagons and pitch camp beneath a cluster of thorntrees, Adam Krotz took leave of Moshesh and the missionaries, and departed with his escort for Philippolis. Two days later Moshesh returned with his retinue to Thaba Bosiu, and the three Frenchmen, their wagon drivers and servants began work on the first missionary home to be erected on Basotho soil.

'It was to be nothing more than a cabin', wrote Casalis in his diary. Built mainly of staves and laths cut in the surrounding woods, it was 'a little larger than the huts of the natives, and in a few days it was completed'. The missionaries made beds of 'reeds placed upon four props driven into the ground ... and an old table and some trunks completed the furniture'. While finishing touches were being added to the roof of the cabin, Molapo, Moshesh's second eldest son, arrived with a squad of helpers. As he and his companions intended remaining some time at Morija, they erected huts for themselves in the bush close by.

As soon as the Frenchmen were settled at Morija, Casalis set out on horseback for Philippolis to fetch the wagon he and his colleagues had left with Kolbe. Along the way he came upon a commando of Koranna driving a herd they had lifted from Tamboekie territory beyond the Orange. Ordered to stop by the leader of the brigands, a foul-mouthed ruffian clothed in greasy skin-trousers, a skin-jacket and sandals, Casalis accused him of spreading terror and misery among the peoples of the interior. He was shouted down and cursed by the brigands, and for a moment he feared he would be put to death. Suddenly, to his great relief, the leader ordered the commando to move on, and poking a horse-whip into the Frenchman's chest, warned him to keep out of the affairs of the Koranna.

'We know that you are going to reside near Moshesh,' he bellowed, 'go and tell him that as soon as our horses are rested we are coming to attack him.'

Casalis spent a week at Philippolis, and taking leave of Kolbe brought the wagon back to Morija under escort of a commando led by Adam Krotz. Assisted by the Griqua he, Arbousset and Gosselin started laying out gardens. They planted wheat and vegetable seeds, as well as a variety of fruit trees given them by Kolbe. Soon afterwards Casalis, with the help of the workers sent by Moshesh, started 'to prepare the materials for a solid and spacious house, and those for a chapel'.

Unlike the Griqua who were invariably lethargic, unco-operative and quarrelsome, the Basotho worked diligently, competing with each other in spite of the fact that the Frenchmen had been ordered by Moshesh neither to reward them for services rendered, nor to 'spoil them with gifts'.

'If you do,' the chief had said, 'they will forget that you are our benefactors, that you are here not for your advantage, but for ours; and they will end by demanding that I also pay them to do anything for me.'

Krotz's men started begging and stealing, and they became so unpopular that when at length they returned to Philippolis, a celebration was held by the missionaries and Basotho at Morija.

Meanwhile some four hundred Basotho under Letsie had arrived at Morija with instructions from Moshesh to erect a kraal near the mission station, and settle there permanently. The Frenchmen were delighted. They could see their new chapel filled to capacity with potential converts.

The missionaries visited Thaba Bosiu at their first opportunity; they were loudly welcomed by the friendly Basotho and taken to Moshesh. The chief was so happy to see them that he fussed around them, and when they asked if they could conduct a service in the *kgotla*, he agreed, adding he had grown impatient waiting to hear them preach.

'Every time you come to teach us,' said Moshesh, 'I shall be there to get my people together, and to see that everybody listens to you with attention.'

The chief packed a huge congregation into the *kgotla*. The service, conducted by Casalis, was the missionaries' most uplifting spiritual experience since leaving France.

Moshesh loved his missionaries, and was quick to reprimand whoever dared criticize them. One day, for example, Casalis was extolling God's great wisdom in creating all men equal and 'of one blood' when suddenly he was challenged by the councillors.

'What!' exclaimed one of them, 'that can never be!' And

pointing to each of the missionaries in turn he cried: 'You are white; we are black; how could we come from the same father?'

'Stupids!' yelled Moshesh, 'In my herds are white, red and spotted cattle; are they not all cattle? do they not all come from the same stock, and belong to the same master?' What of albinos; were they not as worthy to be called Basotho as the blackest of his subjects?

'Black or white,' he continued, 'we laugh or cry in the same manner and from the same causes; what gives pleasure or pain to the one race, causes equally pleasure or pain to the other.' All people irrespective of colour or race were children of God. One God.

During a subsequent meeting with Moshesh and the councillors, Casalis recited the Ten Commandments, emphasizing their significance as a basis for moral behaviour. The chief was amused. There was nothing unique in these laws, he smiled teasingly, for the Basotho although unfamiliar with the white man's Christ knew 'it was very wicked to be ungrateful and disobedient to parents, to rob, to kill, to commit adultery, to covert the property of another, and to bear false witness'. Referring to the sixth commandment—'Thou shalt not kill'—he asked Casalis if the great white nations ever waged war. Told that they did, he feigned surprise. Surely then, he said, Christians must be hypocrites of the first order. The Basotho, he added mischievously, should then not be condemned for the bloody wars they had waged in the past. After all, what more could be expected from a people who since the beginning of time had lived side by side with savage beasts of prey?

For a moment Casalis searched for words. In the time of war, he told Moshesh, Christian soldiers fought not out of hatred for the foe, but out of loyalty to their country. Prisoners of war were not slain by their Christian captors, and the wounded were given medical attention. Moshesh chuckled. 'Then you work this evil without anger,' he gibed, 'mixing wisdom with it?' This he regarded as ridiculous.

Moshesh could never understand why Christians considered the practice of polygamy a sin. One day he challenged Casalis and Arbousset on the subject, but realizing that they were reluctant to enter into discussion with him, lest they cause him embarrassment, he assured them, tongue in cheek, that although 'notoriously the greatest polygamist in the country', he agreed entirely with Christians that one wife was as many as any man could manage.

'Women make us suffer,' he sighed, 'by their quarrels, and the rivalry which they foment amongst our children. Would you believe it,' he added, '[that] with all my herds and all my stocks of grain, there are days when I am in danger of dying of hunger because all my wives are sulking with me, sending me from one to the other, "until," say they, "you get to your favourite, who certainly ought to have a choice morsel for you!"' Women, continued the chief, were a source of frustration to men, and yet he realized they were indispensable. Who other than his wives would fetch his water, grind his corn or sweep his huts? Speaking seriously now, he assured the missionaries that although they might succeed one day in persuading the Basotho to forsake tribal custom, they would never succeed in turning them away from the practice of polygamy. This time-honoured institution, he added, could be likened to a great fortress—it was solid and indestructible.

Moshesh seemed never to tire of his missionaries' company, for even at nights he insisted that they visit him in Mamohato's hut. They would share a platter of beef or venison with him, followed by sorghum bread and curdled milk, and they would chat away until deep into the night, losing all track of time. Eventually, prodded by sleepiness, the Frenchmen would excuse themselves and retire to a hut set aside for them by the chief. They always slept soundly at Thaba Bosiu, despite the orchestration of noises that came out of the darkness—the remote grunting of lions, the coughing of leopards, the whistling of insects and the sing-song voice of Akhosi, the sentinel, announcing that all was well. They always rose at sunrise, for it was then that Moshesh would emerge from his hut and call out loudly, 'Ke bone leseli—I have seen the light'.[1]

Whenever the time came for their return to Morija, Moshesh would beg the missionaries to remain a little

[1] Apparently Moshesh adopted this habit during the *difaqane* wars. Night after night he expected to be slain in his sleep, so every morning on awaking he would greet the rising sun.

longer at Thaba Bosiu. Parting was always an ordeal, and usually the chief found a way to delay their departure. He would only condescend to their leaving when he could see their patience was exhausted. Then he would load their horses with provisions, and wishing them a safe journey, beg them to return soon to Thaba Bosiu. Casalis and Arbousset enjoyed each moment of the visits they paid to Moshesh. In their prayers they never ceased to thank God for the privilege of living and working in the domain of so wise and loving a ruler.

Towards the end of 1833 news reached Moshesh that some ten thousand Barolong, led by Chiefs Moroka, Tawana and Kgontshe, had arrived at Thaba Nchu, the Black Hill. Following closely on the Barolong's heels were three groups of half-breeds—some three hundred Koranna under Jan Hanto, two hundred Griqua under Peter Davids and two hundred Bastards under Carolus Baatje. Heading the entire throng were three white men, Archbell, Edwards and Jenkins, who until recently had superintended the Wesleyan mission stations, Old Boetsap and Platberg near the Vaal river. The Barolong and the half-breeds had been driven southwards by drought and threat of famine. They decided to settle in the country surrounding Thaba Nchu since it was sparsely populated and rich in pasturage.

Chief Moseme who lived with his impoverished followers on Thaba Nchu sent messengers to apprise Moshesh of developments. He refused to meet any of the newly arrived chiefs, and kept clear of the missionaries whose tents had been pitched not far from the footpath leading down from the hill.

When he learned of the strangers' arrival at Thaba Nchu, Moshesh became alarmed, fearing they might attempt to invade the Lesotho. But told they were accompanied by their missionaries, he sent messengers to Casalis and Arbousset with a request that they investigate the situation on his behalf. Later, at their recommendation, he gave permission for the strangers to remain permanently at Thaba Nchu in return for some cattle, sheep and goats. He even drew a cross at the foot of a document giving the Wesleyan missionaries and their charges exclusive owner-

ship over specified tracts of land. He was happy at the
thought that three more white men should choose to settle
so close to Thaba Bosiu. Before long he learned that the
Wesleyans were building four new mission stations for their
followers—New Platberg for the Bastards, Merumetsu for
the Koranna, Lishuane for the Griqua and the Thaba Nchu
station for the Barolong. Told in July 1834 that the Wesleyans had founded a fifth station called Imparani in the
territory of the Wild Cat People, Moshesh was offended. He
said he had been led to believe they would devote their
labours solely to the hordes they had brought from Old
Platberg and Boetsap, and whom he now considered his
vassals. Not once had they mentioned settling near his
enemy, Sikonyela.

On 13 October Moshesh received news from Casalis that
a convoy of wagons, accompanied by thirteen white men
and a large body of Hottentots had arrived at Morija. Next
morning, dressed in European clothes given him by Arbousset, he set out for the mission station at the head of a party
of horsemen. Arriving there during the late afternoon, he
ordered his men to fire their muzzleloaders in salute. Casalis and Arbousset came out of the mission house followed
by the leader of the visiting white men, Dr. Andrew Smith,[1]
whom they presented to the chief and his party. Moshesh
took Smith by the hand.

'My heart,' he said, 'is full of joy.'

The chief, the missionaries and the visiting white men
spent a happy afternoon together, exchanging anecdotes in
the shade of the thorntrees. In the evening they dined together in the doctor's tent.

'[Moshesh's] demeanour at table was most respectable,'
wrote Smith in his diary later that night, 'he kept constantly

[1] Later Sir Andrew Smith K.C.B., Director-General of the
Medical Department of the British Army. At the time of his
visit to the Lesotho, he was the leader of a scientific expedition
organized by the Association for the Exploration of Central
Africa, to collect information about the peoples, geographical
features, flora and fauna and natural resources of central South
Africa.

handing portions of food to a few of his retainers who were
seated round the door of the tent. He complimented us
upon our taste in cooking, and said the English food was
good.'

After dinner Moshesh, an accomplished narrator, en-
thralled the white men 'with a history of the misfortunes of
himself and [his] people'. Smith found him fascinating
company, and chuckled inwardly at his 'rather awkward'
appearance 'in European clothing'. Moshesh's jacket was so
large and heavy that he could barely bend his arms, and for
most of the time was obliged to hold them stiffly at his
sides.

On the following morning, 15 October, the chief had an
ox slaughtered and dismembered, and distributed it among
the white men and their servants. He had breakfast with
Casalis and Smith in the mission house, and during the rest
of the day roamed about Morija with them, enjoying every
moment of their company and responding to Smith's occasional witticisms with hearty laughter.

Moshesh went hunting eland on the 16th, and on his
return to Morija during the late afternoon, he found Danster, the ill-famed Koranna brigand awaiting him. Moshesh
hated this cutthroat. Poking him in the chest with a sjambok, he asked him what he wanted at Morija.

Cringing before the chief, the brigand said he was the
bearer of unhappy tidings. South-east of Morija, he continued, in the vicinity of the Orange river lived a small
colony of Basotho whose leader, a relative of Moshesh, had
long been regarded as a prosperous and friendly patriarch.
In recent times, however, this man had undertaken a series
of cattle-raids into Xhosa territory. As success had followed
success, he had become so avaricious that eventually he and
his robber band had raided a Boer farm in the Cape Colony,
driving off cattle and horses. Pursued by a Boer commando
they had been overtaken and butchered. Moshesh's relative
had managed to escape, but was heavily wounded. That was
why he, Danster, had come to Morija. He had come to
conduct Moshesh to the wounded man's hideout.

Moshesh considered his relative's dilemma with cold
indifference. This man, he told the brigand, had deserved to
be punished and was not worth visiting. If anyone should be

comforted, he added facetiously, it was the Boer whose
cattle and horses had been stolen. Calling Casalis, Moshesh
had him write to the Boer 'to inform him of his sorrow for
the circumstances, and that he would take care to prevent
such occurrences in the future'. Always suspicious of Danster's duplicity, the chief turned again to him and told him
to get out of Morija. There was no place for a polecat
among human beings.

Andrew Smith's assessment of Moshesh's character,
especially as compared with other tribal rulers he had met
in the course of his travels, is worthy of repetition. He saw
in the chief a kindly person imbued with uncommon insight
into human relationships. He marvelled at the reverence
shown to Moshesh by his subjects despite his gentle, un-
assuming and convivial disposition. Most tribal potentates
ruled by fear, Smith reflected, commanding the allegiance
of their subjects under a constant threat of death. His mind
harked back to 1832, when he had visited Dingane, King of
the Zulu: He saw Dingane as a ruthless despot, one who
thought nothing of 'murdering, torturing and destroying
even hundreds of his own subjects in the course of one day'.
Smith had been unable to muster even the slightest 'attach-
ment for such a monster'.

Moshesh, on the other hand, had won the doctor's
admiration from almost the first moment of their meeting.
This chief was in every way superior to Dingane. In fact he
was superior to all chiefs so far visited by the expedition.

Moshesh decided to return home on Saturday 18 October,
and taking leave of Smith and his party, insisted they call in
at Thaba Bosiu before proceeding northwards, as planned,
to the realm of Mzilikazi, King of the Matabele. Smith's
impending visit to the tyrant troubled Moshesh, for news
had just reached him that a Griqua hunting party had been
massacred by a Matabele patrol. Peter Davids, leader of the
ill-fated hunters, had got away, but the Matabele had kid-
napped Truey, his daughter, and Willem, his nephew. Moshesh pleaded with Smith not to venture north of the Vaal
river, but realizing the doctor was determined to meet
Mzilikazi, he advised him never to permit the Matabele
closer than a javelin throw from the wagon. The Matabele

were unpredictable people, and might attack without provocation.

Smith dismissed Moshesh's warnings, concluding that as the chief had once been exposed to the horrors of *difaqane*, his mind was plagued by a lingering fear of enemies both actual and imaginary. Moshesh was a man of indisputable calibre, but his judgment of tribal rulers could not be considered reliable.

The expedition, accompanied by Casalis, left Morija on the following Monday, and reaching Thaba Bosiu on the morning of Wednesday the 22nd, pitched camp near the Khubelu pass. Casalis and Smith were summoned by Moshesh in the afternoon, and were met halfway up the pass by a body of warriors, many of whom were heavily marked with battle scars. More warriors joined them on the summit, and in the vicinity of Moshesh's kraal they were mobbed by youths and maidens, some singing and others dancing.

Inside the settlement Smith and Casalis were hailed from every side, and as they strode to the *kgotla* where Moshesh awaited them, their ears filled with the thud of drums and the yapping of dogs. Brought before Moshesh, Smith explained that he had come not only to pay his respects to the great chief of the Hill at Night, but also to deliver a parcel sent him by the governor of the Cape Colony, Sir Benjamin D'Urban. Taking a medallion attached to a delicate chain from a casket, the doctor hung it round Moshesh's neck. It was to serve as a symbol of friendship, he said, between the Basotho and the people of the Colony. Fingering the gift, his eyes streaming tears of happiness, Moshesh addressed the *kgotla* 'with great feeling'.

In recent months he said, he, chief of the Basotho, had been condemned by some of his elders and councillors for permitting the settlement of white men at Morija and north of the Caledon. Foremost among his critics was his own father, Mokhachane, who feared and hated all strangers, and who considered Casalis, Arbousset and Gosselin as evil men sent by sorcerers to destroy the Basotho. This was ridiculous and wrong, he cried, for who but the Frenchmen had opened the road travelled by Smith and his party, and who but they had 'called forth the friendship and sympathies' of such eminent men as Sir Benjamin D'Urban? Henceforth the missionaries would be honoured and obeyed by all, for they alone could purge the Basotho of the time-worn 'notions and prejudices' which stood in the way of their advancement. Smith, he concluded, could continue his journey knowing that Moshesh, chief of the Basotho, welcomed all law-abiding white men to Thaba Bosiu.

CHAPTER TWELVE

THE GREAT TREK

Moshesh fears an attack by Danster's commando—A Basotho force secretly goes in search of the Koranna, and is intercepted by Moshesh—Moshesh leads an army against the Tamboekies—The Trekkers arrive— They clash with the mighty Matabele

THE new house at Morija was completed during the early Summer. Arbousset visited Cape Town in January 1835, and Gosselin moved temporarily to Bethulie near the Orange, a mission station in the charge of a Frenchman named Jean Pellissier. Casalis was alone with the Hottentots and Letsie's subjects at Morija.

One evening in February a messenger arrived at Morija with news from Moshesh that a Koranna commando, presumably led by the notorious Danster, had been spotted near Thaba Bosiu. Fetching his horse Casalis set off to confer with Moshesh. He reached the hill-top after midnight where he found the chief and his commanders 'in great consternation'. They were expecting the brigands to attack in the morning. However, scouts arrived at sunrise to report that although they had scoured the surroundings for two days, they had found no sign of the Koranna. Moshesh had been misinformed. Greatly relieved the chief and his commanders retired to their huts to sleep. Casalis, his eyes heavy with fatigue, jogged back to Morija. He arrived at the mission house just before sunset and went to bed.

That night, no sooner had he dozed off, than he was roused by a violent banging on the kitchen door. 'Open,' cried a voice, 'light a candle quickly, the Koranna are upon us, and this time we are dead men if we do not defend ourselves.'

Imagining for a moment that Thaba Bosiu had been taken and Moshesh slain, Casalis flung open the door. Before him stood a councillor, his face screwed up with fear and his hands trembling violently. Questioned by the mis-

sionary, the councillor confessed that neither he nor any of
his colleagues had actually seen the Koranna. He had just
come from a diviner named Theko, whose magic bones had
revealed an impending clash between the Basotho and Koranna. He had therefore come to alert Casalis and his
people. Casalis chuckled good-humouredly. He advised the
councillor to banish all fear from his mind. God, he said,
would protect the Basotho from harm.

About a week later Eugene Casalis emerged from his
house to find the men of the mission station preparing for
battle. Some were sharpening assegai blades, some repairing
war regalia and several others were decorating their faces
with white, yellow, red and grey clay as was the custom on
the eve of a battle. Letsie and Molapo arrived with a large
platoon bearing assegais, shields and clubs. Most of the men
wore antelope or leopard skin capes, and their heads were
adorned with multicoloured plumes. Questioned by Casalis,
Letsie and Molapo explained that they were accompanying
their warriors on a hunting expedition. At about midday the
entire force moved off, cheering, whistling, whooping and
chanting as it filed past the mission house.

News of these events reached Moshesh by messenger late
that night, and at dawn next morning he set out on horseback for Morija. On arrival at the mission house the chief,
catching sight of Casalis, flew into a rage, and storming into
the kitchen flung himself into a chair.

'What have you done with my children?' he growled,
staring menacingly at the missionary.

'They have gone hunting,' replied Casalis.

'What!' exploded the chief, 'gone ahunting? They have
gone against the Korannas. My sons have deceived me.'

Moshesh buried his face in his hands and wept.

'Let us go after them,' he pleaded, 'come with me; you
are their father; they will obey you, and you will bring them
back by gentle means.'

At first Casalis was reluctant to accompany Moshesh for
there were many jobs at the mission station requiring urgent
attention. In any case, he felt that Moshesh alone should
settle what was in fact, a domestic affair. But told by the
chief that a force of four hundred warriors was standing by,

poised to attack should Letsie's column refuse to return, Casalis agreed to go. He would use whatever influence he had to prevent the spilling of blood.

Moshesh, Casalis and a small retinue of horsemen headed south-westwards during the afternoon, and towards sunset next day caught up with Letsie's force camped on a hill-slope. Dismounting beside a shallow stream the chief sent a messenger to summon Letsie and Molapo, while he himself knelt at the water's edge to drink. At that moment some scouts who he had sent to reconnoitre the area arrived, but instead of reporting promptly to their chief, they hung around the horsemen gossiping with them as if unaware of Moshesh's presence. Moshesh waited impatiently, then suddenly he jumped to his feet, 'his eyes flashing with rage', and drawing a pistol, fired it 'point-blank' at one of the scouts. Luckily the weapon misfired, and was snatched from his hand by a warrior before he could fire a second shot.

The scouts fled. Captured a few minutes later and brought before him, Moshesh first ordered their execution, but on second thoughts had them flogged instead. The chief was in an ugly mood. Eventually when Letsie and Molapo appeared he ordered them to return without a moment's delay to Morija. He would deal with them there.

About twenty minutes later the chief's two sons crossed the stream, followed by their warriors and set out for home. They resented Moshesh's interference in their affairs, for he had denied them the opportunity of defeating the Koranna and gaining recognition as military leaders. What riled Letsie most was the fact that his father had belittled him in the presence of Casalis and the warriors.

That night as Moshesh and his missionary friend sat at a camp fire beside the stream sipping coffee, a scout arrived with news that the Sixth Frontier war had been declared in the Cape Colony. A British army was advancing swiftly into Xhosa territory.

'What do you think,' said Moshesh to Casalis, 'if I were to aid the king of the white men to reduce them [the Xhosa] to subjection?'

Casalis looked at the chief incredulously.

'My sons [Letsie and Molapo],' continued Moshesh,
'have as yet no renown; they wish to distinguish themselves
in war; and it seems to me that present circumstances
afford an excellent opportunity of ensuring for myself the
friendship of the white people, and of gratifying the desire
of my sons.'

Casalis was shocked. The chief and his sons, he retorted,
had no right to interfere in the political affairs of the
Colony. By taking part in the conflict they would merely
involve the Basotho in unnecessary bloodshed and heartache, and reduce them to poverty.

The matter was pursued no further. Moshesh and his
party returned to Morija on the following morning.

By the time he reached the mission station Moshesh's
anger had disappeared, and instead of reprimanding Letsie
and Molapo he forgave them. Two days later he set out for
home, and arriving on the hill-top, he learned that a herd of
cattle pastured by him near the Orange had been lifted by
Tamboekie raiders. Next morning, heading a force of two
thousand warriors, some of whom were mounted, he struck
out southwards, reaching Tamboekie territory four days
later. During the following two days they razed eight of the
largest Tamboekie kraals to the ground, dispersing the inhabitants and capturing some four thousand head of cattle.
On the morning of the third day they captured over three
thousand sheep and goats, and in the afternoon they set off
homewards.

Meanwhile the Tamboekies had mustered in the hills and
were following Moshesh's force at a distance. At nightfall
they bypassed the spot where the Basotho were encamped,
and took up positions in a chasm close by. Next morning at
dawn the Tamboekies silently encircled the raiders, and
attacked at sunrise just after Moshesh and his councillors
had mounted their horses. Leaping quickly to the ground
the chief joined his men in hand-to-hand combat against the
Tamboekies. The horses reared and bolted, the booty cattle
deserted by their herdsmen, scattered, and Moshesh, realizing suddenly that the Basotho were about to be cut down by
a blast of poisoned arrows, fled with his followers into the
hills.

1 Eugene Casalis, founder of the French Evangelical Mission Station at Thaba Bosiu. He played a dominant role in Moshesh's career.

2 Evening service at the Morija Mission Station, 1834.

3 Basotho War Dance on Thaba Bosiu, in honour of Sir Andrew Smith, 1834.

4 A Boer commando on patrol in the vicinity of Moshesh's domain.

5 Sir Harry Smith, High Commissioner of the British Cape Colony, 1847-1852. Moshesh found his eccentricities entertaining, but was both baffled and annoyed by his extreme impetuosity.

6 Sir George Cathcart leading the British into battle against Moshesh's army in 1852.

7 Josias Hoffman, first president
of the Orange Free State.

8 Moshesh at the age of seventy-four.

The Khubelu Pass taken by the author from the summit of Thaba Bosiu. Rocks used by Moshesh's forces for hurling onto approaching enemies can be seen on either side of the pass.

10 Sir George Cathcart at the time of the British invasion of the Lesotho.

11 Advocate Jan Hendrik Brand, president of the Free State Republic during the twilight of Moshesh's life.

12 The Boer hero – Louw Wepener (*left*) a few years before he was slain on the slopes of Moshesh's stronghold. Photographed with him is his son.

13 An artist's impression of the Khubelu Pass during the second Boer-Basotho war.

14 The author identifying the graves of Basotho dignitaries on the summit of Thaba Bosiu. The black cross in the background marks Moshesh's grave. Note the Maluti Mountains on the horizon.

15 The author's guides, Tseliso and Albert Khalema, at Moshesh's grave.

The Tamboekies recaptured their stock and headed southwards. Moshesh collected his dispirited warriors and continued the journey back to Lesotho. He was jaded and dejected, blaming himself for the setback his men had suffered. He vowed never again to enter the field of battle.

The year 1835 closed without further incident, but it heralded the most complicated period of Moshesh's life. Soon thousands of white men, together with their families, Hottentot servants, multitudes of cattle, sheep and horses would be streaming northwards through the Colony, crossing the Orange river into the vast territory embracing Moshesh's domain. For in the Cape, parties of Dutch-speaking farmers, known colloquially as Boers, had decided to free themselves of British rule and trek to a Promised Land said to be situated in the remote interior of South Africa.

During the past decade, traders, hunters and travellers, venturing north of the Orange river had returned to the Cape with reports of vast expanses of uninhabited and fertile territory found awaiting occupation.

At about the time of Moshesh's ill-fated clash with the Tamboekies, two parties of Boers were reconnoitring territories beyond the borders of the Colony. The first, under a farmer named Scholtz, travelled as far as the Zoutpansberg along the upper limits of the Transvaal, and the second under Petrus Lafras Uys had reached the Tugela river, southern boundary of Zululand, domain of King Dingane. Both parties returned, to inspire their countrymen with fascinating reports of those far-off lands. The Colonial Boers, later to become known as Trekkers, came together and made final arrangements for the exodus northwards. They agreed to trek in separate parties, and rendezvous at Thaba Nchu—the Black Hill.

The van of the Great Trek, a convoy of thirty wagons headed by Boer leaders Trichardt and Van Rensburg were seen by the Basotho crossing the Orange river in the Spring of 1835. These two parties stopped briefly at the Black Hill, and moving on, crossed the Vaal river towards the end of the year. Five months later they reached the foothills of the Zoutpansberg range.

A second party of Trekkers appeared on the southern

horizon during early 1836, and headed for Thaba Nchu.
Arriving at the Wesleyan mission there its leader, Hendrik
Potgieter was cordially received both by the Barolong chief,
Moroka, and the missionary Archbell.[1] After a brief so-
journ at Thaba Nchu, the Trekkers moved farther north as
far as the kraal of Makwana, chief of the Bataung or Lion
People, on the south bank of the Vaal river. The Trekkers
were welcomed by the friendly Makwana, who begged their
protection against the marauding regiments of Matabele
tyrant, Mzilikazi. In exchange for cattle he gave them the
territory bounded by the Vet and Vaal rivers.

At the beginning of October rumours of impending war
between Potgieter's Trekkers and the Matabele reached
Thaba Bosiu. Soon afterwards, Moshesh learned that
several Boers encamped along the south bank of the Vaal
had been butchered by a Matabele patrol. Potgieter, apparently fearing a second attack, had ordered the rest of his
people to draw up in two laagers—one on the banks of the
Vet and the other, under Potgieter himself, on a knoll between the Wilge and Renoster rivers. In October came the
news of a great battle between the Boers and Matabele at
Potgieter's laager. This was followed by the most startling
news of all. The mighty Matabele army had been decimated
and put to flight! More news poured into Thaba Bosiu. The
Matabele had regrouped, and throwing caution to the
winds, had swooped down on the Trekkers' cattle and sheep
driving them unchallenged over the Vaal. The attack on the
white men, Moshesh was told, although disastrous at first,
had therefore ended successfully.

In the meantime, coinciding with this battle, a third party
of Trekkers led by Gerrit Maritz of Graaff-Reinet, had
arrived at Thaba Nchu. Told of Potgieter's plight, Maritz
hurried northwards with draught-oxen supplied by his followers and Chief Moroka. He returned to Thaba Nchu a
week later, bringing Potgieter's Trekkers with him.

So far Moshesh had had no dealings with the Trekkers,
but he was kept informed of their movements by his vassal,
Chief Moroka. In November he learned they were planning

[1] Among the children in Potgieter's party was a little boy
destined to win fame as a President of the South African Republic. His name was Paul Kruger.

to attack the Matabele whose military kraals were scattered over a vast area stretching from Mosega, near present-day Zeerust to eGabeni, Mzilikazi's capital near the Marico river.

A large commando of Boers set out for Mosega in January 1837, accompanied by an auxiliary force comprising Griqua, Koranna, Barolong and Wild Cat People. Moshesh awaited developments with interest. He learned in February that the Boers had sacked Mosega, decimated its inhabitants, and recapturing some seven thousand of their cattle had returned to Thaba Nchu. Apparently their horses had been in too poor a condition to attempt an attack on eGabeni and Mzilikazi's other military kraals. The Boers had therefore decided to postpone operations until the end of the year.

In April Piet Retief, best known of all Trekker leaders, arrived with his party at Thaba Nchu, and then moved on to a site on the banks of the Vet river. At a general meeting of the Trekkers, Retief was elected commandant-general of the combined Trek, and among the first proclamations he issued was one prohibiting the Boers from interfering in the affairs of the local tribes. He sent messages of goodwill to all chiefs in the neighbourhood, including Moshesh, and in a letter to Sir Benjamin D'Urban, governor of the Cape, he stressed his determination to foster peaceful coexistence between his own people and the tribes and clans of central South Africa.

In spite of Retief's good intentions, he was not trusted by most of the elders at Thaba Bosiu. The defeat of the Matabele by the Boers had filled the Basotho with apprehension. Moshesh's father, Mokhachane, his uncle Libe and several councillors predicted a similar fate for the tribe, unless something could be done to appease the belligerent Boers. Moshesh did not share their fears, for Chief Moroka had sent him good reports of their conduct. In any case, he believed the Boers had no intention of remaining permanently at Thaba Nchu. They would be trekking northwards, he told his people, to a hinterland far removed from the Hill at Night.

CHAPTER THIRTEEN

CASALIS MOVES TO THABA BOSIU

The Lesotho in 1837—Gosselin builds a mission station at Thaba Bosiu—Casalis marries Sarah Dyke—He is insulted by some of Moshesh's dignitaries—Moshesh has cause to fear the Boers—James Backhouse visits Thaba Bosiu—One of Moshesh's wives commits suicide.

THE Lesotho had no fixed boundaries in 1837, in fact, not even Moshesh could describe precisely the extent of the territory over which he ruled. Roughly, his domain included the mountainous regions extending southwards from Thaba Bosiu to the Orange, and westwards to this river's confluence with the Caledon. It also included the south-western grasslands flanking the Caledon as far as Beer-sheba;[1] the undulating highveld reaching out to Thaba Nchu; the cornlands south of the upper Caledon and the three patches of land occupied in 1834 by the Griqua, Koranna and Bastards under their Wesleyan missionaries. Moshesh also claimed ownership over the Tlotsi and Butha-Buthe districts, cradle of the Bamokoteli clan, but so did Sikonyela, chief of the Wild Cat People. For the time being he preferred to avoid raising the issue with his old enemy. He would wait for a more appropriate moment, when his army was more powerful.

So great had been the influx of *difaqane* victims and other tribesmen in past years that the Basotho numbered approximately twenty thousand at the time of the Great Trek. In 1837 Moshesh was joined by a section of the war-like Bataung or Lion People, under Chief Moletstane. He gave them land near Mekwatleng, a mission station in the care of a youthful Frenchman named Daumas. In many ways 1837 was an important milestone in Moshesh's life. Most important of all, it marked the founding of a mission

[1] A mission station established in 1835 by the Rev. Samuel Rolland of the Paris Evangelical Missionary Society.

station at Thaba Bosiu itself by his friend and mentor Eugene Casalis.

On numerous occasions since their arrival in the Lesotho, the Frenchmen had begged Moshesh to abandon Thaba Bosiu and settle near Morija. But he had always refused, saying that as the stronghold was his mother he dared not forsake her. He loved Thaba Bosiu, and in return Thaba Bosiu loved him. Had it not been for this mutual devotion, both he and his people would have been wiped out, if not by Matiwane or Mzilikazi, then certainly by the Griqua or Koranna. He could see no great advantage in moving his capital to Morija, however much he cherished the friendship of Eugene Casalis. On the contrary, in his mind's eye he could see troubled times ahead, hence the importance of governing his tribe from the hill-top.

'You think that war is at an end,' he said to Casalis one day.

The missionary nodded.

'I don't believe it,' replied the chief.[1] No, if the Frenchmen really wanted him near them, they would have to move to Thaba Bosiu.

A site for the Thaba Bosiu mission station was selected by Casalis near the northern base of the hill, roughly midway between the Khubelu pass and the Phuthiastana river. As soon as the bricks had been made, the timber fetched and the reeds and grass cut for thatching, Constant Gosselin laid the foundations and building began. Gosselin worked at a steady pace during the rest of that year and well into 1838. Casalis, meanwhile, had journeyed to Cape Town, where he had met and married Sarah Dyke, daughter of a former London jeweller. Returning to Morija accompanied by his bride, he visited Thaba Bosiu regularly, where he preached and watched his mission station taking shape.

Casalis and Sarah moved to Thaba Bosiu in June 1838, bringing with them their baby son, whom they had named Eugene after his father. Their arrival caused a stir in the neighbourhood, for few of the Basotho had seen a white woman before, let alone a white baby. They were welcomed by Moshesh 'with lively demonstrations of joy', and when

[1] E. Casalis, *The Basutos*, p. 78.

for the first time they entered their new five-roomed home,
they prayed long and earnestly for they had never felt happier, nor more deeply indebted to the Lord they served.

Not all Moshesh's subjects approved of the mission
station at Thaba Bosiu. Libe, the chief's uncle, openly condemned Casalis, demanding his removal from Basotho soil.
Moshesh, growing weary of the old man, told him that if
he disapproved so strongly of Eugene Casalis he himself
should consider moving to some other part of the territory.
One day old Libe, collecting his belongings and family, left
the hill-top and settled near Korokoro. He was convinced,
as were many other Basotho, that Eugene Casalis had an
evil influence over Moshesh.

During his first week at the new mission station, Casalis
was visited daily by Moshesh. The chief, he learned, was
troubled by the presence of the Trekkers so near the Lesotho. Lately disturbing news had reached him about Boer
activities in tribal territories, and like most of the dignitaries
of Thaba Bosiu, he wondered what fate awaited the Basotho. In the Summer of 1837, for example, a commando
under Potgieter and Uys had finally crushed the mighty
Matabele tribe, driving its fugitive king, Mzilikazi, into the
Kalahari desert. In February 1838 almost a hundred Boers
under Piet Retief had visited emGungundlovu, royal kraal
of Dingane, King of the Zulu. They had been taken
prisoner at the king's command and clubbed to death on the
slopes of a nearby hill called kwaMatiwane. Ten days later
a huge Zulu army had swooped on Trekker encampments
between the Bushman and Blauwkranz rivers, killing some
three hundred whites and two hundred coloured servants.
Since then Moshesh and his people had lived on tenterhooks. There were whispers that the Boers would avenge
the slaughter of their comrades by clearing Zululand and all
central South Africa of tribesmen.

But in November, to the great delight of the Basotho,
large convoys of Trekker wagons were reported moving
away northwards across the Vaal, under Hendrik Potgieter.[1] However, hundreds of Boer families were still to be

[1] These Trekkers settled on the banks of the Mooi river where,
in due course, they founded the village of Potchefstroom.

found in the territory stretching from Philippolis to the Caledon, and thence to the Vet river as far as the newly founded hamlet called Winburg.[1]

In February 1839 Moshesh learned that King Dingane had been overthrown and driven from his royal kraal, emGungundlovu. Two months before, Dingane's army under command of Ndlela, *induna*-in-chief of the tribe, had been defeated by a Boer commando near the Ncome or Blood river. Warned that the white men were advancing on emGungundlovu, Dingane had fled northwards, taking a great horde of subjects with him, as well as a multitude of cattle and sheep. Reaching the dense fever-stricken Hluhluwe bushveld, Dingane had headed farther northwards bound for the mountains overlooking the Pongolo river.

All these events startled Moshesh and the dignitaries of Thaba Bosiu, and some of them developed a deep-rooted fear of white men. A few of the elders, recalling old Libe's clash with Moshesh, became suspicious of Eugene Casalis, and in the Autumn of 1839, the diviners of Thaba Bosiu protested against his friendship with the chief. The Frenchman, they claimed, was polluting Moshesh's mind with undesirable matters, and unless checked would cause his downfall by magical means known only to himself and his God. Old Mokhachane pointed out that no less than four hundred Basotho, including Moshesh, attended church services conducted by the missionary. Some of them, he complained, were being taught to read and write. There were times when Casalis was publicly humiliated by this 'scoffing and sceptical old man'. On rare occasions when he dared protest, he was reprimanded by the councillors and reminded that in Basotho society young men, and especially

[1] The Boers scattered over this vast territory comprised three distinct groups: firstly, those in the south near the Caledon river, who had not taken part in the Great Trek, but had crossed the Orange in search of grazing for their stock. They were loyal to the British government. Secondly, two hundred and fifty-eight Boer families under Michael Oberholzer living between the Modder and Riet rivers. They too remained loyal to the British government, and were firmly opposed to the Great Trek. Thirdly, there were the Trekkers who had decided to settle permanently in the Winburg district under their leader, Jan Mocke.

strangers, respected their elders. Often Mokhachane would twist Casalis's nose or pinch his ears to the great amusement of all present except Moshesh. The old man hated the missionary, hated the Boers and, indeed, hated all white men. White men must be kept out of the Lesotho, he warned Moshesh and the councillors, lest in due course they crush the Basotho in much the same way as they had crushed the Matabele and the Zulu.

Two more white men came to live at Thaba Bosiu in 1839. They were David Webber, formerly a private in the 72nd Seaforth Highlanders, and a journeyman named Murphy. Webber arrived with a letter from 'a very respectable individual'[1] recommending him to Moshesh as an outstanding carpenter and mason. He was engaged by the chief to erect a large stone house on the hill-top similar to the one built by Gosselin for Eugene Casalis. On its completion Webber and Murphy would be given forty-five oxen. Should they remain at Thaba Bosiu and continue to turn out 'useful things' they would be generously rewarded. The two men started work on the stone house in June, and whereas Moshesh considered their presence as a happy act of Providence, his father condemned them as sorcerers. Moshesh's reasoning, the old man cried in a fit of rage, was clouded by the influence of evil spirits.

Little progress was made by Webber and Murphy in June, for Thaba Bosiu was swept continually by fierce freezing winds and lashing rain. Snow fell on 8 July, and although next day the clouds began to disperse and the sun broke through, the inhabitants of the hill remained indoors, snuggled beneath their *karosses*. Informed by Casalis that a party of white men had arrived at the mission station and had asked to see him, Moshesh went down the Khubelu pass to the missionary's home. In his friend's modest living room Moshesh met the leader of the party, James Backhouse, a traveller who had landed recently at the Cape, after completing an extensive tour of Australia, Van Diemen's Land and Mauritius. Backhouse, Casalis explained, was a member of a welfare organization called the Society of Friends, and had come to South Africa to visit mission

[1] Moshesh's report to the governor of the Cape: Theal, *BR* i.

stations. In May he had completed a tour of Xhosa territory, and crossing the Orange had called on Griqua, Koranna and Sotho-speaking settlements. He had come into
contact with a number of chiefs, some influential and others
insignificant, and he came now to meet the illustrious
founder of the Basotho tribe, and extend to him a hand of
friendship. Backhouse was keen to visit Moshesh in his
kraal on the hill-top, and asked to be shown round his
magnificent fortress.

Welcoming the white man to the Lesotho, Moshesh said
he could come onto the hill whenever he chose. It pleased
him to have visitors on Thaba Bosiu, especially if they were
friends of Eugene Casalis. He returned to his kraal in the
evening, and next morning sent messengers to summon
Backhouse and Casalis. Told that the white men followed
by a retinue, were coming up the Khubelu pass, he fetched
his best European style suit from a kist given him by
Arbousset, and started to dress. He was not ready when
they arrived on the hill, so he sent Ratsiu to show them
around the kraal.

Backhouse found Moshesh's settlement fascinating, and
was particularly interested in the straw-huts which, he
reflected, resembled sparrow-pots. He marvelled at their
tiny entrances, their smooth, clay floors and the tall, circular reed-screens which provided each family with a com-
pact yet cosy courtyard. He and Casalis were examining
some of the uncommon utensils in one of these huts, when
they were summoned to the *kgotla* by Moshesh. They found
him seated on a stool in the shade of the *kgotla*-tree,
surrounded by hundreds of dignitaries.

After the customary exchange of greetings, Moshesh related at great length the dangers faced by himself and his
subjects since the founding of Thaba Bosiu. Makwanyane
and Ratsiu spoke next, and then Casalis and Backhouse
were invited to address the *kgotla*. To the annoyance of
many of the dignitaries, the white men took turns in
condemning the intemperance and indolence that prevailed
among tribal men. Women, they said, were overworked,
oppressed and kept wrongfully in subservience by overfed,
underworked bullying husbands. Most women would enter
the portals of heaven without question, while their domi-

neering patriarchs were destined to be punished by God on
the Day of Judgment.

Old Mokhachane interjected, loudly accusing the white
men of lying, and had Moshesh not taken command of the
situation, the meeting might have ended abruptly in chaos.
Repeatedly Moshesh called his noisy subjects to order, but
they continued to protest declaring that as most of the men
present were unable to understand the white men's reasoning, they never believed nor trusted them. Casalis and
Backhouse were not welcome at Thaba Bosiu. Keeping his
composure Moshesh addressed the *kgotla*.

'You say you will not believe what you do not understand,' he smiled, shaking his head derisively. 'Look at an
egg, if a man break it, there comes only a watery and yellow
substance out of it; but if it it placed under the wings of a
fowl, there comes a living thing from it. Who can understand this? Who ever knew how the heat of the hen
produces the chicken in the egg? This is incomprehensible
to us; yet we do not deny the fact.'

The white men, continued Moshesh, extending a hand
towards Casalis and Backhouse, had come from afar to
spread enlightenment among the Basotho. Admittedly they
had offended the men of the *kgotla*, but this was the result
not of lies they had told, but the painful truth they had
spoken. Was it not true, for example, that Basotho patriarchs looked upon work as beneath them? Did they not
compel their womenfolk to toil in the fields while they
themselves gossiped in the shade of the *kgotla* trees? Tribal
men had become lazy and soft-limbed at the expense of
their wives. Not many months ago, when an epidemic of
measles had swept the Lesotho, he had noticed how diligently the women had nursed their stricken husbands and
children. But he had also noticed that when they were laid
low by the disease, their husbands left them to fend for
themselves. No, the white men had not spoken falsely. He
was pleased they had drawn attention to some of the less
admirable aspects of tribal tradition.

Beckoning Casalis and Backhouse, Moshesh led them to
a hut close by where a meal of cooked chicken and tea
'served in earthen basins of English manufacture' awaited
them. A little later he and the white men called on David

Webber and inspected the stone house he was building.
Leaving Webber, they strolled to the western buttress of the
hill, and visited Mokhachane in his kraal. And so they
moved from one section of the hill-top to another, admiring
the magnificent view of the purple Malutis, and inspecting
the various passes, the boulder ramparts, Moshesh's cattle
and, finally, the horses, firearms and saddles captured from
the Koranna. Towards sunset the white men took leave of
their host and returned to the mission station in the valley.
This had been a most pleasant day for Backhouse. He
considered it a privilege to have spent so long a time with
Moshesh, 'a man of unusual intelligence' and charm.

During that night, not two hours after the white men's
departure from the hill-top, tragedy struck Moshesh's kraal.
Mantsane, one of his wives, flung herself from a krantz
onto a jumble of rocks lining the eastern slopes of Thaba
Bosiu. During the previous week Mantsane, heavy with
child, had contracted measles, and laid low by a fierce fever
had given birth prematurely to a lifeless baby. She had been
grief-stricken, and yet no one, not even Moshesh, had sensed
that she intended taking her life.

Told next morning about the tragedy, Casalis hurried
back to the hill-top taking Backhouse with him. They found
Moshesh's kraal thronged with squabbling men, wailing
women, wide-eyed children and a great herd 'of cattle
collected in idolatrous reverence of the deceased'. As was
the custom among Sotho-speaking peoples, the corpse had
been bound in a sitting position, and a grave had been dug
beneath the wall of the cattlefold. Moshesh, his body draped
in a heavy *kaross* was addressing an angry group of councillors headed by Ratsiu. Apparently the chief had decided
that the corpse should be laid to rest by Casalis in the new
cemetery on the hill-top, while the councillors insisted it be
buried with traditional rites under the cattlefold wall.

After lengthy argument Ratsiu and the councillors
yielded, and the ceremony was conducted by the missionary
a little before noon. During the singing of the final hymn
Mokhachane, 'greatly incensed at the departure from the
customs of the nation', suddenly burst from the crowd, and
poking a fist at Casalis, demanded he be put to death. Taken

aback, the mourners started drifting away, but Moshesh, boiling with indignation, brushed the old man aside and headed for home followed by the white men and a retinue of worried councillors.

Reaching the outskirts of his kraal, Moshesh paused briefly to bid Casalis and Backhouse farewell. Then turning about he retired to the seclusion of a nearby hut. Backhouse left the Lesotho on the following day, and continued his journey inland.

CHAPTER FOURTEEN

TREATY WITH THE BRITISH

*A party of Boers intrudes during Moshesh's absence—
Adele Casalis is born—The United Voortrekker Re-
public is founded—Moshesh persuades the Cape
Governor to pardon David Webber—He visits Boer
farms in the south—Dr. John Philip's false report—
Moshesh interviews Hendrik Potgieter—He weeps in
church—He enters into a treaty with Sir George
Napier*

THE rains came in October, and throughout the Caledon
Valley and surrounding territories tribesmen set to work in
the sorghum fields. The Boers too were busy. Using single-
furrow ploughs drawn by long spans of oxen, they prepared
virgin lands for corn and maize. And while this activity was
taking place, more rain fell, heralding a season of plenty.

Plain-living, hard-working and accustomed to the auster-
ity of country life, the Boers were fortified with an intense
Calvinistic devoutness. They left the course of their destinies in the hands of their beloved God. Most of them were
living in tents or small, rectangular shacks built of timber
and daub. Thatched with grass or reeds, these pioneer
homes were simple by Colonial standards, and yet they
were not uncomfortable. Bedrooms and living rooms were
invariably tiny and crowded with oddments of period furniture, copper, iron and wooden utensils and glass, china
and porcelain heirlooms. Floors were made of a clay and
cowdung mixture, and covered with pelts and *karosses,* or
in some cases reed mats woven by Sotho-speaking clansmen.

The Boers dressed simply as befitted the rustic life they
led. The men wore broad-brimmed hats made of felt or
straw, shoes and jackets of cured hide, leather flap-trousers
and linen shirts. The women wore wide long-sleeved
dresses, handmade skin shoes, shawls and bonnets.

In November when the crops around Thaba Bosiu were

about ankle high, Moshesh went hunting in the Valley at the head of a party of horsemen. He had not been away a week when twenty-seven Boers mounted and armed with muzzleloaders arrived at Thaba Bosiu. Questioned by Moshesh's councillors the leaders of the party, David Joubert and Daniel Pieters, said they had come in search of two Bastards known to be living in the Lesotho. They were Kiewiet Witbooi, a notorious cattle thief and Joseph Solomons, an escapee from a Colonial prison. The white men demanded to be taken to the place where the men were hiding. When Ratsiu told them they would have to get permission from Moshesh, Joubert and Pieters grew angry, threatening to kill whoever was responsible for harbouring the criminals. Ratsiu became afraid. He promised personally to lead the Boers to the fugitives. Next morning Witbooi and Solomons were captured by the Boers on a nearby hill, and put to death.

Learning of the incident towards evening, Moshesh came racing back to Thaba Bosiu, where he conferred with Ratsiu and the councillors. He sent for Eugene Casalis, and together they compiled a letter to the Lt. Governor of the Cape Colony, Andries Stockenström, deploring the Boers' 'unwarranted act of self revenge'. In assuming 'the right to act as Judge and Executioner', the Boers had become a threat to the chief's authority, the letter continued, and a threat to the safety of the tribe as a whole. Moshesh would not tolerate their interference. They had placed him in the most 'difficult circumstances', and had damaged the hitherto happy relations between himself and the Bastards.

Stockenström's reply came as a shock to Moshesh. The Lt. Governor professed to have little interest in the movements of the Boers north of the Orange; they were beyond the precincts of British authority. It was Moshesh's prerogative to keep law and order in Basotho territory, and he alone could punish Joubert and Pieters for 'the acts of cruelty and murder' they had committed. Stockenström's ruling was ridiculous. Moshesh had neither the authority nor the power to punish the Boers. The matter was therefore reluctantly dropped.

Since the founding of the mission station at Thaba Bosiu,

Moshesh had visited Eugene and Sarah Casalis regularly. The sympathy and support he had always received from Casalis in times of trouble had drawn the two men steadily closer together. When the councillors had been emotional or irrational, Casalis had remained placid, dignified and helpful. His insight into the ways of white men was an invaluable asset to the chief, especially as the Frenchman kept him informed of developments beyond the limits of the Lesotho. Moshesh was pleased with Casalis, and pleased with many Basotho, both young and old, who were receiving instruction in reading, writing and religious matters at the mission station.

It was Casalis who told Moshesh of the final defeat of Dingane, King of the Zulu, in January 1840. Routed by the army of his half-brother, Mpande, the Root, Dingane had fled across the Pongolo river into the forest regions of presentday Swaziland. Mpande had then ascended the Zulu throne, pledging allegiance to the Boers who meanwhile had taken possession of the entire belt of country stretching from the Tugela in the north to the Umzimvubu in the distant south. It was also Casalis who told Moshesh of the founding of the United Voortrekker Republic in October. Boer territory now included Mzilikazi's former domain in the north occupied by Potgieter's followers in 1838; a slice of central South Africa reaching southwards as far as the Vet river and eastwards beyond the Drakensberg to incorporate Zululand, Natal and what is today Pondoland. The country between the Vet and Orange rivers, populated by pockets of Basotho, Griqua and Boers loyal to the British government did not fall within the confines of the new Republic. Known later as Transorange, it was meant to serve as a buffer between the British Colony and the United Voortrekker Republic.

Towards the end of 1840 a happy event took place at Thaba Bosiu—a daughter was born to Sarah and Eugene Casalis. When he heard the news Moshesh hurried down the hill to rejoice with his friends, and he fussed about the crib, repeating the baby's name—'Adele! Adele!' Moshesh, Casalis had said to himself on that memorable day, 'possessed among other qualities a great love for children'. He

also recalled the many times he had seen Moshesh play
with his infant sons and daughters about the huts or fondle
them while conferring with his councillors or visiting envoys. It was this side of Moshesh's character—his tender,
loving and simple disposition—that won the missionary's
admiration. Casalis could hardly imagine the other great
tribal rulers of the era—Shaka, Dingane, Mzilikazi—dis-
playing such deep affection for children, let alone in full
view of dignitaries, warriors and menials.

The longer he knew Casalis the more Moshesh relied on
him for guidance, both in tribal matters and the affairs of
the Boers. The Frenchman, by nature a modest man, gives
little indication in his writings as to the extent of his influence on important decisions taken by the chief. Moshesh,
on the other hand, never tired of praising the missionary
for his wise, friendly and unstinting counsel. In April 1841
Moshesh discovered that David Webber, whom he employed as a builder was a deserter from the British army, so
he sent for Casalis and asked him what he should do.
Advised by the Frenchman to inform the governor of
Webber's presence, thereby avoiding possible discord with
the British authorities, he dictated a letter to Sir George
Napier, D'Urban's successor, explaining why the renegade
Englishman had been allowed to settle at Thaba Bosiu.

According to Moshesh, Webber had arrived on the hill-
top at the time when the Basotho were 'just awakening
from a wild state and were trying to be civilized'. He,
Moshesh, had been looking out for a law-abiding white man
who was prepared to settle temporarily at Thaba Bosiu and
instruct the younger men of the tribe in masonry, carpentry
and other important skills. David Webber had done much to
uplift the Basotho, and should he be pardoned by the
governor and remain at Thaba Basiu, he would continue
building operations on the hill-top. Moshesh needed Webber; he had become part of the Basotho tribe.

Attached to Moshesh's letter was a note from Casalis
supporting Moshesh's plea, and vouching both for Webber's
impeccable behaviour and also 'his great usefulness among
the Basutos [sic] in promoting civilization'. Not long afterwards a reply arrived from Napier. Webber had been par-

doned and could remain at Thaba Bosiu. Clasping the missionary's hands in his own, Moshesh confessed he could no longer do without him. Casalis meant more to him now than any of the councillors.

Since the founding of the United Voortrekker Republic, Moshesh had often considered visiting Transorange, and assessing at first hand the extent of Boer encroachment on Basotho grazing land. He had been told that white farmers in those parts had been robbed of cattle, sheep and horses, and were planning a retaliatory attack on Basotho kraals. One morning he set out southwards on horseback accompanied by mounted warriors. Three days later he reached a Bamonaheng settlement near Koesberg, where he stopped for a meal, and moving on entered a vast region dotted with Boer encampments and teeming with their cattle, sheep and horses. In due course he reached Verliesfontein, a farm owned by a prosperous Boer named Jan de Winnaar.

Moshesh spent several happy hours with de Winnaar, and shown around the farm he marvelled at the superb conditions of the Boer's heavy-humped oxen, his stabled milch cows and fat-tailed sheep. The chief took special interest in the fowl-runs, duck-pens and pig-sties, and he was thrilled at the sight of de Winnaar's tools and implements stored neatly in a large rainproof shed. Before leaving Verliesfontein Moshesh is said to have expressed delight at the presence of white men in Transorange, adding that he knew he could count on their help should the Griqua or Koranna attack Thaba Bosiu. He suggested that the Boer should 'plant trees and a vineyard'[1] on Verliesfontein and erect whatever buildings he still required. There was no question that de Winnaar and his fellow-Boers would be ordered out of Transorange.

The chief visited other farms in the area, and was treated with kindness and respect by every farmer he met. After two weeks he returned to Thaba Bosiu, and addressing a sitting of the *kgotla* reported that 'peace ... prevailed in the land'.

In 1842 Thaba Bosiu was visited by Dr. John Philip, the influential and controversial superintendent of the London

[1] de Winnaar's testimony: Theal, *BR* ii.

Missionary Society. Of all Colonial white men, none was
better liked in some circles, and more ardently hated in
others. He was a fiery champion of the Negro, Malay and
Hottentot peoples of Cape Town, but generally he was mis-
trusted by Boers and Englishmen alike. Only a handful of
his closest friends seemed able to fathom his complex
character, and they considered him kindly, rational and un-
impeachably honest. The majority of his associates regarded
him as hot-headed, obstinate and hypocritical, and a medd-
ler in the political affairs of the Colony. One of the Cape
governors, Lord Charles Somerset, called him a deceitful,
'dangerous man' who interferred with 'everything that gave
him political importance'. Most of his political opinions
were said to be 'full of disgusting evasion and perversion of
facts'.

A bitter critic of Colonial native policy, Philip was also
bitterly opposed to the Boers whom he indicted not only in
the Colony, but also in countries abroad as the prime pro-
pagators of racial disharmony. Although past sixty when he
visited Moshesh, he seemed as robust and energetic as ever
he had been.

Philip's humanitarian ideals, however plausible in es-
sence, were sometimes devoid of logic, and therefore im-
practical. On occasions his integrity was open to question.
This did not jeopardize his influence in certain government
and philanthropic circles. On the contrary, Napier valued
his opinions as much as those of the Secretary of Native
Affairs.

During his visit to Thaba Bosiu, Philip discussed many
topics of interest with Moshesh, including Britain's supremacy on land and sea, her magnanimity in dealing with
undeveloped peoples and the respect commanded by her
monarch throughout the length and breadth of the earth.
When the time came for his return to the Cape, he advised
Moshesh to cultivate Britain's friendship, and warned him
to keep clear of the Boers. He promised to report favour-
ably on Moshesh in Cape Town, and to pave the way for a
happy relationship between the Basotho and the British.

Reaching Cape Town in July, Philip discussed his visit to
the Lesotho with Sir George Napier dealing, among other

things, with the settlement of white men in Transorange. He also presented the Cape government with a lengthy and distorted report on political affairs north of the Orange. It is a pity this document ever came into existence, for it set the stage for a most unhappy era in Moshesh's life, one crowded with interracial tension, strife and bloodshed.

According to Philip, the Boers were planning an invasion of the Lesotho, realizing it was free of horse-sickness and therefore ideal for horse-breeding. He predicted they would 'carry their ambitious designs into execution' without delay, and urged Sir George Napier to take immediate action.

A proclamation was issued by Sir George Napier in September warning the Boers against attempting 'to molest, invade or injure any of the native tribes' north of the Orange. Should they ignore the proclamation they would 'forfeit all claims to Her Majesty's protection', and evoke her 'liveliest indignation'.

In January 1843 Moshesh learned from his scouts that a British army had arrived on the south bank of the Orange, and was about to round up the Boers of Transorange and take them back to the Colony. British envoys arrived at Thaba Bosiu with a message for Moshesh to prohibit his subjects from entering the impending struggle. The British commander had been led to believe that the Basotho intended massacring Boer women and children. Moshesh was indignant. He had no desire to be drawn into a clash between white men, and it was certainly not his habit to wage war against defenceless noncombatants. The visit of the envoys was followed by the delivery of a letter from the Boer leader, Hendrik Potgieter, inviting Moshesh to an urgent meeting at Thaba Nchu. The chief was nonplussed, but eager to know what was going on, he set out for the Black Hill accompanied by a small commando. Arriving at Chief Moroka's village he was hailed by a large gathering of Boers headed by Potgieter.

'Are you my friend?' asked Potgieter, as he led Moshesh to a chair.

'Yes, I am your friend,' replied the chief, 'and also the friend of the English.'

Referring to the presence of a British army on the banks

of the Orange, Potgieter suggested that Moshesh prohibit it
from entering Transorange.

'I cannot do that,' exclaimed the chief, explaining that
the British had come to take their people, the Boers, back to
the Colony.

'We are not their people,' retorted Potgieter.

'Were you not their subjects?' questioned Moshesh.

'Yes we were,' barked the white man, 'but they oppressed
us.' The Boers, he continued, were poised to attack the
enemy the moment it set foot in Transorange. They were
determined to die rather than submit to British rule.

Back at Thaba Bosiu, after his meeting with Potgieter,
Moshesh sent scouts to watch the movements of the British
army. He was relieved to learn, a few days later, that for
some unknown reason it had broken camp and was returning to the south. Looking back on his meeting with Potgieter he realized that his subjects would have to keep on
friendly terms with the white men of Transorange. They
dared not risk antagonizing the Boers.

Autumn floated quietly into the Lesotho tinting the sorghum fields with bronze hues, filling the days with luxurious
warmth and fanning the nights with icy breezes. Autumn in
the Caledon Valley was known as 'leisure-time'—a time for
rest, gossip and debauchery, and the time for extolling the
spirits upon whom depended the fate of the harvest.

Moshesh spent most mornings in the *kgotla* interviewing
messengers, scouts and discontented subjects, or presiding
over the tribal court. Occasionally in the afternoon, after a
short nap, he would visit Casalis. Leaning heavily on a
long, black stave, and accompanied by Makwanyane or
Ratsiu, he would amble down the Khubelu pass. Reaching
the foot of the hill, he would stop a while at Rafutho, the
smithy's kraal, and moving on, would follow the dusty
track to the mission station. Usually he was met along the
way by Casalis himself or by Hamilton Dyke, a young missionary appointed recently as the Frenchman's assistant. He
seldom remained longer than an hour, but there were times
when he arrived unexpectedly for breakfast, and did not
return home until before sunset. Invariably on Sundays he
attended the children's Sunday school in the morning and,

straight afterwards, the church service for adults.

In his memoirs Casalis recalls the morning he chose the story of the Good Shepherd as the topic for his sermon. He had started by explaining how a young man had gone in search of his lost sheep. His heart heavy with grief, his cheeks moist with tears, the shepherd had scoured the countryside—every cranny, *donga* and hill-top—but the sheep were nowhere to be found. Undaunted, the young shepherd had continued the search, plodding through marshes and forging an agonizing path through a jungle of thornbush. Body aching, feet bruised, torn and bleeding he had struggled on and on until, eventually, overcome with fatigue, he sank to his knees and wept. The sheep he had learnt to love so much had gone forever. Suddenly, through the haze of his tears, the shepherd had caught sight of them, and rising laboriously, staggered towards them with outstretched arms. But they turned and fled. He fell to the ground, sobbing. What was he to do now?

At this stage of the sermon, Casalis suddenly realized that the children in the congregation were weeping, and as he continued his doleful story, both women and men joined in, and soon his voice was drowned in a deafening din of wailing, sniffing and coughing. Casalis paused, waiting for silence, but when the noise grew louder he sat down in the pulpit and looked on in amazement. Nearby sat Moshesh, weeping pitifully, his face buried in a handkerchief, his body trembling gently. After a short while Casalis climbed down from the pulpit, and crept unnoticed out of the church.

Mosesh missed no more than two services during the reaping season, and one in July when the weather was so bad he dared not venture down the hill. He attended church throughout the Summer, and usually he stayed for lunch. Sarah Casalis always gave him a basket of delicacies to take home with him—biscuits, preserves, sugar, tea or coffee, and when he returned on the following sabbath, he would bring her eggs, a loaf or two of sorghum bread and, occasionally, a shoulder of venison.

One Sunday in December 1843 Moshesh was introduced by Casalis to a visiting government official named Walker.

This man, explained the missionary, had been sent by Sir George Napier to negotiate a treaty between Basotho and the British.

A month before, Walker told Moshesh, a similar treaty had been concluded with the Griqua, Adam Kok. As it was Dr. Philip's belief that the Boers were planning to destroy the Basotho, Napier recommended that Moshesh should follow old Adam's example without delay. After conferring with Eugene Casalis, the chief agreed to the treaty and drew his cross at the bottom of a document placed before him by Walker. In terms of the agreement he would receive a yearly grant of £75 or the equivalent in arms and ammunition. In return he was to keep order in the Lesotho, arrest and deliver criminals and fugitives to the Colony, and keep the British government informed of subversive activities aimed at undermining British authority at the Cape. In future the British government would recognize Moshesh's domain as extending from the junction of the Caledon and Orange rivers in the west to Butha-Buthe in the east; from the Orange river in the south to an imaginary line thirty miles north of the Caledon, and running parallel with it as far as Wild Cat territory.

The document was countersigned by six witnesses, one of whom was Moshesh's army commander, Makwanyane.

Napier's treaty caused immediate unrest north of the Orange. Firstly, Moshesh demanded that his northern boundary be extended to include Thaba Nchu and Merumetsu; secondly, Davids the Griqua, Baatje the Bastard and Taaibosch the Koranna, challenged the validity of the document, on the grounds that they did not recognize Moshesh as their chief. Thirdly, the Boers of Transorange, finding to their horror that they had been placed under the authority of Moshesh and Adam Kok, protested to the Colonial governor, warning him that unless his ridiculous treaty were rescinded, it would lead to bloodshed.

As the months passed the outcry against the treaty mounted, and Dr. Philip was accused by Colonials, the Transorange Boers and Wesleyan missionaries of deliberately misleading Sir George Napier. They held him responsible for planting the seeds of war among the peace-loving peoples of the interior.

And at Thaba Bosiu the tempers of Moshesh and his councillors rose to boiling point as daily they debated what action to take against the protesting Griqua, Bastard and Koranna living within the borders of the new Lesotho. Questioned by Casalis, Moshesh admitted giving them the right to plant and reap their crops, to graze their stock, but never to consider the land they lived on their own exclusive property.

'Nothing will induce me to relinquish my right to the country in which you live,' he wrote in a circular letter to Davids, Baatje and Taaibosch. He was not angry with them, he continued, only amazed at their ingratitude. He was keen to remain their friend and protector. The half-breeds scoffed at Moshesh, and the quarrel continued, reaching such ugly proportions in April 1844 that the Basotho felt obliged to call upon the governor to arbitrate.

With Casalis's assistance Moshesh wrote to Napier asking for help, but the letter never left Thaba Bosiu. For at that very moment the chief received startling news from the Cape. Sir George Napier had been recalled to England, and his place was filled by a newcomer to the Colony, an elderly military commander named Maitland.

CHAPTER FIFTEEN

SIR PERIGRINE MAITLAND

Basotho dignitaries clash with a posse of Boers—Moshesh meets Maitland at Touwfontein—He has problems with his sons—Sir Perigrine has faith in Moshesh's integrity—Poshuli's clan is joined by the riffraff of central South Africa—Moshesh is suspected of duplicity

LIEUTENANT-GENERAL SIR PERIGRINE MAITLAND, formerly the lieutenant-governor of Nova Scotia, had arrived at the Cape aboard the *Zenobia* in March. Almost seventy, his rangy, stooped frame bore signs of many hardships suffered during fifty years of active military service. He was soft-spoken, reserved and intensely religious, and although a man of uncommon charm, he had two conspicuous failings: he was a poor judge of character, and tended to turn the proverbial blind eye to the inadequacies of his subordinates. Most of his colleagues considered him far too soft-natured for the post of governor of the Cape Colony.

When Maitland took office at the Cape, said Moshesh jocularly in 1844, he trod on a snake's tail, implying that the new governor had stepped inadvertently into an unpleasant situation. Among the first of his problems was a complaint by Adam Kok that the Boers of Transorange had challenged his authority and were, in fact, preparing to attack Philippolis. Apparently Kok had had a farmer named Van Staden arrested on an allegation of murder and the Boers, although agreeing he should be brought to trial, had protested against old Adam's interference in the matter. Kok, they argued, had no jurisdiction over white men. Van Staden had to be tried by a Boer magistrate and no one else.

Refusing to be drawn into the argument, Maitland ignored Adam Kok's complaint. Neither would he comment on the dispute between Moshesh and the half-breeds for, in his own words, he was far too inexperienced in the political affairs of central South Africa to provide a satisfactory solution to the problem.

Eugene Casalis informed the Colonial government in October that despite the Napier Treaty, the Boers of Transorange refused to acknowledge Moshesh's authority. Many of them were selling farms and erecting homesteads and outbuildings without his permission Hundreds of newcomers had settled on land which, in terms of the Treaty, belonged to the Basotho. Maitland ignored the Frenchman's letter, and gradually relations between the Boers and the Basotho deteriorated.

Unfortunately, although most of the Boers of Transorange were God-fearing, law-abiding people, there was also a handful of rogues among them who did much to antagonize Moshesh. One such person was Piet Botha, a bullying ne'er-do-well who was known to almost everyone between the Orange and Vet rivers. One afternoon in December, he arrived in the Koesberg district with a flock of sheep he had lifted from a Boer named du Toit. Looking around for a place to sleep, Botha came upon a farm owned by Thomas Bailey, one of the few white men whom Moshesh had allowed to settle in the area. Botha drove Bailey off the farm at gun-point, and taking over his modest reed-house converted the garden into a sheep-pen. For several days he kept guard over the stolen animals, a loaded musket in one hand and a bottle of brandy in the other.

When news of Bailey's ejection reached Thaba Bosiu, Moshesh sent Chief Letele and three other dignitaries to order Botha off the farm. North of Koesberg, as they entered a deep valley, Letele and his companions were intercepted by a party of Boers under Field-cornet Fouche. They were ordered, under threat of death, to return to Thaba Bosiu. They had no authority to deal with Botha, Fouche told them, and if Moshesh himself should dare to set foot in Transorange, and interfere with Boer affairs, he would be 'received with loaded muskets'.[1]

Moshesh complained bitterly to Maitland, but again no action was taken.

As a result of Sir Perigrine's apparent indifference, Moshesh turned more and more to Casalis for political advice.

[1] Report by Moshesh to Montagu, Sec. to the Government.

From that time on the Frenchman was drawn into all important discussions concerning the British and the Boers. He would have preferred not to become involved, realizing that by assuming the rôle of Moshesh's political mentor, he was exposing his evangelical career to outside interference. But he had little option. He felt morally bound to stand by the chief and share his burdens.

Moshesh was now about fifty-seven and although slightly more fleshy than in days gone by, he was as erect and agile as most men ten years younger. In the twenty years since arriving at Thaba Bosiu, his wives had increased considerably in number, and it is said that his children were so numerous that if brought together, they could fill the largest cattlefold in the land. Often he would jest with herdboys and ask after their fathers, not realizing they were his own children. He is said to have met a woman drawing water from a spring one evening after sunset, and after flirting with her for several minutes he asked her good-naturedly the name of her husband.

'Moshesh,' she replied, bursting into laughter, 'Moshesh, the chief with far too many wives.'

Invariably when asked how many children he had, Moshesh would say 'five', meaning the four sons—Letsie, Molapo, Masuphu and Mayara, and the one daughter Nthe, born of Mamohato, his senior wife. Most of his grown-up sons were still living either on Thaba Bosiu or in the neighbourhood, and they often caused him unhappiness. They were forever squabbling with, or besmirching each other in the presence of their kindly, over-tolerant father. Most of the councillors looked upon his sons with scorn and delighted in running them down beyond earshot of the chief. According to old Libe, Moshesh's sons were as much a source of irritation to their father, as the swarms of flies that infested the kraal. He vowed that had they been his sons, he would have flogged them publicly in the *kgotla*.

Of all the 'princes' Masupha and Sekhonyana were the most reliable, capable and intelligent, and on Casalis's advice were sent by Moshesh to Cape Town to learn reading, writing and English. This was to prove a happy move, for in years to come when they returned to Thaba Bosiu, they would assume the rôles of interpreters, scribes and special envoys.

Adam Kok and the Boers squabbled during most of 1844, and in January 1845, when it was reported in Cape Town that they were skirmishing near Philippolis, Maitland sent a British force to intervene. A Boer commando, mustered by Jan Mocke on the farm Touwfontein, clashed with the British in May, and was put to flight. Disbanding the commando the Boers returned moodily to their farms. They vowed to get even with Kok the moment the British returned to the Cape.

No sooner had news of these events reached Thaba Bosiu, than Maitland himself arrived in Transorange, and invited Moshesh to meet him at Touwfontein farm on the last day of June. When the time drew near, Moshesh set out southwards in a horse-drawn wagon, and arriving at Maitland's camp, he discovered that all neighbouring chiefs, as well as the various Griqua and Koranna leaders, had also been invited and had already arrived. There was one notable exception. Sikonyela, chief of the Wild Cat People, had not turned up.

In spite of the presence of so many tribal dignitaries at Touwfontein, the meeting with Maitland was devoted mainly to the political affairs of the Griqua of Philippolis, the Basotho and the Boers. After lengthy discussion it was decided to divide Kok's territory into two distinct districts, one where European ownership of land would be strictly prohibited, and the other where farms could be bought or leased by white men either from Kok himself or from his subjects. Both districts would be served by a resident magistrate named Rawlins, who would cooperate closely with the Griqua.

Turning to the problems of the Lesotho, Maitland said he and his government had been surprised to learn that Davids, Baatje and Taaibosch had refused to acknowledge Moshesh's authority. Moshesh interrupted. The dispute between the petty-chiefs and himself, he said, was not important enough to warrant discussion at a meeting such as this. The greatest problem facing the Lesotho was the presence of white men in Transorange. He and his councillors wanted all white men to move back to the Colony whence they had come, but as this was bound to cause dissension, he was prepared to compromise. After all he, chief of the Basotho, was a peace-loving, considerate person. As a token of his sincerity, he continued, he had decided to set aside a tract of land between the Orange and Caledon rivers exclusively for occupation by white men. In return he expected Maitland to have all foreigners removed from Basotho soil, be they British or Boer; the missionaries alone would be welcome to stay. Returning to the question of the petty-chiefs, Moshesh said he would leave the matter in the hands of the governor.

In reply to the chief, Sir Perigrine, somewhat bewildered, promised to convene a further meeting of tribal heads as soon as he had made a closer study of the political situations in central South Africa. He discreetly omitted to mention the land grant made by Moshesh to the Boers. The territory was so small, so inadequate for the white men's needs that he could not decide whether the offer had been made in jest or in earnest.

A month after the Touwfontein meeting, Moshesh was visited at Thaba Bosiu by Gideon Joubert whom he had met three years before. The Boer had been sent by the Colonial government to look into the squabbles between Moshesh and the petty-chiefs. He had already called on the Wesleyan mission station north of the Caledon, and had been amazed to discover how intensely unpopular Moshesh had become in those parts. This he attributed to interference by both the French and Wesleyan missionaries in tribal affairs. Moshesh refused to discuss his problems with Joubert, saying he was far too busy. In any case Eugene Casalis was away in Colesberg. Joubert would have to wait for his return.

Informed that Casalis had arrived at Morija on his way home and would be staying a few days with Arbousset, Moshesh, accompanied by his councillors, Joubert and Moletstane, chief of the Bataung, set out for the mission station on 9 August. There he was met by a large gathering of subjects and chiefs as well as the missionaries and a handful of Boers. As the 10th was the sabbath, Moshesh and his retinue attended holy worship conducted by the

Frenchmen. On the Monday morning Casalis called all the people together, and invited Moshesh to address them.

'Moshesh made a long speech,' wrote Joubert in a report to Maitland, 'he explained to his people the substance of the Napier treaty ... praised the British government, spoke of its power and the happiness they the Basotho would enjoy under the protection of its mighty laws.' When the chief had finished speaking Joubert asked him to consider increasing the size of the territory he had given the Boers as it was far too small. After careful consideration Moshesh agreed. He said he would extend the south-eastern boundary from the mouth of the Kraai river to Kommissie drift. The remainder of the territory would stretch westwards as far as the junction between the Caledon and Orange.

'I endeavoured to insist on a higher more easterly boundary line,' continued Joubert, 'and I put it to his feelings that a great number of Boers to whom he had given places, farms which they had built up and planted, would now with grief be obliged to leave them.'

Moshesh had been offended, and refused to discuss the matter further. Later he promised to visit and inspect the area personally, and if necessary reconsider his decision.

The meeting closed a little before noon and most of the people started leaving for home. As Joubert was about to go he was called aside by Moshesh and advised not to expect any further grants of land to the white men. If the Boers were not satisfied, he said, they could move to some other part of South Africa, any part, as long as it was far from the borders of the Lesotho. Joubert was dumbfounded. Three years back he had considered the chief 'the most fit, sensible and stately' tribal ruler he had met. Now it struck him that if ever Moshesh became supreme ruler over the territories north of the Orange, as was presumably his aim, he would be a 'puffed up dangerous and troublesome neighbour' to the Colonial government. Of all chiefs in the area he was the least worthy of British support, and the last to be trusted.

On his return to Cape Town, Joubert found little support for his opinion of Moshesh, least of all from Sir Perigrine Maitland. In fact, the governor dismissed his report as

biased, and spoke out in defence of the chief, describing him
as a 'superior man whose great and increasing influence
over neighbouring Native tribes ... was likely to prove very
serviceable in preserving peace beyond the Cape border'.
Admittedly Moshesh was illiterate, and unenlightened by
European standards. But he was imbued with admirable
qualities, not the least of which was a determination to
protect the Basotho against exploitation by the Boers. In the
eyes of the British government Moshesh was an honourable
man; a ruler of unquestionable calibre.

An army captain named Sutton was appointed 'British
Resident among the Native Tribes to the North East of the
Colony' in October, with headquarters at Philippolis. He
resigned in January 1846 and was succeeded by Capt. H. D.
Warden of the Cape Mounted Rifles, a conscientious
student of tribal affairs. Warden moved to a site he had
selected between the Riet and Modder rivers, not a mile
from the wagon-track to Winburg. Nestled in the shadows
of a wooded range of hills, his camp became known as
Bloemfontein, after Jan Bloem, the Koranna marauder.

Meanwhile Maitland had sent a report to the Colonial
Secretary in London, Lord Stanley, outlining developments
north of the Orange, and predicting that peace would prevail between Moshesh and the Boers. But as events were
about to reveal Maitland was out of touch with Basotho
affairs, and unaware that Moshesh, although a wise and
capable ruler, was surrounded by influential dignitaries.
And while some were almost as wise as he, others were
bigoted, suspicious and hot-headed. There were trouble-
makers like Poshuli who had not the least respect for the
chief, and whose reputation as a brigand compared with the
worst of the Griqua, Koranna and Bergenaar cutthroats. In
1846 he was living with his followers at Thaba Tseu, but
more often than not he could be found at Thaba Bosiu
laying a charge against some chief or another, demanding
favours from Moshesh and generally stirring up trouble.
Poshuli had considerable influence over Moshesh and the
councillors. In February he decided to move his people
from Thaba Tseu to Vechtkop, a mountain stronghold in

the heart of Boer-occupied Transorange. Not a murmur of protest was heard in the *kgotla* at Thaba Bosiu.

Poshuli and his followers fortified Vechtkop in much the same way as Moshesh had fortified Thaba Bosiu. News of their arrival spread swiftly in all directions, and soon hordes of riffraff—the dregs of the surrounding tribes— drifted in to Vechtkop. Welcomed to the stronghold, these strangers were told they would have to recognize Poshuli as their only chief, and carry out his orders promptly and zest- fully. They would have to accompany him on cattle raids, steal for him and, on occasions, kill for him. They would have no claim to booty lifted in neighbouring territories, for Poshuli alone decided which of his raiders deserved to be rewarded and which deserved to be flogged for cowardice.

Towards the end of February, Moshesh acting under pressure from the councillors, sent Molapo together with three hundred handpicked subjects to occupy a large stretch of territory near the Tlotsi stream. No sooner had the Basotho arrived in the area than they were attacked by a commando of Wild Cat People which they put to flight after a fierce skirmish. The presence of Molapo and his people so unnerved Sikonyela, chief of the Wild Cat People, that he appealed to Davids, Baatje and Taaibosch for help. But they refused, firstly because they distrusted this chief, and secondly because they realized that by entering the dis- pute they might antagonize Sir Perigrine Maitland. Sikon- yela turned in desperation to Captain Warden for help, and was assured that the matter would be placed 'in the hands of the British Government'. The Basotho, however, could remain in the Tlotsi district until further notice. They were not to be molested by the Wild Cat People.

The Axe War, the seventh in a series waged in the Cape Colony between the Xhosa and the British, broke out in March, and in April many thousands of Xhosa refugees, driving a multitude of stock before them, came pouring into the territory between the Orange and Tees rivers. Not many months before, this same territory had been occupied by Chief Moorosi and his Baphuthi clan. It was inevitable that sooner or later the Baphuthi, who were vassals of Moshesh, should clash with the trespassing fugitives.[1]

Determined to keep on good terms with the British, Moshesh sent envoys with orders for the Xhosa to return to the Colony. Told that they had refused to move, and were planning to settle permanently north of the Orange, he threatened to exterminate them. Moshesh reported the matter to the civil commissioner of Colesberg, assuring him that provided the Basotho were supplied with arms and ammunition, they would enter the war on the side of the British.

Four months passed and the refugees continued to hang about Moorosi's settlements. Suddenly at the beginning of Spring, they fled, taking thousands of Baphuthi cattle with them. Throughout the Summer, Moorosi's commandos, supported by a force from Thaba Bosiu, hounded the Xhosa in the surrounding hills. Eventually the banks of the Tees became strewn with Xhosa corpses, and its water ran red with blood.

Meanwhile hordes of refugees continued to stream in from the Colony, and by the Autumn of 1847 they numbered an estimated fifteen thousand, and their cattle no less than three hundred thousand. The Xhosa herds surged hungrily through the Wittenberg and Koesberg districts, overrunning Boer and Basotho grazing lands, crowding the drinking-pools and polluting the springs. Stock-theft became rife. In one night Poshuli lost a quarter of his cattle, and Cochet, missionary-in-charge of the new station at Hebron, had all his stock lifted in the course of a week. Complaints poured into Bloemfontein. Action was demanded from the British Resident.

Warden headed southwards in October accompanied by a hundred and thirty mounted Boers, his own tiny standing army and a small contingent of Basotho. Reaching Koesberg and later the Wittenberg districts, he discovered the Xhosa had fled, leaving not a beast behind them. Warden tracked the Xhosa across the Tees, skirting Moorosi's settlements, but after a week's fruitless search, he decided to abandon the chase and retrace his steps to Bloemfontein.

[1] Moorosi had occupied this stretch of Cape Colonial territory without the permission or knowledge of the British government.

The captain was troubled, but calling on Moorosi's kraal on his way home he made a discovery which caused him far greater concern. Since the outbreak of the Axe War, tremendous supplies of firearms, ammunition, swords and bayonets looted by the fleeing Xhosa from the British, had fallen into the hands of Chief Moorosi, and were being delivered to Thaba Bosiu. Apparently Moshesh, far from disapproving of the refugees, had given them sanctuary in Moorosi's territory in return for the loot.

Warden believed Moshesh had deceived him. The old jackal was not to be trusted.

CHAPTER SIXTEEN

BRITISH INTERVENTION

Moshesh apologizes to the British Resident on Po-shuli's behalf—One of his wives dies believing she has been bewitched—Sir Harry Smith succeeds Pottinger and visits Winburg—Moshesh is amazed at his eccentricities

SINCE his appointment as British Resident, Warden had striven to foster an harmonious relationship among the peoples north of the Orange. Called upon constantly to settle squabbles and petty disputes between chiefs and between farmers and tribesmen, his life was fraught with problems. A lesser man could never have endured so demanding a position. He had to remain calm and dignified even in the face of unrelenting criticism by chiefs, white settlers and government officials. True, he was sometimes rash in his judgment of situations and people, but he was quick to admit his mistakes and equally quick to seek the pardon of whomever he offended. Sir Henry Pottinger, newly appointed governor of the Cape in the place of Maitland, decried his abortive pursuit of the Xhosa refugees, and he was accused of complicity in the 'perfidious' schemes of Moorosi and Moshesh. Warden could not deny the futility of his recent expedition into the Wittenberg and Koesberg districts, but he objected to the false accusations levelled at him by someone as ignorant of the facts as Sir Henry. He wrote to Pottinger, vindicating himself and stressing he had no real proof that Moshesh had received firearms, ammunition or any other items of loot from the Xhosa. He therefore assumed that the Chief of the Basotho was 'an honest and straightforward' man. He expected Sir Henry and other members of the government to share this opinion.

Stock-theft was becoming rife in Transorange during the second half of 1847, and though most of the raiders were known to have come from the Vechtkop stronghold, both farmers and government officials held Moshesh, not Poshuli, responsible and demanded compensation from him. In actual fact Moshesh had neither organized nor authorized the raids, and was deeply troubled at the thought of the repercussions that were bound to follow.

'I need not say how much I lament such conduct on the part of my people,' he told Warden. He promised to send all stolen cattle found in the Lesotho to Bloemfontein.

No one was more concerned about these new developments than Eugene Casalis. Fourteen years had passed since his arrival in the Lesotho, and in all that time his friendship with Moshesh had been as firm as the very krantzes that crested Thaba Bosiu. He had unwavering faith in Moshesh's integrity, often expressing profound admiration for his dignified manner, the temperate way of life he led, and his extraordinary love for children. Perhaps what he admired most in Moshesh was his gentle, unselfish and even-tempered disposition and, above all, his humility. It did grieve him sometimes that in spite of all these admirable qualities, the chief had not been converted to Christianity. He knew that Moshesh approved of the work being done by the missionaries. What he did not know was that the chief considered much of tribal custom and religion beyond the comprehension of white men, and therefore beyond reach of Christianity. He had been attending church on Sundays not out of devoutness, but out of respect for his friend Casalis. In 1847 Casalis could claim only one hundred and twenty-eight members for his church. Few tribesmen living beyond the immediate vicinity of Thaba Bosiu ever attended services.

There were times when Moshesh, confronted by great misfortune, turned not only to the spirits, bonethrowers, medicine men or witchdoctors for help, but also to his faithful, uncomplaining missionary friend. Casalis was usually a pillar of strength when members of his kraal fell ill. For example, Manaile, one of Moshesh's wives was laid low with sickness, and was said to have been bewitched by a female Xhosa refugee. At one time Manaile had been his favourite wife and was therefore disliked by many of the chief's less privileged women. She was continually sland-

ered by the agitators of the kraal. Manaile is said never to
have caused her husband unhappiness or undue annoyance.
She revered him, extolled him, saw assiduously to his comforts. When he was downcast, she had the knack of uplifting him.

But when her health failed, Manaile became rotund,
lackadaisical and listless. A diviner summoned by Moshesh
maintained she had been bewitched, and gave her protective
decoctions to drink and charms to wear. Later, as the
malady prevailed, he gave her even more potent medicines,
including a mixture prepared from Moshesh's own *lenaka*
or medicine horn. But nothing would bring relief. Next a
witchdoctor was summoned. First he cut a deep incision
into Manaile's arm, and as the blood oozed out he placed a
small antelpe horn, opened at both ends, over the wound
and sucked. In this way he bled her, declaring eventually
that the evil influence had been extracted.

As days passed and Manaile showed no signs of recovery,
Moshesh had more diviners brought to Thaba Bosiu. One of
them, casting his magic bones, said her illness had been
caused by a hyena whose chuckle had haunted the residents
of Thaba Bosiu in recent months. Only if the evil beast were
killed would Manaile's health be restored.

A second diviner attributed her illness to a monkey given
Moshesh by Casalis, and a third, refuting the claims of the
others, said that his magic bones clearly revealed the presence of a sorcerer on the hill-top. Unless Manaile was removed from Thaba Bosiu she would never be cured.

One morning Moshesh sent the ill-fated Manaile, accompanied by her aged mother, to a cave in hills twelve miles
away. Two weeks later he sent Casalis to comfort her and
present her with gifts of food and clothing. The missionary
found her curled up on a bed of straw, her body wrapped in
tattered skins and her head, crowned with a confusion of
matted, unwashed hair, resting on a block of wood. He
could see at a glance 'she had all the symptoms ... of
dropsy', and he suggested that she should return with him
to Thaba Bosiu for treatment.

'What!' cried the stricken woman, her eyes suddenly
wide with fear, 'into the midst of my murderers? Never!'
And pointing to the roof of the cave, she added: 'I will die

under this rock.'

To Casalis's consternation Manaile flew into a wild rage, threatening to tear him to pieces if he remained longer in the cave. Bidding her a hasty farewell, Casalis retreated through the mouth of the cave into the silver-bright sunshine. Mounting his horse, he hurried back to Thaba Bosiu.

During the following month Casalis pleaded with Moshesh to have Manaile brought back to the hill-top, but the chief refused, claiming he was afraid of antagonizing both her relatives and the ancestral spirits. One night he changed his mind. He sent a party of warriors to fetch her, and she was smuggled into a hut near Casalis's church where she was given medicines and nourishing food.

Before long Manaile started regaining a little of her erstwhile strength, and with the help of her old mother she would venture outside into the reed enclosure and bask in the sun. Then one day a mysterious change came over her. She refused to leave her bed, refused to take her medicine and refused to eat. Bewildered, Casalis remonstrated with her.

'Manaile,' he cried, 'I see you have no confidence in me!'

'Do not speak so,' she whimpered, 'my heart says, Thank you! Thank you! Even though I am silent, my heart says, Thank you!'

'This hut is killing you. Why do you refuse to go out of it?'

'Because the Basutos [*sic*] are very wicked; they have put a fountain in my body!'

'How so?'

Manaile was weeping now.

'When I returned from the fields one day,' she sobbed, 'some of the chief's wives offered me some beer to drink and death was in the vessel!'

'Why do you think so,' asked the Frenchman, 'what reason had they to hate you?'

At that moment Manaile's brother entered the hut. She was once a beautiful woman, he told Casalis, the envy of all but a few of Moshesh's wives. That is why some of them sought to kill her.

'My friends,' smiled the missionary, 'God alone can cause life or death,' and turning to Manaile he said: 'Unless there was poison in the vessel, the beer given you by the wives of Moshesh has done you no harm.'

'No!' retorted Manaile, 'there was no poison, but the vessel was bewitched!' She begged him to help her. Her life was drawing slowly, tormentingly to a close.

'Yesterday when I was resting outside the hut,' she quavered, 'a raven perched upon me!'

'Well?' queried Casalis.

'It was sent,' she wailed. It had come to remind her that death was about to claim her tormented soul.

The more Casalis tried to comfort her the more emotional she became, for confused visions of impending disaster crowded her mind, and her eyes bulged with fear. Moshesh never came near her, and everyone expect her anguished mother considered her mad and possessed by an evil influence. One night she was whisked away by relatives, and deposited in the cave she had formerly occupied. Again the noble Casalis attended to her, and 'after a few months of severe suffering she expired in the arms of her mother!' Her death evoked little comment at Thaba Bosiu. Not even Moshesh seemed upset.

On a dank, sweaty afternoon in December, Casalis was summoned by Moshesh, and arriving on the hill-top was given a letter from Warden to read and interpret. Among other things, he told the chief and councillors that Sir Henry Pottinger had been transferred to Madras, and his place had been taken by Sir Harry Smith, newly appointed High Commissioner over Her Majesty's dominions in South Africa. Casalis was summoned again to the hill-top in January 1848, this time to confer with the chief on a matter of extreme urgency: News had just been received that Sir Harry was coming to central South Africa, and had invited Moshesh to meet him at Winburg. At the missionary's advice the chief sent word to the Cape, expressing delight at the news. He looked forward to meeting the High Commissioner, as there were many important matters to discuss with him.

Sixty-year-old Sir Harry George Wakelyn Smith was no ordinary man, as Moshesh was soon to discover. Son of a country doctor, he was born in the parish of Whittlesea, Cambridgeshire, and had spent all but the first fifteen years of his life in the British army, rising to the rank of Lt.-General. In many ways he was a peculiar person—a source either of intense admiration, intense annoyance or intense amusement to all who knew him. He was endowed with a granite-hard constitution, the strength and energy of a dray-horse, and a childlike zest for adventure.

Smith was essentially an extrovert—domineering, boastful, conceited, contradictory, and both envious and acutely critical of his rivals. A compulsive conversationalist, he had an overbearing and often bewildering effect on his staff, family and friends. Among the elite of Colonial society he was considered eccentric, and somewhat a joke. However, a number of people, mindful of his distinguished military career, were honoured to know him and win his favour. He had seen active service in most parts of the world—South America, India, Africa and in Europe against the armies of Napoleon.

Sir Harry had been sent to the Cape Colony in 1829, and six years later as the colonel and chief of staff of the Colonial army, he had won renown for his gallantry against the Xhosa in the Sixth Frontier War. He had been a popular figure then both in Cape Town and on the frontier among the Boers, large numbers of whom had served under him and looked upon him as their friend. He had lost some favour in Britain following the killing of Hintsa, a Xhosa chief, by one of his officers. Transferred eventually on promotion to India, he little guessed that he would return one day to South Africa as High Commissioner.

He was no less energetic, enthusiastic or ebullient in 1848 than he had been a decade before. Admittedly he had grown visibly older. His torso once solid and square, was softer and wide-girthed now; his face was rutted and heavy-jowled; his hair crystal white; his huge aquiline nose, perfectly chiselled in former days, was rough and fleshy; his eyelids were minutely puffed; his cheeks elegantly whiskered and his tawny lips crested with a long melancholy moustache. This was how Moshesh would see him at Winburg.

Smith reached Philippolis on 24 January, followed by an exhausted retinue, and two days later, after a tempestuous quarrel with Adam Kok, whom he threatened to hang in public, he moved on across the Orange, heading for Winburg, the sleepy Boer hamlet north of the Vet river.

Moshesh, accompanied by Casalis and a small party of councillors and warriors, set out on the 25th, and reaching Thaba Nchu at nightfall pitched camp about six miles from Chief Moroka's settlement. At three in the morning two dragoons arrived with orders for Moshesh and his party to proceed at once to Winburg. They dared not be late for the meeting with Sir Harry in the morning. Saddling their horses, the Basotho followed the dragoons into the night, and reaching Winburg next day a little after noon, discovered to their amazement that the High Commissioner had not yet arrived. Apparently Smith had been delayed as a result of his clash with Adam Kok. Moshesh was told that he had stripped the Griqua of all authority over the Boers, believing that peace could never prevail while white men were ruled by a coloured chief, and especially one known to have as shady a past as Kok.

Moshesh and his followers spent the night on the outskirts of Winburg, and next morning, learning that Sir Harry had been spotted not five miles to the south, they saddled their horses, and linked up with a party of Boers sent by the local commandant to escort the illustrious visitor into the village. They met Sir Harry and his large entourage in the veld, and a noisy exchange of greetings took place. With a wide sweep of an arm the High Commissioner signalled the crowd to follow, and spurring his horse struck out at a canter for Winburg.

Complimenting Moshesh 'on his skill in horsemanship', Sir Harry said he was delighted to meet the chief whose name he had heard mentioned so often in Cape Town. As a token of friendship he had brought Moshesh four gifts—two new saddles, a marquee tent and a gold watch.

Catching sight of Winburg, Sir Harry called a halt, and holding his hat aloft cried out: 'I salute you gentlemen of

Winburg!' The procession moved on amidst cheers from the Boers, and as it entered the village, clattering slowly along its solitary dust-clad road, the air was filled with the crackle of musket-fire, the animated voices of farmers and the yapping of dogs. Harry Smith, hero of the Frontier Wars, friend of the Boers had arrived!

'Moshesh!' cried the High Commissioner, turning in his saddle to face the chief, 'that musket-fire is the sound which war generally makes, but today it is the sign of peace.' Pausing a short while, he then continued: 'I bring peace; I have fought much, but I declare that there is not a man in all the world who has as great a horror of war as I have. It is a horrible thing.'

Moshesh agreed. Peace, he said, was a great benefactor, the mother of all nations. He was happy that Sir Harry, like himself, abhorred the evils of war.

The procession drew up now, and as he dismounted Sir Harry was welcomed by a large gathering of Boers, many of whom had known him since 1835. Addressing the crowd, the High Commissioner said he had come 'expressedly to place everything on a solid footing' north of the Orange. He was determined to establish, once and for all, 'a durable peace between the natives themselves, and between the natives and the Colony and all British subjects', including the emigrant Boers. He had 'minutely examined' the political situation in Transorange, and had decided that the Boers should be left unhindered on the farms they occupied. He promised personally to prohibit further encroachment by white men on Basotho territory.

'Therefore,' cried Sir Harry, ignoring an effort by Moshesh to speak, 'with a view to assuring a durable peace between all parties, in order to preserve intact the hereditary rights of the Chiefs and in order to oblige the Boers to remain within the locations at present occupied by them, I will at once proclaim the sovereignty of the Queen of England over all lands now held by the Boers.... I see no other way of coming out of the dilemma in which I find the country.

'Trust me,' continued Smith observing a look of surprise on Moshesh's face, 'and no one will dare raise his hand against the Great Chief of the Basutos [sic].'

In recognition of Moshesh's 'understanding and friend-ship', he added, he would send him 'a valuable present of English manufacture' from Cape Town. In fact, he would arrange for a gift to be sent each year by the Colonial government.

Suddenly catching sight of a Xhosa named Makhomo who had accompanied him from the Cape, Smith ordered him to tell the gathering how he, Sir Harry, had brought the Axe War to a successful close. Obviously embarrassed, Makhomo began by extolling his illustrious master's prow-ess as a soldier, but he was interrupted continually by Smith who, presumably intending to improve the narrative, was uttering irrelevant Xhosa catch-phrases and unintelli-gible Zhosa-sounding exclamations. When the unfortunate Makhomo had completed his task, all eyes turned to Sir Harry for he had pretended to fall asleep, his head cush-ioned in his hands, and according to Casalis 'he began to snore with all his might'. Sitting up suddenly with a jerk, a mischievous grin spanning his moustachios, he turned to Moshesh.

'Everyone is to sleep in this way now,' he said, meaning that as the Axe War had ended, and peace had been restored to Xhosa country, both tribesmen and Colonials could retire at nights without fear of attack.

In the meantime Makhomo was padding back to his companions.

'Come here, come here, Sir,' bellowed Sir Harry, 'come here, shake hands with the Great Inkosi chief of the land.'

Makhomo swung round in his tracks, timidly took Mo-shesh's hand, and then fled from the scene.

In the afternoon after lunching with Moshesh and his white hosts, Sir Harry called all the people together saying he had some further important announcements to make. Standing on a table and looking onto the myriad of faces below him, he vowed that should the Boers even encroach on the territories either of Moshesh or any of the other chiefs, he 'would follow them up, even though it were to the gates of the infernal regions!' His voice tense with emotion, he implored the white men to help him create a haven of peace and prosperity in central South Africa.

'We must get to work at once and begin to build a church,' he cried, and extracting twenty-five sovereigns from his purse, poured them onto the table before him.

'There is £25 for my share,' he continued, 'you are living without divine worship, without schools. What a state of degradation!'

Calling upon Eugene Casalis to lead the gathering in prayer, Sir Henry 'came forward ... knelt reverently' on a stone, and began praying on his own. Suddenly he rose and gazed impassively before him, tears meandering over his creviced cheeks.

'Let us go,' he croaked, beckoning Moshesh and Casalis. And as they walked away he buried his face in a handkerchief and sobbed bitterly. Directed by a Boer to a house in the village, Sir Harry entered the living room with his two companions and flung himself into an armchair. Wiping away his tears, he confessed that presenting the Boers with a donation for the church had been his most joyous experience.

Moshesh and Casalis seated themselves on either side of the High Commissioner, and immediately he besieged them with questions, overwhelmed them with anecdotes resurrected from the distant past, and drove them to bewildered boredom with an exposition of his philosophy of life.

'What a man!' exclaimed Casalis, when at length he and Moshesh succeeded in withdrawing from the company of the untiring greybeard. He had 'never met one with such a diversity of character', and could think of no one more eccentric. And Moshesh? He had found Sir Harry overpowering and far too domineering to win his affection, but he chuckled with Casalis over his unusual manner. Her Majesty had certainly appointed an extraordinary person to keep watch over her South African dominions!

CHAPTER SEVENTEEN

RUMBLINGS OF UNREST

Sir Harry places a price on Pretorius's head—The Boers are dispersed by the British at Boomplaats—The British army gets rations from Moshesh—Moshesh and Sikonyela quarrel in Warden's company—Tribal unrest north of the Orange—Drawing of boundaries

SIR HARRY left Winburg on the morning of 28 January, convinced that Moshesh and the Boers were in favour of a British takeover north of the Orange. Travelling due east he reached the Drakensberg a week later, and crossing into Natal headed for the Tugela river where he had arranged to meet Andries Pretorius, the Boer leader responsible for the defeat of the Zulu at Blood river.

No sooner had they met than Smith presented Pretorius with a draft proclamation outlining the impending declaration of sovereignty. It had never occurred to him that the Boers might oppose the idea. He suggested that Pretorius should return immediately to his followers, and break the good news to them. Andries Pretorius boiled. The Boers, he said, would have no dealings with the British, and would fight to the very last man, rather than agree to so absurd a proposal. Smith remained calm, suggesting that the Boers should consider the matter for a while. He promised to leave things as they were, pending a reply from Pretorius. The two men parted on friendly terms, but a few days later the High Commissioner, becoming suddenly impatient, officially proclaimed central South Africa north of the Orange and south of the Vaal a British possession. This vast new dominion would henceforth be known as the Orange River Sovereignty. The Sovereignty was to be divided into three districts—Bloemfontein, Caledon River and Winburg.

News of Sir Harry's duplicity came as a shock to the Boers, and during the following five months there were rumblings of unrest on every farm and in every village.

Mustering a large commando in July, Pretorius advanced on Bloemfontein and captured the British fort without resistance. A few days later the Boers moved southwards, and pitched camp on the banks of the Orange. When Smith received news of these developments, he placed a price of £1,000 on Pretorius's head. Then at the head of a powerful force consisting mainly of cavalry, he hastened to Colesberg, took command of the British garrison there and struck out northwards.

Smith and his men crossed the Orange in August, and locating Pretorius's commando on a farm called Boomplaats, fought and put it to flight. Withdrawing to Bloemfontein, the High Commissioner scribbled a note to his 'friend, [the] great Chief Moshesh ... faithful ally of Her Majesty of England'. The British, he wrote, had crushed 'the rebels under that vile man Pretorius'. However, he had since encountered a dreadful problem: His army had run out of rations. Perhaps Moshesh would send 'slaughter bullocks and sheep a great many, also all sorts of grain, wheat, barley and Kaffir corn [sorghum]'. He also wanted Moshesh to meet him at Winburg in September.

Dressed in gold lace trousers, a faded blue coat of a British general and a large forage cap pulled rakishly over his thick greying hair, Moshesh rode into Winburg on the appointed day. He was accompanied by Casalis and seven hundred horsemen and footmen. Next morning he visited Sir Harry's camp on a hillside overlooking the village. He was surprised to find the High Commissioner in conference with numbers of other chiefs, including Sikonyela of the Wild Cat People. He was given a hearty welcome by Sir Harry and shown to a seat beside him.

As was his custom when in the company of people he liked, Sir Harry dominated the conversation, keeping his audience spellbound with an account of the wars he had fought. The chiefs found him entertaining, enjoyed his flattery, and marvelled at his ability to pour forth a deluge of words, seemingly without even pausing for breath. On the afternoon of the 10 September they were treated to a parade of the infantry and a display of horsemanship by the cavalry. No one was more impressed than Moshesh, and according to Sir Harry he 'was much amused ... and particularly astonished at the Artillery, these being the first regular troops that had been so far into the interior'. On the 11th, the High Commissioner reviewed Moshesh's force— a disorderly procession of horsemen bearing old-fashioned muzzleloaders, and footmen armed with clubs and assegais.

'A fine body of men for savages,' thought Smith, 'undisciplined as they were.' What really impressed him was a war-dance performed by the Basotho in his honour at sunset. After dark he feasted with the chiefs and warriors. This had been one of the happiest days of his life.

Next morning Sir Harry set out for home aboard a mule wagon. Not a mile out of Winburg, he and his party were overtaken by a horseman bearing a letter from Moshesh.

'I desire again to express ... my sincere and respectful esteem for Your Excellency, the Great Chief of the British in South Africa,' he read. 'It is my constant wish ever to live in peace and fellowship with all under your Government. ... Go, Great Warrior of your Nation, go under the shield of your mighty God Jehovah, by whose help, you tell me, you have been able to do such great things in this country. Go, Great Leader of the Soldiers of the Lady your Queen, tell Her Gracious Majesty, in my name that I love her Government. I love her Warriors whose deeds of valour have filled me with wonder. Tell Her Majesty that I am sensible to the great debt I owe to the brave General and her troops, who has in a few days driven back and scattered the host of the wicked Rebels.'

Sir Harry was elated. He could not have wished for a more pleasant surprise than a letter such as this, and especially one from so illustrious a dignitary as Moshesh, chief of the Basotho.

Moshesh had been back at Thaba Bosiu less than three weeks when Sikonyela and his Wild Cat commando burst into the Tlotsi districts and set fire to the Basotho kraals. As soon as news of the attack reached the Lesotho, powerful commandos under Letsie, Makwanyane, Sekhonyana and Moshesh himself, set out for Wild Cat territory. Reaching the first of Sikonyela's kraals two days later, the Basotho attacked 'mercilessly slaughtering' eighteen Wild Cat

People, among whom was the wife of Mota, the chief's brother.

The Basotho advanced on Joalaboholo—the Great Beer, Sikonyela's capital kraal, meaning to raze it to the ground. But coming suddenly upon a multitude of cattle, goats and sheep swirling towards them out of a valley, they changed their minds, and capturing the animals retraced their steps to Thaba Bosiu.

News of the upheaval reached Warden[1] in October. He went first to Thaba Bosiu and then to Joalaboholo, and persuaded Moshesh and Sikonyela to meet him on 7 November. They chose as the rendezvous, the premises of an English trader named William Prynn, near the Caledon river.

Moshesh and Sikonyela, each accompanied by a large commando, met the British Resident as arranged, but they refused to speak to each other, or to sit together with Warden at the same counsel table. After considerable persuasion by the white man, Moshesh condescended to proffer his old enemy a hand, and Sikonyela accepted it halfheartedly. In this way Warden was able to get the meeting started. But the chiefs soon started quarrelling, the one blaming the other for the upheaval in the Tlotsi district. Again after much perseverance Warden persuaded them to postpone discussion on past events, and consider what steps should be taken to promote peace between the two tribes. Neither of the chiefs had much more to say. They undertook to settle their differences in future not on the battlefield, but in the *kgotla*. Taking leave of the British Resident they returned to their homes.

In December, Moshesh received a letter from Southey, secretary to the High Commissioner, summoning him to Smithfield, a village recently founded on a farm called Waterval, five miles north of the Caledon. Learning that the purpose of the meeting was to fix a boundary line in Transorange, between the Basotho and the Boers, the chief refused to go. He sent Sekhonyana in his place, and asked the Rev. Rolland to stand in for Casalis who had left on a visit to France a week before.

A fortnight later, having conferred with Southey, Sek-

[1] Now Major Warden.

honyana returned to Thaba Bosiu with news that a line had
been fixed provisionally to extend from the source of the
Modder river, along the Langberg range, to the junction of
the Caledon and Orange. Moshesh was 'filled with grief and
astonishment'.

Should the British attempt to mark the line with beacons,
as had been suggested by Smith, the chief would call the
Basotho to arms. Sir Harry's skull would be used to adorn
the first beacon erected, and the blood of warriors, both
black and white, would 'run as large as the Caledon river'.

Meanwhile rumours had reached Thaba Bosiu that the
Wild Cat People were planning to invade the Lesotho. In
January 1849 Sikonyela sent messengers to Moshesh demanding that his daughter, Nthe, be delivered to Joalaboholo—The Great Beer, as compensation for the eighteen
people slaughtered by the Basotho four months before.

'If this be not done,' Sikonyela had said, 'then I declare
there shall be war.'

Moshesh did not wait for Sikonyela to act. Mustering a
large commando under Molapo and Chief Moletstane, he
sent it against the Wild Cat People. The Basotho charged
into Sikonyela's domain, burning down kraal after kraal,
driving women and children into the hills, and cattle,
horses and sheep into the valleys. Reaching Imparani, they
set fire to the Wesleyan mission station, tearing down its
flimsy cattlefold and trampling its vegetable garden under
foot. Challenged by a party of herdsmen, the Basotho sent a
volley of slug into their midst, killing two and wounding
ten. Then, as swiftly as they had come, they streaked
homewards.

A week later, Sikonyela stole into the Tlotsi district at the
head of some five hundred horsemen and engaged Molapo's
people in battle. Day after day they skirmished, sometimes
north of the river and sometimes to the south. At the same
time bands of brigands—renegade Koranna, Griqua and
Sotho-speaking warriors—took advantage of the situation
by pillaging defenceless settlements in Wild Cat territory.
Moving north-westwards they fell upon Boer farms, sacking homesteads, outhouses and unreaped crops, and loading
their horses with loot. One of the brigand bands came unexpectedly upon members of a land commission sent by the

High Commissioner to erect beacons along the new boundary line. First the ruffians caught and bound them, then cuffed and whipped them and, finally, drove them at musket point into the hills. Boers in the neighbourhood, fearing for their safety, took shelter in a chain of laagers formed by Field-cornet Wessels in the Caledon River district. Complaints and appeals for help poured into Bloemfontein, but Warden was powerless to act. His garrison was ill-equipped, and far too small to risk an encounter with the brigands.

In the meantime the Wild Cat People had been joined by Taaibosch's Koranna, and withdrawing from the fight on the banks of the Tlotsi, had attacked the Bataung near the Mekwatleng mission station. Moletstane, chief of the clan, appealed to Warden for help, and when the British failed to come, he reported his dilemma to Moshesh.

Moshesh was furious. What was the use of a British garrison, he complained, if it failed to keep law and order, and if its guns remained silent while innocent people were butchered?

'You bound our hands behind our backs,' he wrote to the British Resident, 'and strangers cut our throats.'

About two weeks later, told by a party of Griqua that Moshesh was preparing a full-scale invasion of Wild Cat territory, Warden appealed to Sir Harry for reinforcements. Smith's reply came three weeks later: Warden was to remonstrate with Moshesh, but should he fail to persuade him to abandon the attack, he was to muster a force of Boers, Barolong and Griqua and invade the Lesotho.

'If Moshesh [should] shut himself up on his mountain, Thaba Bosigo [sic],' concluded the High Commissioner, 'I believe some howitzer shells may be thrown upon him.'

Warden invited Moshesh to meet him at Platberg, but the chief refused, saying he would send Makwanyane instead. He then suggested that Moshesh should meet him at Beersheba, and although this time the chief agreed to come, he would not budge from the hill-top when the appointed day arrived. So Warden called a meeting of all the chiefs, purposely excluding Moshesh, and entered into an agreement with them to combine forces against any tribe responsible for disrupting the peace.

On his return to Bloemfontein, Warden learned that

Moshesh had called off the invasion of Wild Cat territory. According to his informant there had been heavy storms over the Lesotho and the chief considered the rivers and streams too swollen for his commandos to cross. The British Resident chuckled happily. His plan to unite the chiefs against Moshesh had worked!

Warden summoned Moshesh to Bloemfontein to discuss the new Boer–Basotho boundary line with him, but the chief refused to come. He therefore sent Moshesh a map indicating the line he intended recommending to the High Commissioner. The chief was to sign and return it to Bloemfontein provided, of course, he approved of the boundary line.

Moshesh drew his customary cross at the bottom of the map, but he was bitterly dissatisfied, for the new line cut off not only a hundred or more Basotho kraals from the Lesotho, but also Poshuli's stronghold at Vechtkop. He would have rejected the map had he not feared this would lead to unpleasantness. He would protest later, he told his councillors, when the dust had settled.[1]

Warden's line came into force in December 1849, and both he and Sir Harry predicted the dawning of an era of peace in the territories north of the Orange. But in January 1850 violence broke out in several parts of central South Africa: Chief Moletstane's Lion People attacked and sacked Barolong kraals near Thaba Nchu, threatening to kill the missionaries if they dared interfere. The Koranna led by Taaibosch also swooped on the Barolong, destroying their fields of ripening sorghum, and returning laden with booty to their grimy village at Merumetsu. Poshuli, heading a commando under cover of darkness, raided Boer farms in Transorange, driving off many thousands of cattle and sheep.

But of all the plunderers who moved into action in 1850, none was as ruthless, destructive and daring as the 'Free-

[1] Warden's line extended roughly from the junction of the Kornet and Orange rivers to Vechtkop, and thence to Leeuwkop, Jammersberg Drift, the source of the Modder and north-eastwards to Thaba Nchu. From there it travelled southwards along a spruit as far as the great Leeuw river.

booting Chief, Sikonyela'. His commandos razed tribal
settlements and Boer homesteads to the ground. They even
slaughtered bands of impoverished Bushmen found living in
caves on the hillslopes.

Asked by the Boers to drive Sikonyela back to Wild Cat
territory, Warden refused. He had received not a single re-
inforcement from the Colony, and the Bloemfontein garrison was hopelessly inadequate. Bringing to mind the various chiefs of central South Africa, it suddenly struck him
that Moshesh had been uncommonly quiet of late, and it
pleased him to think that he and the dignitaries of Thaba
Bosiu seemed satisfied with the new boundary line. He
would write to Moshesh, inviting him to Bloemfontein as a
guest of the British government. Should the chief find it
difficult to undertake the journey, he, Warden, would
gladly go to Thaba Bosiu. The venue was unimportant.
What really mattered was that they should meet as soon as
possible.

CHAPTER EIGHTEEN

TRIUMPH AT VIERVOET

Thaba Bosiu in 1850—J. J. Freeman supports Moshesh against the High Commissioner—War-clouds loom over the south-eastern horizon—Casalis returns from France, and tries to prevent war—Chief Moletstane triumphs over Donovon's force at Viervoet

WARDEN'S note could not have been worse timed, for Moshesh had not the slightest desire to meet the British Resident, considering him a hypocrite and prime protagonist in a plot to crush the Basotho. If he never saw Warden again, so much the better.

In years gone by Moshesh would have been less obstinate, but now at the age of sixty-three, he was easily riled, and dwelt at length on even the most trivial incident. And yet, physically he had not weathered much in the course of his stormy life. His hair, although grey and bereft of the lustre of his youth, was still woolly-thick; his face while leathery, was sparsely furrowed, and his modest, short-cropped moustache and beard, streaked with white embraced a firm thick-lipped mouth. True, his hands, corded with veins, had become calloused and gnarled, his chest a little shrunken and his waist flabby. But clad in a military uniform, with a capacious mantle draped over his shoulders and a top hat cresting his forehead, he still cut an elegant figure.

In the twenty-six years since Moshesh's arrival at Thaba Bosiu, striking changes had taken place in the surrounding countryside. As a result of the rapid growth of the tribe, the once sparsely populated valley had become closely studded with kraals both large and small, and the plains, hill-slopes and river banks, formerly the haunts of a great variety of game, now teemed with cattle, goats and sheep. Most of the dark-soiled sorghum land nearest the base of the hill had been washed away, and as far as the eye could see huge, gaping *dongas*, some two hundred feet wide, meandered like monstrous serpents down to the mud-choked Phuthi-astana river.

Contact over the years with missionaries, white traders, hunters, travellers and farmers, had presented the Basotho with a new and exciting material culture. Soon most of the tribe, and especially the younger set, clamoured for European clothing, firearms, horses, farming implements, household furniture and utensils. Even the traditional grass huts, once the only type known to Sotho-speaking peoples, went out of vogue, and were replaced by small, rondavel-type stone houses similar to those built for Moshesh on Thaba Bosiu.

The most imposing Basotho dwelling in 1850 was Moshesh's large, thatched, rectangular stone house built by David Webber some three hundred paces from the top of the Khubelu pass. Situated slightly to the right of the kraal entrance, it could be seen from far off by travellers approaching the western slopes of Thaba Bosiu. Two dome-shaped rocks planted five yards apart in the main pathway, marked the spot beyond which no stranger could pass without Moshesh's consent.[1] Before entering the kraal visitors were required to drop a stone or two on to a nearby cairn, as a token of reverence for the chief.

Moshesh's 'great house' was furnished mainly with items of European manufacture. The interior was dark, dingy and cluttered with an agglomeration of personal belongings. The furniture, subjected over the years to constant use by visitors was soiled, and in some cases, dilapidated.

In the Spring of 1850, while most of his subjects were away preparing the fields for planting, Moshesh remained confined to his home. He had been unwell lately, laid low by an attack of influenza, and his mind was fraught with troubles. Since signing Warden's map, he had been slated by his father, accused of weakness by his sons, ignored by many of the elders, and warned by Poshuli and others that if he allowed the boundary line to remain unchallenged, they would invade and devastate Boer farms. His sons particularly continued to cause him grave concern. He no longer interfered in their squabbles, realizing that they

[1] Three rocks planted in line are to be found on Thaba Bosiu. The addition was made after Moshesh's time.

neither welcomed his opinions nor recognized his authority. He had one comforting thought: Masupha and Sekhonyana were back from Cape Town having completed
their schooling. They were kind to him and had advised
him assiduously on all matters demanding a knowledge of
reading and writing. It also pleased him to think that some
of his younger sons were receiving similar instruction at
Casalis's mission station.

In September Thomas Arbousset brought two white men
to Thaba Bosiu—J. J. Freeman, Home Secretary of the
London Missionary Society, and Robert Moffat, veteran
missionary of Kuruman. Learning of their arrival at the
mission station, Moshesh sent them his greetings. The following day was the sabbath, so dressing in his best European clothes, he went down the Khubelu pass to meet them.
Freeman, he discovered, was a man of influence, a close
friend of Dr. Philip and an ardent opponent of both Sir
Harry Smith and Warden. He was delighted to learn that
this friendly white man considered Warden's line unjust
and contrary to British colonial policy. Freeman promised
to contest the line on behalf of the Basotho, on his return to
England. He would do his utmost to restore the territory
appropriated by the British Resident to the Lesotho. Moshesh's heart filled with renewed hope. Later, joining the
white men at worship, he offered prayers of thanksgiving to
the Molimo.

On the following Tuesday morning Freeman, Moffat,
Arbousset and Dyke, Casalis's assistant, paid Moshesh a
visit on Thaba Bosiu. They found the old chief in the
kgotla, dressed only in a loin-cloth, and he was discussing
with his councillors a clash reported to have taken place
between Poshuli and the British Resident. Catching sight of
the white men, the chief came forward to greet them. They
followed him into the kgotla and sat down on either side of
him.

At Arbousset's request Moshesh recalled the highlights of
his career since his flight from Butha-Buthe, stressing the
horrors of difaqane, the founding of Thaba Bosiu, the
arrival of white men in the interior and, finally, the emerg-
ence of the Boers and British as a threat to his power.

Learning that Arbousset was offended that the chief should have received his guests in a state of seminakedness, Moshesh withdrew apologetically in order to change into European clothing. He had not intended causing his missionary friend embarrassment.

While Moshesh was away the white men strolled about the hill-top and viewed the magnificent panorama stretched out in the valley below. Summoned by Moshesh, they were ushered into the stone house by a councillor, and entering the living room were told to be seated on a sofa draped with leopard skins. Moshesh joined them a little while later, and the room filled with dignitaries. So unbearably hot did the house become in the blaze of the morning sun, so heavy with the fetid reek of sweaty bodies, that one of the white men, feeling faint, suggested the meeting should be held in the *kgotla*. But Moshesh refused. He preferred to entertain his guests in his home. Turning to Arbousset, he asked him the purpose of Freeman's visit to Thaba Bosiu.

Freeman, began the missionary, had come to South Africa two years before, on a tour of inspection to mission stations throughout the area. He had since covered the entire Cape Colony, and after Thaba Bosiu would be visiting the missionaries of central South Africa and Natal. He would then rejoin his ship in Cape Town and return to England. Freeman and Moffat, continued Arbousset, were men of God, filled with love for non-white peoples and driven by an urge to spread spiritual enlightenment among all who were living in ignorance.

Recalling that at their first meeting Freeman had condemned Boer and British policy in central South Africa, Moshesh outlined the political situation as it had developed since the arrival of white men in the interior. He spoke for two long hours, pausing only to wipe his sweaty brow and neck. In spite of the stifling heat, 'his people listened with intense interest', taking in each word, nodding occasionally in agreement or interjecting with exclamations of approval.

'These people have a keen sense of the just and the unjust, the true and the false,' Freeman thought as Moshesh continued to speak, 'and they deeply feel that they have been unjustly and most untruly dealt with, and that too by a Government professing higher and nobler things. They therefore feel helpless against the power of the British, and they are helpless as to obtaining justice.' On his return to England, he told himself, he would inform the Colonial Secretary that Sir Harry Smith was unsuited to the task of determining the destinies of tribal peoples. He would blame the High Commissioner for depriving the Basotho of a 'large and valuable portion' of territory. This was a heinous act 'against which ... the chieftain Moshesh and his people bitterly, indignantly and justly complain'. Small wonder the chief looked upon white men as 'rapacious and unjust'.

It was well past noon when Moshesh came to the end of his address, and after sharing a pot of coffee with his guests, he accompanied them to the mission station. At Freeman's request, he and Hamilton Dyke drew up a report stressing Sir Harry's and Warden's incompetence in handling the political situation in central South Africa. Freeman would take the document with him to England, and bring it to the attention of both the government and Her Majesty, Queen Victoria.

Unknown to Freeman, at the time of his visit to Thaba Bosiu, bands of mounted Basotho were rampaging across Boer farms in the Caledon River district, pillaging, destroying newly planted crops and taunting the farmers with jeers and threats of annihilation. Several of Moshesh's vassal chiefs, including Moletstane and Letele joined the marauders in October, and Warden, convinced that the Basotho were preparing for war, appealed to Sir Harry for help. He could count on the Griqua, Koranna, Barolong and Wild Cat People to send him troops and provisions, so provided Sir Harry sent reinforcements at once, he believed he could crush the Basotho.

Warden was stunned by the High Commissioner's reply. He was not to involve the British in a war with the Basotho, and was to wait for Casalis's return from abroad, and then get him to talk to Moshesh. Meanwhile Warden would have to maintain law and order as best he could.

Eugene Casalis and his family returned to Thaba Bosiu in December, and were given a great welcome by a large gathering headed by his old friend Moshesh. But the missionary, although overjoyed to be back at last with his flock was filled with despair at the war clouds looming over the south-western horizon. It broke his heart to learn that his congregation had dwindled to less than half. Many of the staunchest converts were said to have forsaken Christianity, and had joined the trouble-makers of the tribe in urging the councillors to rid central South Africa of white men.

The missionary could see a considerable change in Moshesh. The chief seemed to have aged unduly and had lost some interest in the affairs of the tribe. Admittedly he had little control over his sons and vassal chiefs, and seemed never to tire of bewailing the presence of white men so near his borders. How was he to prevent the depredations of such forceful and headstrong chiefs as Poshuli, Moletstane, Letele and Moorosi, he would ask, recalling complaints received from Warden. Was he to have them flogged or executed, or was he to sack their kraals and decimate their followers? This was the practice in Zulu territory when lesser chiefs defied the authority of their awesome rulers. No. He, Moshesh, would not use fear as a means of maintaining order. Frightened men were unhappy men, and therefore dangerous subjects. Why else had Shaka and others been assassinated by their own followers. The vassal chiefs had resorted to brigandry, he assured Casalis, not because they were by nature evil men, but because they feared the white man. Not until all the Boers had returned to the Colony could there again be peace in central South Africa.

By the Autumn of 1851 skirmishing between Basotho and Boer commandos had reached such alarming proportions that Warden called a meeting of all chiefs of the Sovereignty, hoping to win their support in preventing a full-scale war. But with the exception of Moroka and Taaibosch the chiefs cold-shouldered him, Moshesh declaring he dared not undertake so long a journey for fear of attack by the Wild Cat People.

'It is utterly impossible for me to go to Bloemfontein,' he added, 'for the greatest confusion prevails about me, and my absence from home would most certainly create still more.'

Warden wrote to Sir Harry for advice. Learning that arms and ammunition were being smuggled into the Leso-

tho from across the Orange, he decreed that anyone found
guilty of this 'illicit trade' would be jailed or heavily fined.

At the beginning of June, Warden received a reply from
Garvock, Sir Harry's secretary, authorizing him to call the
Boers and chiefs to arms 'so as to smite down the turbulent
and refractory' subjects of Chief Moshesh. Two weeks later
another letter arrived, this time from the High Commissioner himself, urging quick and drastic action against the
Basotho. Moshesh must be humbled, Smith demanded, and
in future 'the peaceable and exemplary Moroka' was to be
recognized as the supreme chief of the Sovereignty.

Warden started preparing for the invasion of the Lesotho. He sent messengers with orders for the Boers, the
Barolong, Batlokwa, Bastards, Griqua and Koranna to join
him at Platberg. On 20 June he reached the mission station
heading one hundred and sixty men, among whom was a
British contingent under Major Donovon. By the following
evening the allied force had grown to two thousand. There
were three hundred Boers, and as many Griqua and Koranna, all mounted and armed with muzzleloaders. Sikonyela had come specifically to witness Moshesh's overthrow,
and old Moroka, fearing an attack on Thaba Nchu, had
brought several hundred women and children along with
the Barolong contingent.

In the meantime Warden had written to Moshesh suggesting they should meet for discussions at Platberg. But the
chief refused, and sent Casalis and Dyke in his place. The
missionaries pleaded with Warden to disband his fighting
force. Moshesh, they said, was 'most desirous for peace',
and had promised to restore the many thousands of cattle
stolen by his subjects from the Boers and neighbouring
tribes. He had wanted to visit Platberg, but had been 'afraid
to leave his mountain'. In any case, he had been prevented
'by his people from doing so'.

On their departure for Thaba Bosiu, the missionaries
promised to bring Moshesh to Platberg. Four days later
when neither they nor the chief had turned up, Warden sent
a letter to Moshesh demanding the immediate delivery of
six thousand cattle and three hundred horses to the allied
force encamped at Platberg.

Reconnoitring the surrounding countryside on 28 June, Warden's scouts discovered large numbers of Basotho on most of the hills close by. Moletstane's stronghold, a flat-topped hill named Viervoet, swarmed with cattle under guard of a powerful commando. Warden convened a council-of-war, and it was decided to occupy Viervoet as a prelude to the invasion of the Lesotho. Donovon was to take charge of the operation.

At daybreak on the 30th the British force set out along a wagon trail for Viervoet, and though pestered by snipers, it reached the base of the hill safely by sunset. Weary after the long march from Platberg, Donovon's troops bivouacked, swallowed a scanty meal and retired to their tents. No sooner had they lain down to sleep, than bullets came zipping into camp from the top of Viervoet. Most of the firing was far off the mark, for the camp was in total darkness, but at about two in the morning a sentinel was struck in the chest by a stray bullet, and came staggering towards the tents screaming for help.

All was quiet on the following day, Sunday the 1st of July. During the morning, Donovon and most of the troops attended divine worship in camp, and in the afternoon they hung about the tents discussing the impending clash with the enemy. Meanwhile large numbers of Bataung, or Lion People, had been creeping silently up the opposite slope of Viervoet, and had occupied strategic positions in the cliffs. Thousands of warriors lined the hill-top all day waiting to sound the alarm should Warden's force emerge from the camp. They started singing and dancing towards sunset, and when night fell and their fires had been lit, they could be seen warming themselves against the freezing Winter air or roasting beef in the flames.

The night passed without incident but at dawn the Lion People awoke to the booming of a British six-pounder, followed by the rattle of musket-fire. A cry of panic went up from the hill when suddenly they realized that the enemy had climbed to the summit under cover of darkness, and was advancing swiftly to destroy them. The Lion People scattered, some on foot, others on horseback, and they scrambled down the southern passes. The cattle started stampeding now, rolling across the hill-top, swerving, dodg-

ing and rearing as suddenly they came to the edge of the
summit, and struggled to retrace their steps to safety.
Donovon and his men came surging forward, and locating
batches of fugitives in the upper passes mowed them down.
Realizing that the bulk of the Bataung army had slipped
through his fingers, Donovon decided to abandon the operation and return to camp. He left a contingent of seven hundred Barolong to round up Chief Moletstane's cattle and
drive them to Bloemfontein.

Reaching the bottom of Viervoet the Lion People regrouped and joined forces with two commandos that had
arrived on the scene under Molapo and Mopeli. After a
brief discussion the leaders decided to re-occupy Viervoet
and prevent Moletstane's cattle from falling into the hands
of the enemy. So the combined force climbed the hill singing and chanting war cries, and locating the Barolong, discovered they had been gorging beer abandoned by the
Bataung, and were incapable either of fighting or fleeing.
The Bataung and Basotho pounced on the helpless Barolong, and would have annihilated them had not a party of
Boers under Comdt. Erasmus arrived and engaged them in
battle. And although at first they held their ground, they
soon fell back towards the passes and retreated down the
hill, leaving the Boers to rescue the Barolong and conduct
them, together with Moletstane's cattle, back to Donovon's
camp. During this short skirmish, one hundred and fifty-
two Barolong were killed and almost as many wounded by
the Bataung and Basotho.

Now while Erasmus and his men were retracing their
steps down the hill, their attention was arrested by the
sound of gunfire coming from the camp. Some minutes
later they were met by a messenger with orders from
Donovon to hurry. A huge force of horsemen under Chief
Moletstane had arrived at the base of Viervoet and was
expected to attack at any moment.

Indeed, Moletstane had been awaiting this opportunity.
Three weeks before a female seer, named Mantshupa Makhetha, had predicted he would defeat Moshesh's enemies at
Viervoet hill. The woman had said the struggle would be
short and sharp, and so fierce and decisive that it would be
remembered always as *Ntwa ya sefako*—the Battle of Hail.

Donovon took two horse-drawn six-pounders, under escort of a party of Boers, Griqua, Koranna and troops of the Cape Mounted Rifles, into a nearby coppice. Molet-stane's force opened fire, but with no effect for the enemy was out of range. Just as the six-pounders were being brought into position, about a hundred yards apart, Molet-stane and his followers charged, guns aloft—three thousand whooping, whistling, cat-calling horsemen. Blasted by the allied force they came racing on, firing volley after volley into the coppice. Some of them galloped recklessly to with-in fifty yards of the nearest six-pounder, sending the Cape Mounted Rifles scurrying for shelter amidst a flurry of musket-fire.

A deluge of slug cut viciously into the coppice now, driv-ing the defenders back to the second field-gun and head over heels into a rock-strewn thicket beyond. Suddenly the chief called a halt. The terrain had become too treacherous for the horses, and he would not risk following the enemy on foot. And so the Battle of Hail came abruptly to an end. Moletstane's force withdrew to a safe place, plucked off a few Barolong spies seen clambering over the rocks above the thicket, and retired eastwards. Donovon's party crept cautiously back to camp during the late afternoon. Casualties had been surprisingly light; but of one thing the crestfallen major was certain: If ever he was to defeat Moshesh's tribe, he would need not only a larger army, but one trained and equipped for guerrilla warfare.

During the remaining hours before sunset, Donovon, Warden and leaders of the various contingents conferred. At dusk scouts returning to camp reported that Molet-stane's commandos were bivouacked on a hill-slope several miles to the east, and were unlikely to resume operations until the following day. But there was to be no further fight-ing at Viervoet. Next day Donovon's force withdrew to Thaba Nchu, and after a short rest it dispersed.

CHAPTER NINETEEN

WAR WITH THE BRITISH

*Warden loses the support of the Boers—Sir Harry
Smith is slated by Lord Grey—He is replaced by Sir
George Cathcart—Cathcart invades the Lesotho—The
British blunder at Berea hill—Moshesh's extraordinary
act of diplomacy*

ALTHOUGH Moletstane's success was celebrated at Thaba
Bosiu, Moshesh was troubled. He realized Warden would be
more determined than ever now to crush the Basotho. He
hated Warden but dared not reveal this to him. He was
anxious to establish a lasting bond of friendship between the
Basotho and the mighty British, and would allow nothing
to foil his efforts. Reflecting on the Boers, it pleased him to
know they were not all antagonistic towards his tribe. Those
who had fought under Warden and Donovon at Viervoet
deserved to be punished. As for the British Resident's
demand for six thousand cattle and three hundred horses,
this seemed ludicrous in the light of recent events.

Warden returned to Bloemfontein on 6 July, and after
sending Sir Harry a report on the fiasco at Viervoet, set
about recruiting an army. He would bring the Basotho to
their knees, he told himself, before the arrival of Spring.
But the British Resident found himself faced with a serious
problem. He could persuade few of the Boers who had
fought at Viervoet to enlist for a second spell of active
service. Most of them had lands to reap, and in any case,
while they had been away on commando, their lands had
been pillaged by avenging Basotho. The wags among them
scoffed at the idea of fighting again on the side of the
British, adding facetiously that they would prefer to join
forces with Moshesh.

Of the six hundred Boers Warden had hoped to recruit,
only seventy-five came forward. The situation was desperate. What hope had he now of overthrowing Moshesh?

And to add to his dilemma, reports reached Bloemfontein that hordes of Tamboekies, many of them experienced in Colonial warfare, were streaming across the Orange to support the Basotho.

Towards the end of July, Warden had a reply from Sir Harry, ordering him to speed up preparations for Moshesh's overthrow. If necessary, he was to threaten to punish the Boers should they persist in cold-shouldering him. And what of the Griqua, Koranna and Barolong? They should be forced to join him. Furthermore, continued Sir Harry's letter, Warden was to make sure the Bloemfontein fort was adequately stocked with supplies. But he was not to invade the Lesotho unless he and Donovon were sure of victory.

'Partial success,' he added, 'would be little thought of, while failure would be attended with disastrous results.'

The following months were the most difficult and frustrating Warden had known since arriving in central South Africa. He could see no hope of collecting an army capable of defeating the Basotho, who in 1851 numbered approximately 70,000; the only British reinforcements he could count on were a small party of regulars and five hundred native levies under Capt. Parish of the 4th Regiment. These had been promised him by Sir Benjamin Pine, Lt. Governor of Natal.

Meanwhile J. J. Freeman, who had visited Moshesh in September 1850, had returned to England, and in a letter to Lord Grey,[1] Secretary of State for the Colonies, had made a scathing attack on Sir Harry's native policy. Smith's ignorance in the political situation north of the Orange, he said, had deprived Moshesh of valuable territory and, in addition, had heralded an era of inter-tribal conflict, exposing the Colony to 'extreme peril'. Freeman could foresee 'nothing but anarchy, bloodshed and ruin to the Colony'. He begged Grey to implement the necessary legislation for restoring 'tranquillity and confidence' among the tribes of the Sovereignty.

Grey acted fast. He appointed two special commissioners, Major W. S. Hogge and C. M. Owen to investigate matters, and sent reinforcements to the Cape lest the Colony be

[1] Albert 4th Earl of Grey.

threatened. He also wrote to Sir Harry, accusing him of sending 'imperfect information' to Downing Street, of acting rashly in his dealings with the Basotho, and of misleading the British government into believing there was a need for the establishment of the Sovereignty. For example, it was not true that British rule was 'generally desired' by the peoples of the interior, as a means of preventing 'disorder and bloodshed'. Grey also questioned Smith's 'prudence and propriety' in attempting to overthrow Moshesh. The British government would no longer tolerate interference by either Sir Harry or his subordinates in the affairs of the Basotho and neighbouring peoples.

Warden's plans for the invasion of the Lesotho were abandoned, and gradually Boer–Basotho relations improved. Admittedly the Basotho continued to raid Boer farms, but their activities were directed solely against those who had fought under Warden and Donovon at Viervoet. Farmers unaffected by the raids refused to assist their less fortunate countrymen, fearing they themselves would become implicated. Two of the leaders, Jan Vermaak and the influential Andries Pretorius, assured Moshesh that should the Basotho become involved in a war with the British, the Boers would observe a strict policy of neutrality. In contrast, relations between Moshesh and the petty-chiefs living near the various Wesleyan mission stations deteriorated.

Attacked incessantly by Basotho commandos the Barolong fled from Thaba Nchu to a hideout near the Modder river. Taaibosch fled with his Koranna to a cluster of hills overlooking the Vaal, and the Bastards reduced now to no more than a hundred impoverished wretches, withdrew westwards, settling after months of privation on a pinch of unoccupied land near Bloemfontein.

In January 1852 Moshesh was summoned to Winburg by Hogge, the special commissioner, but he refused to go lest the Wild Cat People should invade the Lesotho during his absence. Some days before, Sikonyela's commandos had made a surprise attack on Basotho kraals east of Thaba Bosiu, carrying off thousands of cattle and sheep, and slaying twelve herdsmen. On 5 February Moshesh sent Mopeli, Molapo and Masupha to confer with Hogge. Learning on their return that they had been cordially received, he agreed to meet the special commissioner himself, provided a venue was selected south of the Caledon.

Moshesh, accompanied by a Basotho commando, and another under Chief Moorosi, met Hogge near the Orange river on the 22nd. He liked the young white man from the start, especially his forthright unpatronizing manner, and it soon became clear to him that he and the special commissioner shared similar views on local political matters. The old chief felt a sense of calm, a welcome relief from the troubles which had crowded his mind in recent months. He was delighted to learn that Warden had been removed from office. In addition, the boundary line introduced by him and approved by Sir Harry Smith would no longer be recognized by the British government. The territory occupied by Poshuli, now incorporated in the Sovereignty would be restored to the Lesotho. According to Hogge, from now on the Basotho could look forward to living in peace with the white men of the interior. All that remained was to determine a new line, by mutual agreement, in the Caledon River district. Moshesh, of course, would have to surrender whatever stock his people had stolen from the Boers.

Moshesh returned to Thaba Bosiu a far happier person than he had been in many a year. In April he learned that Sir Harry had been sacked, and his post filled by Sir George Cathcart, a soldier of great repute. He welcomed Sir George's appointment, little guessing that this white man was fated to be a more formidable enemy than even Smith or Warden.

From the moment he took office in Cape Town, Cathcart showed little tolerance either for Moshesh or his vassals. He was suspicious of Moshesh's integrity, declaring all documents bearing the chief's cross as 'political frauds'[1] conceived by Casalis, Dyke and other allegedly meddling missionaries. He would not be hoodwinked by this wily chief, and far less by white agitators.

Warden's place was taken by Henry Green, a little-known commissariat officer of the British army. Hardly had he taken office than bands of mounted Basotho stole into the

[1] Letter from Sir George Cathcart, to the British Resident.

Winburg, Caledon River and Bloemfontein districts, looting, terrorizing farmers and butchering their servants. Chief
Moroka who had returned with his clan from the Modder
river to Thaba Nchu, hastened to Bloemfontein and pleaded
for protection. Moshesh, he told Green, was preparing for
war. He was determined to clear the Sovereignty of the
Boers, British and Barolong before the arrival of Spring.
Rumours spread that thousands of Basotho were massing
along the southern banks of the Caledon. And then came a
disturbing development. Basotho servants employed on
Boer farms vanished overnight. It was assumed they had
been summoned by Moshesh for military service.

Henry Green acted promptly. He scribbled a note to
Cathcart informing him of the crisis facing the inhabitants
of the Sovereignty. A reply arrived quicker than he had
expected—the High Commissioner was coming to investigate the situation himself. He would be bringing a powerful
force comprising reinforcements from England, and a contingent of seasoned fighters drawn from the strife-torn
Cape Eastern Frontier. Green was to pass the news on to
Moshesh, for then the chief and his subjects would be loath
to invade the Sovereignty.

Cathcart was right. When news of his impending visit
reached Thaba Bosiu, the menacing warclouds lifted and
drifted away, cattle-raiding ceased overnight and an uncanny quietude pervaded central South Africa. On 2 December a British messenger arrived on the hill-top with
news that Sir George had just crossed the Orange at the
head of two thousand infantry and five hundred cavalry.
The High Commissioner was anxious to confer with Moshesh, and would expect him at Platberg in two weeks'
time.

Cathcart arrived at Platberg on the 13th, and was met by
Letsie and Molapo acting on behalf of their father, who was
said to be indisposed. But the High Commissioner refused
to see them, declaring he would not hold discussions with
anyone but the chief himself. Next day Letsie and Molapo,
accompanied by Owen, the special commissioner, returned
to Thaba Bosiu with a letter from Sir George. Finding
Moshesh in the *kgotla* with his councillors, they told him
about the snub they had received. Moshesh fumed, and

cutting them short told Owen to interpret Sir George's letter.

'I have been told,' read Owen, 'that you [Moshesh] are a great chief, and a good man; but I find that . . the Basuto [*sic*] people under your rule have become a nation of thieves. This state of things must not be, and I have come to put an end to it, and to restore peace between you and your neighbours, if I can.... I will not, therefore, stop to talk, but ... demand of you ten thousand head of cattle and one thousand horses, to be delivered to the British Resident at this place within three days' time.... If this be not done I must go and take either cattle or other things from you and your people ... and if resistance be made it will then be war between us, and I must then take three times the amount of cattle, as well as kill many of your people and destroy their dwellings and kraals, which I should be very sorry to be obliged to do.... Now chief ... it is for you ... to save yourself and your people from ruin, or else prepare for war, for on the fourth day, I must bring you to an account.'

Moshesh and his councillors were shocked. They had expected a message of goodwill from the High Commissioner, not threats and talk of war. They would have to appease this angry white man without delay, or face destruction by the greatest army ever to come north of the Orange. It was decided that Moshesh should journey in haste to Platberg.

The chief set off on horseback early next morning, reaching Platberg in the afternoon. He was taken immediately to the British camp where Cathcart awaited him.

'I am glad to see you and make your acquaintance,' said Sir George, extending a welcoming hand.

'I am glad to see the Governor,' replied Moshesh, 'as since his arrival in this country I have been expecting him.'

Cathcart then said he had come in peace to meet Moshesh whom he considered the greatest chief in South Africa. Moshesh smiled approvingly.

'Peace,' said the chief, 'is like rain which makes the grass grow, while war is like the wind which dries it up.'

'I will not now talk much,' continued Sir George, 'but wish to know whether you received my message yesterday, in which I made the demand of cattle and horses. I have nothing to alter in that letter.'

'Do you mean the letter I received from Mr. Owen?'

'Yes.'

'I received the letter, but do not know where I shall get the cattle from. Am I to understand that the ten thousand head demanded are a fine imposed for the thefts committed by my people?'

'I demand but ten thousand head, though your people have stolen much more, and consider this a just reward, which must be paid in three days.'

'Do the three count from yesterday or today?'

'Today is the first of the three.'

'The time is short, and the cattle many. Will you not allow me six days to collect them?'

'You had time given you before. . . .'

'That is true, but I have not now control enough over my people to induce them to comply with this demand, however anxious I may be to do so.'

Cathcart's patience was running out.

'If you are not able to collect them,' he cried, 'then I must go and do it; and if any resistance be made it will then be war, and I shall not be satisfied with ten thousand head, but shall take all I can.'

'Do not talk of war,' Moshesh retorted, 'for however anxious I may be to avoid it, you know that a dog when beaten will show its teeth.'

This was a tactless remark, the chief reflected, one spoken in a moment of anger. Cathcart was not a man to be threatened.

'I wish for peace,' said Moshesh regaining his composure, 'but have the same difficulty with my people that you have in the Colony. Your prisons are never empty, and I have thieves among my people.'

Cathcart was furious now. 'I would then recommend you catch the thieves, and bring them to me,' he bellowed, 'and I will hang them.'

'I do not wish you to hang them, but to talk to them and give them advice,' replied the chief, 'if you hang them they cannot talk.'

'If I hang them they cannot steal, and I am not going to

talk any more. I have said that if you do not give up the cattle in three days I must come and take them.'

'I beg you not to talk of war.'

'I have no more to say.... I therefore advise you to go and collect the cattle as quickly as possible.'

This brought the meeting to an abrupt close, but before Moshesh took leave of Sir George, he promised to pay the colossal fine demanded of him. 'Perhaps God will help me,' he was heard to say as he strode to his horse. Turning suddenly, he asked Cathcart to extend the expiry date just one more day. Sir George nodded condescendingly. The old chief climbed onto his horse and rode away.

The following three days passed quickly, and although on the 18th Moshesh could send no more than a third of the cattle and half the horses, he was not unduly worried. He said he was 'too old to be frightened by threats'.

On the evening of the same day Moshesh learned that Cathcart, on receiving the animals, had divided them among Moroka, Baatje and Taaibosch. Told that the remaining seven thousand beasts and five hundred horses had not yet been collected, Sir George sent envoys to Thaba Bosiu with a message to prepare for war.

On Sunday 19 December, Basotho scouts discovered the British army encamped on the north bank of the Caledon, so they hurried to Thaba Bosiu and broke the news to Moshesh. The chief sent Mopeli to plead with Cathcart to wait a little while longer. He had almost collected the cattle and horses demanded by Sir George. There was no need to invade Basotho territory.

Next morning the scouts saw Mopeli returning home, and they learned he had been snubbed by the High Commissioner. About an hour later they beheld the British army crossing the Caledon, and realizing it was heading for Berea, a flat-topped hill crowned with cliffs, they again hurried to Thaba Bosiu to alert Moshesh. Two days before, following the chief's return from the meeting with Cathcart over thirty thousand cattle, together with women, children and herdsmen had been taken by horsemen on to the summit of Berea hill.

Splitting into three divisions Cathcart's army converged
on Berea. The first division under Lt.-Col. Eyre climbed up
the hill along a cattle track, the second under Col. Napier
and the third under Cathcart himself moved slowly southwards on either side of the base. It had been decided that as
soon as Eyre had driven the cattle from the summit, the
three divisions would unite south of Berea, and march on
Thaba Bosiu.

After an arduous struggle over stone-strewn terrain, Eyre
and his men reached the cliffs above, then entering a steep
winding pass, crawled onto the summit of Berea. Catching
sight of the British, the women and children, screaming
hysterically, ran for shelter followed by the herdsmen and
warriors. Abandoned horses, some of them saddled, came
loping towards the British followed by a great rush of cattle.
Eyre and his men fired a volley into the air, driving the
terror-stricken animals back. They then went in pursuit of
the fugitives, who by this time were heading for one of the
southern passes.

With a swift flanking movement Eyre and his men,
muskets firing, intercepted most of the fleeing Basotho and
took them prisoner. In the course of a half an hour thirty-
eight Basotho had been shot dead on the hill-top, almost
three times as many had been wounded, and several were
later 'found dead on other parts of the field',[1] including the
southern pass. Eyre had won a resounding victory, and
had lost not a single man. He had the thirty thousand cattle
brought down from the hill and taken southwards under
escort.

In contrast to Eyre's successful operation, misfortune
had befallen the division led by Napier along the base of
Berea hill. Instead of waiting for Eyre as ordered, Napier
had sent his men in search of stock, and had been taken
unawares by a commando of Basotho under Molapo and
the sons of Chief Moletstane. The Basotho had cut down
first a squad of lancers coming down the hillslope, and then
a pocket of infantrymen found in the sedge of a ravine.
Napier had rallied his scattered force, driving the Basotho
onto a knoll close by. Taking advantage of the situation, he

[1] Eyre's report: Theal, *BR* i.

had then sent messengers to Cathcart for help, and joined within the hour by the 74th Highlanders, he ordered his force to move swiftly southwards in case it could still link up with Eyre's division.

Eyre meanwhile, growing impatient of waiting, and learning that Cathcart was already advancing on Thaba Bosiu, had moved on southwards together with the thirty thousand Basotho cattle. Suddenly Molapo's commando came into sight, its front row dressed in the uniforms and white helmets of Napier's slain lancers and infantrymen. The Basotho charged, and with muskets firing swooped on the vanguard of Eyre's division. The British retaliated fiercely, but the commando stormed onwards, blasting a gap through a platoon of riflemen, stampeding the cattle into the veld and sweeping away Capt. Faunce of the 73rd Regiment, a sergeant and a trooper who were instantly put to death.

At the height of the skirmish Molapo was joined by a second commando, and the British, now greatly outnumbered, huddled together—their guns spewing relentless volleys of slug—in a last desperate effort to avoid annihilation. So keen was the aim of Eyre's division, and so dreadful the devastation it wrought on the attacking foe, that for a moment Molapo's followers hesitated, and losing courage galloped away in confusion. Once beyond range of the British guns the Basotho halted, and turning about, awaited developments.

Eyre, his division concealed in the haze of gun-smoke, snatched the initiative. First he formed his men into 'three companies, in skirmishing order, two in front and one thrown back on [the] left', and then, moving them swiftly to the attack, unleashed a roaring fusillade into the ranks of the enemy. The Basotho recoiled before the vicious bombardment, but after a time they charged again, only to be driven back with heavy losses. Eventually they were so 'daunted by the coolness and steadiness' of the white men that they abandoned the fight and drifted away across the veld towards the Puthiastana river.

As soon as the Basotho were out of sight, Eyre's division moved on southwards, reaching the outskirts of Thaba Bosiu in the late afternoon. It linked up with Cathcart's

column near Casalis's mission station. Napier's force had
not yet arrived.

The presence of the British at the foot of his stronghold
frightened Moshesh. Accompanied by councillors and warriors he trudged to the edge of the hill-top and looked down
into the valley below. Cathcart's army was smaller than he
had been led to believe, but he realized that the Basotho,
however numerous, were no match for this highly trained
force armed with weapons of destruction both large and
small.

About six thousand Basotho horsemen, concealed behind
Qilwane hill, attacked at about four o'clock, but were driven
back sharply by a blast of bullets and shrapnel. Splitting into
groups the Basotho attacked again from several directions,
and for fully an hour Thaba Bosiu echoed to 'the roar of
artillery and the roll of platoon firing ... without intermis-
sion'. Clouds of dust, mingled with smoke, swirled over the
hill-top, and drifted away towards the Maluti mountains.

At the height of the skirmishing heavy banks of cloud
began rolling over Thaba Bosiu, and at about five o'clock
the heavens split open, and rain came cascading down. The
battle came to a sudden end. Everyone hurried away in
search of shelter. Gigantic shafts of lightning, each followed by ear-rending detonations of thunder, zig-zagged
over the valley. The storm raged for over an hour; then a
wind sprang up, brushing away the leaden clouds and
letting through the fading rays of the setting sun. Slowly
the Basotho drifted back into the valley and the British,
drenched and weary, moved off towards the Phuthiastana
river to bivouac for the night.

In his home on the hill-top Moshesh discussed the day's
events with a small group of dignitaries. The old chief was
tense with anxiety. Although less than a hundred of his
people—warriors, women and children—had been killed or
wounded since sunrise, he believed that the morrow would
bring the devastation of Thaba Bosiu, and the destruction of
his tribe. Admittedly many would manage to escape, and as
in the days of *difaqane*, might even find sanctuary in 'high
and almost inaccessible mountains'. But what of the future?

Was this young tribe to be reduced to a rabble of fugitives, wandering wretches driven by hunger to 'carry murder and incendiarism into the Sovereignty'? No, he would rather capitulate before one more shot was fired. The Basotho were powerless against the mighty British, so why expose them further to the horrors of war?

The missionaries, Casalis and Dyke had watched the afternoon's skirmishing with anguished hearts, and when the thunderstorm broke they had offered a prayer of gratitude to God. Until that moment they had 'expected to see the battlefield covered with dead or wounded'. Like Moshesh, they dreaded the events that lay ahead, believing that the valley would become blood-drenched 'should the British troops be ordered to advance'. After nightfall they had prayed again, seeking God's counsel, and beseeching Him to spare the Basotho from peril. They retired late to bed, their minds racing with 'anxious doubts and fears'.

At about midnight Eugene Casalis was awakened by a sharp rapping at the kitchen door. Rising sleepily he found a messenger awaiting him outside. The man had been sent by Moshesh to summon the white man; the old chief was troubled and needed urgent advice.

Arriving on the hill-top Casalis was taken to Moshesh's house where the chief was conferring with his councillors. The first thing he learned, on joining the group of dignitaries, was that a decision had been taken to surrender to the British. The Frenchman was greatly relieved. During the following hour he assisted Moshesh in a carefully worded letter to Cathcart. This the chief had delivered in all haste to the High Commissioner's bivouac.

Sir George had retired early to his tent to consider what action he should take on the following day. At first he had decided to re-engage the Basotho in battle, to crush them and take Moshesh's stronghold. On second thoughts he considered this too great a risk, especially as his force was so greatly outnumbered, and he could not be sure that Napier's division would arrive in time. Tossing his thoughts this way and that Cathcart eventually decided to postpone operations for a day or two. He would move his men back to the camp on the Caledon, and prepare a full-scale attack on Thaba Bosiu.

The British struck out northwards at sunrise next morning, and although harried by snipers they reached the Caledon without mishap at noon. About two hours later Cathcart was given a letter by a Basotho messenger bearing a flag of truce.

'Your Excellency,' he read, delighted that the note was from Moshesh, 'This day you have fought against my people, and have taken much cattle.... I beg you will be satisfied with what you have taken. I entreat peace from you—you have shown your power—you have chastised— let it be enough I pray you; and let me be no longer considered an enemy of the Queen. I will try all I can to keep my people in order in the future. Your humble servant, Moshesh.' Cathcart mused. He could not have wished for a more satisfying surprise. There would be no more fighting, he assured the messenger. As High Commissioner it was his 'duty to accept the chief's submission, without further prosecution of the war'.

CHAPTER TWENTY

AN OMEN OF DOOM

*The Basotho celebrate the cessation of hostilities—
Moshesh puzzles Sir George Clerk—the Wild Cat
People flee to Clerk's bivouac—Moshesh demands the
withdrawal of all white men from central South Africa
—The Sovereignty is dissolved and is replaced by a
provisional Boer government—Moshesh is fêted by the
Boers—He witnesses the removal of the Union Jack
from the fort at Bloemfontein; also an omen of doom*

FOLLOWING the cessation of hostilities rumours swept the
Lesotho that the British had been put to flight with heavy
losses, and were spared annihilation only because Cathcart
had begged Moshesh for mercy. In every kraal, far and
wide, the Basotho sang praises to their old chief, calling
him Peace-Maker! Conqueror! Father of the Tribe!
Crocodile! On the morning of 22 December 1852, all the
warriors were ritually cleansed by Moshesh's medicine men
in the Phuthiastana river. Wearing charms to protect themselves against the vengeful spirits of the white men they had
slain, they went up on to the hill-top, where they were led
by Moshesh in extolling the virtues of the ancestral spirits.

Scouts reported on the 23rd that the British had broken
camp on the Caledon and were marching westwards. Casalis and Dyke visited Moshesh in the afternoon, and 'found
him singing and clapping his hands for joy'.

'I can begin to sleep now,' he told them, explaining that
during the recent upheaval his mind had been so besieged
with anxiety, that he had lain awake night after night.
Owen arrived next day, and was 'received by him [Mo-
shesh] and his councillors with great civility and respect'.
The chief said he felt privileged to welcome a representative
of the Queen to Thaba Bosiu. His heart ached at the
thought of the futility of war. He had been told that Owen
wished to visit Berea and bury the corpses of the British
killed in action. The white man had his permission to go,

and would be accompanied by Sekhonyana, Masupha and a
party of menials who had been ordered to help. This caused
a stir among the councillors, for by bringing his subjects into
contact with enemy dead Moshesh would be exposing the
entire tribe to the destructive influence of evil spirits. Ratsiu, speaking on behalf of the elders, implored him to let
Owen proceed alone. But Moshesh refused, claiming that
the idea had come not from his mind, but from the realm of
spirits.

His task accomplished, Owen left the Lesotho straight
after Christmas, and as little more was heard of the British
during the following months, the Basotho returned gradually to their leisurely, peaceful way of life. Calling a *pitso* in
April 1853, Moshesh warned his subjects against antagonizing the Boers, the Batlokwa and Taaibosch's Koranna.
He condemned the unscrupulous behaviour of some of the
Basotho living in the south. For example, in January a
commando had terrorized Boer families attending church in
Winburg, and in March a tribesman had stoned a Boer near
Beersheba, knocking him senseless from his horse. Acts of
violence such as these, he said, could only lead to further
bloodshed in the Lesotho. He urged his people to direct
their energies to the traditional pursuits of tilling, planting,
reaping and cattle-breeding. By this he did not imply that
the Basotho were to become soft and defenceless. On the
contrary, should the Lesotho be invaded again he, their
father, would call them to arms, and if need be, lead them
into battle.

An atmosphere of quiet pervaded the Lesotho during the
Autumn, and usually Moshesh could be found in the *kgotla*
chatting happily with his ageing cronies. Sometimes he
preferred the solitude of his stone house, and would often
sit in the doorway drinking in the strains of a *lesiba* or
tumo, or some other instrument played by his most accomplished musicians. He had stopped attending church at the
mission station, and challenged by Casalis, he complained
laughingly that his legs were too old and rickety to carry
him down the Khubelu pass.

Casalis and his daughter, Adele, visited him frequently
on the hill. Five years before, at the age of nine, Adele had

been sent to school in Cape Town. She had returned now, forsaking her studies prematurely in order to attend to her sickly mother and keep house for her father. Delly, as Moshesh called her, had always been one of the chief's special favourites, and now at the age of fourteen she was better able to admire his soft, kindly nature, his uncommon dignity and extraordinary wisdom. As in former years she lavished him with homemade delicacies, and nothing pleased her more than to hear him discuss her culinary skills with associates.

In August Moshesh was informed by letter that Sir George Clerk, a high-ranking British official, had arrived in Cape Town some months before, and was heading for central South Africa. He was coming to investigate the political situation in the Sovereignty. Appointed in London to the post of special commissioner, Clerk had studied the many documents relating to the clashes between Moshesh and his neighbours. By the time he reached Bloemfontein in September, he had decided that much of the trouble in the Sovereignty was due to the extreme ignorance of the non-white races. He considered most tribesmen as degenerate, and enslaved by a 'taste for ardent spirits, and a craving to obtain muskets and gunpowder'.[1]

Although in Clerk's opinion the missionaries were 'truly pious men', he regarded their teachings as inconsequential in tribal South Africa. The reason was that black men, although seemingly quick to grasp the rudiments of learning, were equally quick to 'relapse in barbarism, and cattle stealing and nudity', when once they returned to their 'squalid wigwams'. In the eyes of Clerk this was the situation in the Colony, and he could see no reason why it should be different in the Sovereignty.

Told that Clerk had arrived at Platberg on 20 October, Moshesh decided to visit him, hoping to solicit his friendship and support. On the eve of his departure Basotho scouts located the commandos of Taaibosch and Chief Sikonyela north of the Caledon. Apparently they had just returned from raiding Chief Witsi's clan, near present-day

[1] Despatch to the Secretary of State for the Colonies: Theal, *BR* ii.

Harrismith, and were heading home to Wild Cat country
where they would divide the spoils. As it was rumoured that
Taaibosch and Sikonyela were planning a similar attack on
Basotho kraals in the Tlotsi area, the councillors urged
Moshesh to cancel his journey to Platberg.

In spite of these entreaties the old chief left for Platberg
on the morning of the 21st. He found the journey laborious
and fatiguing. In former days he had ridden farther and
faster, had swum the swollen Caledon many a time, but
never had his body ached as it did that evening on reaching
Clerk's camp near the mission station. He had been off-
colour recently, dogged by a persistent weariness. As soon
as he had met Clerk he asked to be shown to the tent set
aside for him, and stretching himself out on a *kaross*,
descended into a deep, noisy sleep.

Moshesh felt no better on the following day, and during
the two meetings he had with Clerk—one during the morning and another in the afternoon—he barely spoke. And he
discreetly avoided discussion on the racial problems confronting the Sovereignty. His reticence puzzled Sir George.
The white man concluded that the chief's mind 'was rather
pre-occupied with concerns of more immediate importance
to him'.

Hardly had Moshesh left Platberg on his journey homewards, when he was met by messengers from Thaba Bosiu,
who urged him to hurry home. Sikonyela and Taaibosch
had been sacking kraals and rustling cattle all day near the
Phuthiastana river. They were bound to capture the chief
should they come upon him so far from home.

Arriving safely at Thaba Bosiu Moshesh found his councillors in discussion with his sons and army commanders.
The Basotho army, he learned, had been mustered, and
would be joined next morning by a Bataung contingent, led
by Chief Moletstane.

Two days later the Basotho and Bataung rode out in
search of Sikonyela and Taaibosch, and locating them on
the outskirts of Joalaboholo—the Great Beer, drove them
into the hills. Next day Sikonyela, heading sixty horsemen,
fled westwards through the flat-topped hills dotting the
north bank of the Caledon. From then on he became a

fugitive, hounded by the Basotho and Bataung over the Highveld plains. Week after week he and his band rode hither and thither, friendless, invariably hungry, scorched by the summer sun and wearied by pounding rain and sleepless nights spent in dank caverns. Eventually, in desperation, they decided to beg Moshesh's mercy. But on 1 December, discovering to his great delight that Sir George Clerk was bivouacked on the left bank of the Vet river, Sikonyela hastened to meet him and ask for protection.

The chief and his sixty followers were cordially received by Clerk and given shelter in the British camp. Two weeks later, following a report that a Basotho commando had been seen watering its horses in the river, they were taken under escort to the fort at Bloemfontein.

Clerk had little liking for Sikonyela, and far less for Moshesh, and he regarded Moletstane, Taaibosch and the other half-breed leaders as incorrigible scoundrels. During the remainder of December and most of January 1854 he probed the political situation north of the Orange, taking evidence from British officials, Boer leaders and some of the less belligerent tribal chiefs like old Moroka. Soon he came to the conclusion that Britain must relinquish its jurisdiction over central South Africa. He would speak again to Moshesh, or better still, he would convene a meeting of all leaders of the Sovereignty, irrespective of colour, and invite the old chief to attend as his special guest.

The meeting took place towards the end of January at Jammersberg Drift, a farm owned by a Boer named Josias Hoffman. Moshesh attended, accompanied by Letsie and the more senior councillors of the tribe. He had refused at first, complaining he was far too old to undertake so long a journey on horseback, or even by wagon. Eventually he had agreed to go, if only to persuade Sir George to settle the boundary question.

In Moshesh's opinion nothing had contributed more to racial disharmony in past years, than this single factor— Warden's line. He considered it unfair, entirely impracticable, and an affront to the Basotho tribe.

The meeting opened in the most cordial atmosphere, and in addition to Clerk and his officials, most of the chiefs

were present, as well as Josias Hoffman, Hendrik Viljoen,
J. G. Landman and other Boer leaders. The first matter discussed was Warden's contentious boundary line, and Moshesh was amazed to hear Sir George describe it as deplor-
ably unfair to the Basotho. The special commissioner ruled
that the line should be reviewed objectively by the Boers and
then adjusted in collaboration with the Basotho.

Moshesh objected, and in so doing released a proverbial
genet among the doves. He said it was ridiculous to expect
the Basotho to recognize boundaries when the entire
country belonged to them alone, and before them to their
ancestors. What right had the white men to complain of
raids by marauders when, in actual fact, they themselves
were living on land they had stolen? Warden's line should
not merely be adjusted, but must be rubbed from the face of
the earth. Henceforth the dividing line between the Basotho
and the Boers would have to be the Orange river. There was
no place for white men in central South Africa.

At this stage of the meeting, with tempers soaring, Clerk
intervened. Moshesh withdrew in anger, and retired to a
tent provided for him by Clerk. Visited in the evening by the
Boers seeking to open discussion on the boundary question,
he stubbornly refused to consider their views.

On the following morning Moshesh took leave of Clerk
and set out homewards. The Boers departed some hours
later, and Clerk headed for Bloemfontein. The meeting had
been far more turbulent than he had expected. He hoped
that some day a suitable solution would be found to the
boundary dispute. Fortunately, by that time, he told himself, he would have returned to England.

February 1854 crept tardily by. Moshesh was ill—laid low
with a heavy, unrelenting fever—and not until the first
week in March was he seen outside his home.[1] He had

---

[1] Mamohato, his senior wife, died at about this time. Facts
concerning her death are vague, but it is known that she was
buried beneath the stone wall of Moshesh's cattlefold, just to the
left of the entrance. Bound in a squatting position, the corpse was
placed in a hollow made in the wall of a large circular grave.
(See James Walton, *Villages of the Paramount Chiefs of Basutoland*, p. 5.)

grown thin and angular, and heavy shadows contoured his
tired, sunken eyes.

At about this time Moshesh was visited by Robert Moffat
Jnr., son of the missionary of Kuruman, who told him that
the Sovereignty had been dissolved by Britain. A provisional
Boer government, headed by Josias Hoffman, had been in
control since 23 February. According to an eye-witness,
Moshesh was 'strongly disquieted', and with Casalis's help
he wrote to Clerk asking for an interview. A few days later
a reply arrived. The special commissioner was too busy to
see the chief. In future Moshesh would have to confer with
Josias Hoffman.

During the middle of March a letter from Hoffman
reached Thaba Bosiu, inviting the chief to Bloemfontein as
a guest of the provisional government. Early one morning
Moshesh set off on horseback accompanied by his sons,
Sekhonyana, Masupha and Majara. Still ailing, he had
wrapped himself in 'a long military cloak', and he rode in
silence, preferring not to talk with his three companions.

Reaching Thaba Nchu, he was joined by Chief Moroka,
and together they covered the last twenty miles to Bloemfontein. Met by Hoffman, he and his sons were conducted
to lodgings prepared for them. In the evening they were
the guests of honour at a 'friendly dinner party' arranged by
the provisional government. During the meal Moshesh was
invited to address the diners. Rising amidst a loud ovation,
the chief said he was overjoyed to learn that Hoffman had
been appointed acting-president of the Boer government.
This man, he said, was not unknown in the Lesotho, and
was considered by many as a friend. Few white men were
as 'intimately acquainted' as Hoffman with tribal law and
custom. It was hoped his followers would seek to emulate
his excellent example, for then the Basotho and the Boers
would progress rapidly towards a happy relationship, un-
blemished by squabbling or bloodshed.

Hoffman was a peace-loving man, the chief continued,
and had played no part in the overthrow of the kings,
Dingane and Mzilikazi. That had been the evil handiwork
of Andries Pretorius and Hendrik Potgieter, both of whom
'had sought to obtain their object by violence and war'.

These two men had never experienced the 'repose and
freedom' enjoyed by a gentle person like Josias Hoffman.
Hoffman was a man of different calibre—a friend of all
races, and the father and protector of the needy. This white
man had refused to take part in Cathcart's invasion of the
Lesotho, and had appealed to Boers and Basotho to lay
down their arms, and settle their problems peaceably. In
return he had been ridiculed, and even threatened with
death by hotheads on either side. And yet, 'in the midst of
all changes and tumults' he had continued to promote peace
and goodwill among peoples of the Sovereignty. Like few
other white men, Josias Hoffman had earned the respect of
the Basotho.

Speaking in reply to the chief's address, Hoffman said
that the Boers, like the Basotho, valued peace and prosperity, and would strive to avoid any situation which might
lead to conflict. Moshesh would always be treated with
'honesty and sincerity' no matter who eventually became
president of the Boers; meanwhile it was hoped he would
consider introducing 'more stringent laws to check disorder
and punish crime' in the Lesotho.

'I shall confidently hope that all will go well,' concluded
Hoffman, 'especially as I have personally known you, Moshesh, for many years to be a man who loves peace.'

On the following morning Moshesh and the Boers gathered outside the fort at Bloemfontein to witness the lower-
ing of the Union Jack, and the hoisting of the Batavian
Tricolour, flag of the new Boer Republic. Just as the ceremony drew to a close, a British trooper collapsed and died.
About an hour later, after the corpse had been laid to rest in
the cemetery close by, Sir George Clerk and his party left
for the Colony. For the Boers this meant the beginning of a
happy new era. But what of the Basotho? Moshesh wondered. Why had the trooper dropped dead during the un-
furling of the new flag, he asked himself, and why at that
particular moment? Was this an omen of doom, a sign of
dreadful events still to come? Time alone would tell.

PART THREE

CHAPTER TWENTY-ONE

THE BOERS TAKE OVER

*The Orange Free State republic in 1854—Josias Hoff-
man is elected its first President—Moshesh predicts the
return of the British to central South Africa—He is
deeply disturbed by the outbreak of violence in the
new republic—He and Joseph Orpen visit a band of
marauders*

THE new Boer republic was called the Orange Free State,
and it covered a vast area bounded by the Orange and Vaal
rivers and the Drakensberg range. It excluded the Lesotho,
of course, as well as the few patches of territory occupied
by the Batlokwa, Barolong, Bataung and other clans. By
1854 the white population of the new republic numbered
roughly twelve thousand, some five hundred of whom were
English and the rest Boers. Farms were generally large,
homesteads small and communications extremely poor. Villages were still undeveloped—hot and slushy in the rainy
season, cold and dust-laden from April to September.
Smithfield, inhabited predominantly by English-speaking
citizens, comprised only forty-two houses, yet this was
more than twice the number in either Dutch-speaking Winburg or the English hamlet of Bloemfontein. Educational
facilities barely existed—there were less than two hundred
children at school—and the only newspaper was the flimsy
Friend of the Sovereignty published in Bloemfontein. Boer
churches were plentiful, and in Bloemfontein the foundations were being laid for the first Anglican cathedral north
of the Orange.

The Orange Free State was a popular haunt for itinerant
Colonial traders peddling a large variety of trinkets, household goods, groceries and gunpowder. It was also frequented by Boers from beyond the Vaal bartering grain,

meal, tobacco and dried fruits for sheep and wool. Crime
was minimal despite the absence of a police force. Almost
without exception the devout churchgoing Boers followed a
strict code of moral behaviour, based on an almost literal
interpretation of the Holy Scriptures. They held their religious and political leaders in deep reverence, attributing to
them a wealth of wisdom gleaned from a life-long study of
the teachings of biblical dignitaries. In everyday social activities the Boers were convivial, uncomplicated folk. But
when involved in political matters they were fiery-tempered
and uncompromising and inclined to split into rival, dis-
senting parties.

The Free State *volksraad* was destined to weather many a
stormy session. Twenty-nine candidates, among whom were
three Britishers, were elected to the first *volksraad* on 28
March 1854, and Josias Hoffman became the first President
in May.

Hoffman was a farseeing politician and a magnificent
orator. Although generally popular, there were times when
his somewhat revolutionary attitude towards racial matters
was bitterly condemned by his more insular-minded political
colleagues. Born in Cape Town, Hoffman was a man of little
formal learning, but he was well-read, well versed in European and local history, and an avid student of the arts. He
was a self-taught yet accomplished harmonium player, and
was fluent not only in Dutch, his mother-tongue, but also
English and Xhosa.

As a boy in 1824 Hoffman had accompanied his father
on an historic expedition led by pioneer adventurer Francis
Farewell, to the military kraal of Shaka, King of the Zulu.
In 1834, while boarding a ship in Table Bay, he had
stumbled and fallen overboard, fracturing his legs in several
places. This accident left him crippled for life.

Hoffman was among the first Boers to settle north of the
Orange. A prosperous farmer at Jammersberg Drift, he was
also a roving trader carrying a large assortment of wares by
oxwagon to villages, farms and Basotho kraals. Of the
twenty-nine members of the *volksraad*, none could claim a
more thorough knowledge of the peoples of central South
Africa, than this genial, stout-hearted Boer. In the light of

past events, he was superbly qualified to head the infant Boer republic.

At the beginning of April the *volksraad* sent one of its members, a twenty-five-year-old Irishman named Joseph Orpen, on a goodwill mission to Thaba Bosiu. A land surveyor by profession, Orpen had worked in most parts of South Africa, and although he knew many of the chiefs, he had never met Moshesh. Calling in at Platberg on his way to Thaba Bosiu, Orpen was joined by Thomas Giddy, son of one of the Wesleyan missionaries. Together they rode southwards, and crossing the swollen Caledon, headed for Casalis's mission station, which they reached in the late afternoon.

Orpen and Giddy spent the night with the missionary and his sickly wife, Sarah, and next morning they were led onto the hill by Sekhonyana. Striding towards Moshesh's stone house, they beheld the old chief coming leisurely to meet them. He welcomed them 'in a very cordial manner', and showing them into his home, sent his servants to fetch refreshments. An elderly woman, presumably Sekhonyana's mother, Moshesh's second most senior wife, brought in a tray of tea and a freshly baked sponge cake. The old chief said his heart had been gladdened by Orpen's visit to Thaba Bosiu. He suggested the two white men should return to the mission station, while he summoned the dignitaries of the tribe. He particularly wanted his vassal chiefs to meet President Hoffman's special envoy.

Three days later Orpen and Giddy were fetched again by Sekhonyana, and reaching Moshesh's kraal, found the old man in the *kgotla*, 'seated in a great circle of his chiefs and people'. Moshesh rose amidst loud applause to greet them. Then he addressed the gathering.

Orpen, he explained, had come to Thaba Bosiu with greetings and messages of goodwill from the leader of the Boers, Josias Hoffman. The Boers, he continued, were eager to live in peace with the Basotho. This was heartening news, especially as it had always been his aim to foster an harmonious relationship between his subjects and white men.

Turning suddenly to Orpen, Moshesh cried out: 'Mr. Orpen, will you please tell me what is your native country.'

'England,' replied the white man, assuming Moshesh had not heard of Ireland.

'You see now,' grinned the chief proudly, 'this is what I have been telling you.' The Free State Boers were to be admired for including a man of British origin in their parliament. In his mind's eye he, Moshesh, could see Queen Victoria seated on the crest of a great mountain. He could see her looking smilingly down on her children, both 'white and black', who were 'playing below and sometimes quarrelling too'.

'She is watching and trying us,' he cried. 'Some day Queen Victoria will come back among us, and on that day I shall rejoice as I rejoice at the rising of the sun.'

Moshesh's admiration for the Queen and her people pleased Orpen. He became enchanted by the chief's eloquence as for fully an hour he spoke on the future of his tribe.

'Old man,' mumbled Orpen to himself, 'great is thy faith.' Perhaps one day the British would realize how great a friend they had in Moshesh.

Thomas Giddy was just as impressed with the chief, and later while refreshments were being served, he ventured to ask, between mouthfuls of sponge cake, if a British agent was to be stationed at Thaba Bosiu. This had been a suggestion made by Clerk.

'Such an appointment might or might not be advantageous,' said Moshesh, 'much would depend on the man.'

'How would I do?' asked Giddy, his face aglow with happy anticipation.

Moshesh paused to think. Squinting mischievously at his youthful guest he said he considered Giddy too young for so responsible a post.

'You are just like one of those sweet little children who Jesus Christ put his hands on and blessed,' he chuckled. No, Giddy was still a fledgling. He would be better advised not to leave his parental nest prematurely.

Orpen and Giddy remained on Thaba Bosiu all day, enjoying every moment of Moshesh's company. They took leave of the chief and the friendly dignitaries towards sunset and returned to the mission station. Next morning at cock-crow they set out homewards.

Arriving in Bloemfontein, Orpen assured the *volksraad* that Moshesh wanted peace with the Boers. During the following three weeks not a single case of stock-theft was reported at Bloemfontein, and this the villagers and local farmers attributed to Orpen's influence over the Basotho chief. But on 7 May violence broke out near Winburg. Moshesh was said to have broken his pledge.

Orpen heard the news at daybreak. He had been roused from his slumbers by a rapping at his bedroom door. Crawling from his bed, he had found Hoffman outside. The President was out of breath and seemed deeply troubled.

'Serious news has just arrived from the border district of Winburg,' cried Hoffman, 'you must start as soon as possible and see Moshesh.'

The sleepy Orpen peered incredulously at the President.

'Basuto [*sic*] Koranna and others have been reported encroaching on farms,' continued Hoffman, 'and stock-thefts have been taking place.'

Orpen was wide awake now.

'How soon can you start?' asked the President.

'As soon as I am dressed.'

'Well, come over then and I shall have coffee ready.'

The rising sun found Joseph Orpen on the dusty wagon track leading to Thaba Nchu. Reaching Thaba Bosiu on the following afternoon he was taken in haste to Moshesh. The chief said he was sad at the news of the outbreak of violence, and asked Orpen to go with him to the kraal of the scoundrel responsible. This man, said the chief, was Witsi, the most cunning cattle-raider east of the Caledon.

Two days later Orpen and Moshesh, leading a large retinue of dignitaries, set out for Chief Witsi's territory. The old man was immaculately attired in a dark blue uniform, a heavy military cape, leather gloves and a new top-hat. Riding a little to the rear of Moshesh Orpen studied him with admiring eyes. He was exceedingly fond of the old chief, and looked forward to the few days they would be together.

They rode slowly, stopping frequently for Moshesh to stretch his legs, steal a quick nap in the shade of a bush or cool his face and feet in a stream. At every stop a servant would brush the dust from his clothes and hat, shine his boots and present him with soap and a basin of water. The old man was always scupulously clean and groomed.

Each morning on rising he would strip naked and lathering himself 'all over his head and body' with a wedge of homemade soap, he would order his attendants to 'pour buckets full of ice-cold water' all over him. Suddenly he would grope his way out of the deluge, snorting and gasping, but from the moment he started drying himself, and while he dressed and combed his hair and white-streaked goatee, he would hum or whistle softly, or even burst into song depending upon his mood. Eventually given a mug of steaming coffee, he would sip it noisily with protruding lips.

Scenes such as these amused young Orpen and drew him constantly closer to his distinguished companion. Moshesh looked far happier than other chiefs he thought, and seemed in complete accord with his subjects including his humblest servants. In contrast to the majority of tribal rulers the white man had met, and especially those enslaved by sorghum beer and *dagga*, Moshesh was alert, open-hearted, self-possessed and dignified. In fact he had all the attributes one would expect to find in a person of his calibre.

On the morning of their third day together Moshesh and Orpen were riding leisurely southwards along the banks of the Tlotsi stream. They had sent a letter earlier to Jan Fick, field-cornet of the Winburg district, asking him to meet them, together with Field-cornet Hattingh of Harrismith at an appointed place near Butha-Buthe. After about an hour's ride they reached the site of Menkwaneng, Moshesh's birthplace. The straw huts, the *kgotla*-pallisade and the encircling hedge had vanished. But Moshesh, brimming over with childlike excitement, was able to locate the tree under which his father and the elders of the Bamokoteli clanlet had always sat in council. He also found traces of hut floors, ash heaps and the cattlefold. Most exciting of all was his discovery of the spot where, 'as a little boy he had played at building miniature kraals', and finding 'the very stones he had used', he clapped his hands for joy.

At about midday they moved on towards the east, reaching Butha-Buthe during the late afternoon. Gazing up into the precipitous slopes of the hill, his mind harked back to the time he defied the armies of the conqueror, Mantatisi, queen of the Wild Cat People. He recalled how he and his followers had fled eventually to Thaba Bosiu—the Hill at Night.

Two more days' travel brought Moshesh and his party to the spot where Fick and Hattingh were to meet them. Climbing the slopes of a semicircular range of hills at sunset, they entered one of the many caverns lining the base of a gigantic sandstone cliff, and settled for the night. Chief Witsi and his commando were encamped close by in a valley.

Next morning, watching the rising sun from the mouth of the cavern, Joseph Orpen saw a Boer approaching cautiously on horseback along the base of the hill. Reaching the cavern the stranger said he had a message from Fick for Orpen and Moshesh. The field-cornet and his colleague, Hattingh, would not be coming as arranged. They had just been told that Orpen intended conferring with the notorious Witsi. They feared the white men would be put to death in much the same way as Piet Retief and his party of Boers had been slaughtered in 1838 at the command of Dingane, King of the Zulu. Fick was not prepared to throw his life away. He would deal with the marauders in the way he thought best.

'Ass!' exclaimed Orpen angrily. It was essential that the field-cornets should attend the meeting with Witsi. He decided to visit Fick himself and induce him to change his mind. In the meantime Moshesh and the councillors would have to visit Witsi without him. He would tell them to warn the chief that unless he returned the stolen cattle, he would be destroyed by a Boer commando.

Moshesh did meet Witsi and he made him promise to keep out of Boer territory. Returning home the old chief was escorted by the marauders for many miles along the Caledon river. But the moment they parted Chief Witsi led his commando towards Winburg and continued raiding in the district. By the time Moshesh reached Thaba Bosiu the marauders had returned eastwards, plundering farms as far as presentday Harrismith, and sending great droves of Boer cattle and sheep into the Drakensberg foothills. Disgruntled farmers converged on Bloemfontein and demanded action.

Suddenly the raiding stopped. Witsi had had enough. He withdrew into the Drakensberg hoping that when the dust settled, he and his people could return to their kraals and start life afresh. Chief Witsi was not a greedy man. He had enough cattle now to keep him contented until his dying day.

CHAPTER TWENTY-TWO

UNHAPPINESS CROWDS MOSHESH'S LIFE

*Sarah Casalis dies during a visit to Morija—Moshesh
comforts Eugene Casalis—President Hoffman is sacked
by the* volksraad*—He is succeeded by Boshof who
clashes with Moshesh—Cattle-disease breaks out in the
Lesotho—Death of Mokhachane—The Boers crush
Chief Witsi's clan*

THINGS were quiet on Thaba Bosiu after Moshesh's return,
for it was harvest time, and almost everyone had flocked to
the lands in the valley. When he was not strolling about his
kraal with Makwanyane, or yarning with his councillors in
the *kgotla*, the chief could be found in his home. Sometimes
he would stretch himself out at leisure on his sofa, all but
his face concealed beneath a *kaross*, or he would sit outside
basking in the mellow Autumn sun.

Occasionally Moshesh would amble to the edge of the hill-
top and watch his people toiling in the fields below. He
always looked down onto the mission station, and if he
caught a glimpse of Casalis or Adele he would cup his
hands to his mouth, and lifting his voice, ask after the noble
Sarah whose declining health was causing so much anxiety
at Thaba Bosiu.

Sarah's fast-ebbing life had brought sadness into the eyes
of Eugene Casalis, Moshesh told Makwanyane. In years
past when death had slunk onto the hill-top, whisking
away a loved one, Moshesh had sought and found solace in
the warm companionship of his beloved missionary. From
now on he would go down to the mission station more
often. Eugene Casalis was in need of comfort!

Visiting the Frenchman one morning in June, Moshesh
found him loading a wagon in preparation for a journey to
Morija. On the previous day news had reached Casalis of
the sudden passing of the Arboussets' infant son. Sarah,
although gravely ill, insisted on being taken to them. Moshesh marvelled at Sarah's courage as he watched her,

wasted away with sickness, being helped by Casalis and
Adele onto the wagon. Somehow he knew he would not see
her alive again.

As the wagon lumbered out of the mission station and onto
the sandy track skirting the base of Thaba Bosiu, the old
chief followed behind conversing softly with Casalis. Reaching a point in the road near Rafutho's kraal, he took leave
of his friends and struck out for the Khubelu pass.

Two weeks later while conferring with a group of vassal
chiefs in the *kgotla*, Moshesh was told that Sarah was
dying. A messenger had just arrived from the kraal of Chief
Letsie. Deeply moved, the old chief sent a servant to saddle
his horse. Within the hour he was heading south-westwards
accompanied by a few of his sons and most of his councillors.

It is said Moshesh wept often in the course of the journey, and although implored by Makwanyane to rest, he refused, dismounting for the first time on reaching Morija.
The mission station thronged with his subjects—greybeards,
horsemen, women with infants and children bunched
timidly together beneath the trees. All were waiting in
morbid silence for the announcement of Sarah's passing.

Told of the chief's arrival Casalis came out of the house,
and taking his arm led him to the stricken woman's bedside.
The room was crowded with Basotho, and a long line of
women filed slowly past the bed, some stooping 'to place a
kiss upon her hand', and others lifting 'their little children'[1]
to bid the kindly Sarah a final farewell. Moshesh had
arrived just in time, for hardly had he greeted her than she
sank into a heavy sleep and floated into the darkness of
death.

A grave was dug in an open space near the mission
house, and besides the missionaries and their children, fully
a thousand Basotho attended the funeral, part of which was
conducted by Arbousset and part by Casalis. After the coffin
had been lowered into the grave, and the final prayer
spoken, 'Moshesh stepped forward and addressed the large
assembly with an emotion which he could not control'.

This day, he said, the Basotho mourned the passing of

[1] From the Memoirs of Adele Casalis: Edwin W. Smith, *The
Mabilles of Basutoland.*

their beloved mother, Sarah Casalis, and their hearts ached
at the sight of the grief suffered by her husband. The
missionaries, he cried, had won the affection of the Basotho, for in addition to their endless efforts to enlighten and
uplift the people they served, they had always called upon
their own God for help, when misfortune had befallen the
tribe.

'Our mother, before dying,' continued the chief, referring
to Sarah Casalis, 'expressed the conviction that the Gospel
would soon triumph in this country. Perhaps that is a
prophecy, and ... she was able to see things which we
cannot perceive.'

Moshesh started weeping now.

'Today you are a man,' he said, addressing Casalis,
'[and] you know all the trials through which a man may
pass.... You believe that because Moshesh is a polygamist
he cannot understand what you suffer. For me there has
never been but one woman, and since Mamohato left me
[died], I walk as a solitary man in the midst of the crowd.'

Pointing to Casalis's children the chief, sobbing loudly,
bewailed the loneliness that awaited them. Arbousset was
moved by the old man's distress and tried to console him.
The children, he said, were not orphans, after all they could
count on their father for love and attention.

'Arbousset,' sniffed Moshesh, 'you forget that little
chickens need the feathers of the hen; Casalis and I, you
know, have but Cock's feathers.'

Moshesh returned to Thaba Bosiu straight after the
funeral. During the following few weeks he went often to
the mission station at the foot of the hill, fussing about
Casalis and entertaining the children with folktales and
riddles. Then suddenly in August he stayed away. He was
expecting a visit from Josias Hoffman.

The President remained with Moshesh for four days,
and together they sought a solution to the unrest caused
by Chief Witsi's marauders in Boer territory. The chief
promised to place Molapo near the Caledon with authority
to arrest and punish all stock-thieves. And he agreed that in
future Basotho wishing to enter the Free State would have
to carry a pass signed by a missionary.

When the time came for the President and his party to leave, they were given a great ovation by a crowd which had gathered to see them off. They were saddling their horses when Moshesh called Hoffman aside saying he had a special favour to ask of him. He wanted Hoffman to send him a keg of gunpowder as compensation for the amount used up four days before in saluting the Boers with gunfire. The President agreed, and bidding the chief farewell left with his followers for home.

On his return to Bloemfontein Hoffman gave an account to the *volksraad* of his visit to Thaba Bosiu, expressing delight at the chief's 'earnest and friendly desire' to cooperate with the new republic 'for the preservation of peace'. One aspect of his visit he discreetly omitted—Moshesh's request for gunpowder. In fact, he had already sent a keg to Thaba Bosiu.

Not all members of the *volksraad* shared Hoffman's good opinion of Moshesh. He was accused by his opponents of bowing and scraping to the chief, when in fact he should be demanding retribution for losses suffered at the hands of Basotho raiders. A small, influential group condemned the President's friendship with Moshesh, suggesting that the Basotho should be crushed for damage done to Boer property. But the ravings of these men were scorned by the majority of *volksraad* members. Hoffman was praised for establishing more friendly relations between the republic and the Lesotho.

In January 1855 a storm was unleashed in the *volksraad*. One of the members had come upon a document revealing Hoffman's gift of gunpowder to Moshesh! The President was immediately forced out of office. A committee of four, under the chairmanship of a farmer named Jacobus Johannes Venter was appointed to administer the government pending the election of a new president.

When the news reached Moshesh he was shocked. How was it possible he asked Casalis, that so trivial a matter could have led to the President's downfall? But in March he received an even greater shock! Eugene Casalis, his constant companion and mentor, was recalled to France, and left Thaba Bosiu for ever. The parting was sad, and it created a void in the old chief's life, one that the new missionary, the Rev. Jousse, could never hope to fill.

Josias Hoffman retired to his farm, Jammersberg Drift, and he wrote to Sir George Grey lamenting and condemning the attitude of the *volksraad* to the gunpowder incident. 'I am a special friend of Moshesh,' he added, 'and dare to recommend this chief to Your Excellency, as one well worthy of your esteem and respect.' The old chief, he concluded, although peace-loving, was surrounding by scores of agitators. If antagonized these men could stir both the Basotho and their neighbours into open hostility against the republic. Moshesh himself would be powerless to intervene.

Contrary to what Hoffman expected, the Free State *volksraad* maintained the friendliest relations with Moshesh. Even during the Winter when reports of stock-theft came pouring in from all parts of the republic, not a shot was fired in retaliation. Farmers were ordered by proclamation to avoid bloodshed, except in self-defence, and deputations went regularly to Thaba Bosiu to seek Moshesh's cooperation. At a sitting of the *volksraad,* Venter, who 'had long experience with tribesmen', advised his colleagues against blaming Moshesh for crimes committed by his vassal chiefs. 'There was something causing dissatisfaction among Moshesh's young nation', and he intended speaking to the old man, 'as a true friend', and offering to help him 'remove the causes immediately'.

Three weeks later Venter reported that he had seen Moshesh and persuaded him to permit a party of Boers to enter the Lesotho in search of stolen cattle. The chief was as keen as any member of the *volksraad* to put an end to the trouble.

In August Venter and his temporary committee were replaced by Jacobus Boshof, newly appointed President of the Free State republic. Unlike Venter and Hoffman who had looked upon Moshesh as a friend, Boshof was suspicious of the chief, accusing him of duplicity. According to several *volksraad* members, the new president was too shrewd a judge of character to be deceived by Moshesh's charm and disarming brand of diplomacy.

Jacobus Boshof was a learned and capable man, whose experience in governmental matters dated back to many a year preceding the Great Trek. Receiving his initial training in the Colonial civil service, he had been posted to Graaff-Reinet in 1836, as clerk to the British civil commissioner. He was later appointed magistrate of Pietermaritzburg and chairman of the Natal republic *volksraad*. He seemed the ideal choice for the presidency of the Orange Free State.

Moshesh and Boshof met for the first time in Aliwal North, at a meeting convened by the High Commissioner, Sir George Grey. They clashed from the start! Accused by the President of encouraging the Basotho to raid Boer farms, Moshesh became furious, saying he would not have attended the meeting had he known he would be insulted. The chief admitted he had lost control over many of his vassal chiefs and headmen, but refused to accept the blame for the crimes they committed. What was he to do, he asked pleadingly, his eyes filling suddenly with tears. What advice had Sir George to offer him?

'Stealing will never cease until thieves are punished,' barked President Boshof impatiently. In the Orange Free State thieves were imprisoned or whipped, and he refused to believe that Moshesh was powerless to do the same. No, the chief was lying, and the Boers were becoming more angry and eager for revenge.

'The sword of the mouth is grievous,' retorted Moshesh, fuming now, and he demanded that the meeting be brought to a close.

'Let us go home,' he cried, 'we can correspond by letter.'

Taking command of the situation Sir George spoke up; he said he was surprised Moshesh should be so impulsive. Boshof had reason to complain, and was merely seeking a way to prevent conflict between the Boers and Basotho.

'I cannot bind myself to say that there will be no more stealing,' rasped Moshesh, 'thieves do not tell me when they come and go.... I have eaten the Governor Grey's meat, and it will be easy for me to vomit it up, but it is not so easy to make thieves disgorge what they have stolen.'

The meeting ended a few minutes later, and Moshesh departed for home. This had been a disturbing experience

UNHAPPINESS CROWDS MOSHESH'S LIFE

for him, one he would toss about in his mind for many days
to come.

Boshof too was troubled, believing Moshesh was in
league with the brigands of the tribe, and therefore unlikely
to cooperate with the *volksraad*. From now on the Boers
could expect more violent and more frequent raids from the
Basotho, he told himself. Every precaution must be taken
to prevent Moshesh inflicting 'grievous injuries' on the
farmers and their families. Sir George Grey had sided with
the Boers at the meeting. He would ask the High Commissioner to help him 'procure four or six small brass field-
pieces with carriages and a supply of ball and grape-shot'.
Also 'one howitzer'.

Disaster struck the Basotho in the Summer. A mysterious
disease swept through their herds, killing tens of thousands
of beasts including most of the cattle stolen from the Boers.
All at once raids into the republic stopped. Now the chiefs
and kraal-heads confined themselves to their kraals, dosing
their stricken animals with potions prepared by the medicine men, or dismembering or burying carcasses in the veld.
It was believed that the scourge had been sent by Boer
sorcerers in revenge for the cattle stolen from them. The
disease raged through the territory for fully two months,
and then suddenly in November it lifted and, according to
the Basotho, drifted away on the east wind.

Gentle rains fell during most of December. By the close
of the year the crops were tall and lush, and the surviving
cattle round, smooth-skinned and strong. An air of optim-
ism pervaded the land and the spirits were said to be
appeased. Then in January 1856 tragedy struck again.
Thaba Bosiu was plunged into mourning. Old Mokhachane,
Moshesh's father, suddenly died.

The Boers, meanwhile, were delighted that the cattle-
raiding had come to an end, and Boshof wrote to Moshesh
telling him so. He also expressed the *volksraad*'s sympathy
in the passing of Mokhachane.

'My wish is that Moshesh may live to be a very old man
too,' the letter read, 'and that when he is called away from
this world of sin and trouble he may find a father in heaven,

where I too shall be glad to meet him and to speak to him of better things than we often have to do in this life.'

Moshesh found comfort in Boshof's letter, and he was pleased that the Boers were no longer angry with him. Over the years his quarrels with neighbours had cost him 'many a restless night'. Now, at last, peace had come.

The old chief's dreams of a prevailing peace were shattered in February when he learned from scouts that the Boers were erecting forts along the Caledon river, and on farms throughout the republic. Why this duplicity, he complained to the councillors, what had Boshof in mind? Was it really peace the President wanted, or was he preparing for war? Boshof had been visited recently by Martinus Wessels Pretorius, the new president of the Boer republic north of the Vaal.[1] Were they plotting to invade the Lesotho?

Only two weeks before, a land commission had been seen in the Caledon Valley district. What were these white men up to? Were they aiming to take more land from the Basotho? The Boers were courting disaster. Sooner or later the land commission would be attacked by tribesmen living along the banks of the Caledon.

Unknown to Moshesh some of his sons and vassal chiefs had been meeting secretly to plan new cattle raids into Boer territory. They were ready at the end of February, and in March bands of marauders rampaged again across the republic, carrying off cattle, firing maizefields and sacking homesteads and barns. Protests and threats reached Thaba Bosiu from Bloemfontein, and Moshesh fearing retaliation by the Boers, pleaded with the marauders to keep away from the republic. But they scoffed at him, saying they would welcome a clash with the white men. It was not peace they wanted—they wanted war!

The first rumblings of war-thunder were heard one misty morning in April when a commando, two thousand strong, belonging to Chief Witsi, came riding into the Wittenberg area—a yelling, gesticulating rabble heavily charged with sorghum beer and *dagga*. Racing from farm to farm they

[1] Martinus Wessels Pretorius was the son of Andries Pretorius, hero of the Battle of Blood River, who died in 1853.

drove farmers off their properties. By May some three
thousand Boers were laagered in tented wagons. Their own
servants and tribesmen coming from beyond the Caledon
occupied the abandoned homesteads.

The Smithfield Boers were faced with a similar plight.
They were attacked by a combined force under the cunning
Poshuli and Chief Letele.

Boshof called the Boers to arms and locating Poshuli and
Letele in June, drove them across the Caledon. Boer com-
mandos headed by Field-commandant Botha pounced on
Chief Witsi's force, blasting it out of the Wittenberg area,
and pursuing it eastwards into the Harrismith district. The
Boers continued into Witsi's domain sacking kraals and
capturing cattle. Reinforcements arrived in July, and soon
Witsi's people were scattered across the lowlands of the
Lesotho, from Butha-Buthe to Thaba Bosiu.

In a letter to Boshof, dated 16 June, Moshesh begged him
to remove his commandos from Basotho soil. Chief Witsi's
clan was crushed, Poshuli and Letele had been driven away,
and the Boers had retrieved their stolen cattle. He depended
on Boshof to staunch the blood-flow in central South
Africa, and to allow the pulse-beat of life to return again to
Witsi's mangled clan. Wars, he said, were cruel and merciless, like 'ravening wolves'.

Moshesh wanted peace. Permanent peace!

CHAPTER TWENTY-THREE

THE FIRST BOER–BASOTHO WAR

Boer envoys, Coleman and Viljoen, deliver a letter to Thaba Bosiu—Moshesh is falsely accused of instigating the National Suicide of the Xhosa—1857 becomes known as 'The Year of Endless plunder'—Boshof sends Moshesh an ultimatum—The Boers invade the Lesotho

ON 5 July two white men from Smithfield set out for Thaba Bosiu by horse-drawn cart. They were Field-cornets William Coleman and Hendrik Viljoen, and they were taking a letter from Boshof to Moshesh. Travelling joltily along a narrow twining wagon-track, their cart struck a boulder on the 6th, damaging an axle. During the next two days while they repaired the cart the white men were assisted by Basotho from a nearby kraal. In discussion with the local headman they learned that Letsie was planning an invasion of the republic. The chief had decreed that the Basotho keep their horses 'constantly prepared for war, and on no account to use them for any other purpose', not even hunting.

Next morning Coleman and Viljoen moved on, and reaching Thaba Bosiu two days later, pitched camp near the mission station. They visited Moshesh for a few minutes on the 10th, and again on the 11th when they found the chief, his councillors and military commanders awaiting them in the *kgotla*.

Reading Boshof's letter to the gathering Sekhonyana explained that the President was bitterly dissatisfied with Moshesh—the chief was not keeping his subjects under control. Stock-theft, for instance, was rife; acts of violence perpetrated by Basotho brigands had become daily occurrences; Boer women and children were kept in constant fear by drunken or *dagga*-crazed ruffians. The President, Sekhonyana continued, demanded that stock-thieves be delivered by Moshesh to Bloemfontein. Should the chief refuse, the Boers would round up the transgressors themselves and bring them to trial. Magistrates had been given the power 'to pass sentence of death' both on habitual thieves and tribesmen found guilty of terrorism.

Boshof's letter shocked Moshesh and the councillors, and the meeting came to an end in rowdy confusion. Told by the chief to return to their tents, and report again at the *kgotla* on the morrow, Coleman and Viljoen withdrew as quickly as they could. The meeting on the 12th was far more orderly, for in the meantime Moshesh had conferred with the councillors and reached what he considered a solution to the quarrel with the Boers. Addressing Coleman and Viljoen in a friendly manner, he said most of the thieving was being done by vassal chiefs over whom he had lost control. He had therefore decided to dissociate himself from them or, as he put it, 'to cast them off' forever. He would send Masupha or a senior chief to enforce law and order along the borders. But he had one important point to make: He was weary of being blamed for every crime committed by the Basotho, and refused to assume the rôle of 'a second Christ and die for thieves and robbers'.

Coleman and Viljoen returned to their tent towards evening, believing Moshesh was genuinely keen to live in peace with the Boers. Next morning as they were about to set out for home, they were visited by one of the chief's sons who gave them a message for Boshof and the *volksraad*. The Basotho, he said, had every intention of destroying the Boers, and there was little Moshesh could do to intervene. No one in the Lesotho favoured peace with the republic, not even the most senile grandmothers or the tiniest babes in arms.

In August Moshesh was accused by the British government of meddling in Colonial tribal policy. He was said to be an arch-conspirator and leading protagonist in the National Suicide of the Xhosa. Foremost among his accusers were Sir George Grey and Charles Brownlee, a renowned commissioner of the Colony.

One of the strangest and saddest episodes in South African history, the National Suicide had started in May, between the Bashee and Kei rivers. This was the domain of

Kreli, chief of the Gcaleka clan, an old acquaintance and admirer of Moshesh.

Apparently one morning while scooping water from a stream, a girl named Nongqwase was confronted by three strangers who claimed to be prophets appointed by the spirits to drive all white men from the Colony. Nongqwase fled in fear to her uncle, Umhlakaza the witchdoctor, and he in turn interrogated the strangers thinking they might have come to harm Chief Kreli. Umhlakaza was soon convinced they were prophets—messengers from the shades of the dead. Thrilled by the message they had brought, he hurried away to confer with his chief. The Gcaleka and, indeed, all Xhosa clans, he told Chief Kreli, were on the brink of liberation from British rule. But first they had to follow the advice of the three great prophets. Henceforth until their emancipation, all Xhosa-speaking people were to destroy their harvests, slay their herds and abandon the practice of witchcraft. They were not to plant crops in the Spring or drink either fresh milk or curdled. Sexual intercourse would be strictly taboo.

Then, in due course the day of glory would dawn! Two balls of fire would rise in the east, causing the earth to rumble, and suddenly the British would be whisked away in the coils of a mighty tornado and scattered over the sea. Next the ancestral heroes of all Xhosa clans would rise from the grave, driving a multitude of cattle before them. Crops would come to life in the untilled fields, and granaries would be replenished overnight.

Chief Kreli was so delighted that he ordered his subjects to obey the behests of the prophets to the very last detail. The Gcaleka embarked on an orgy of destruction in June, and as the prophets' message spread swiftly along the east coast, from kraal to kraal, other clans followed their example. By the end of Winter almost all Xhosa territory reeked of decaying carcasses. Great clouds of vultures patrolled the skies, and the hills and valleys crawled with hyenas and jackals.

Determined to save the Xhosa from impending disaster, British officials toured the Colony, remonstrating with chiefs, headmen and kraal patriarchs. But their efforts were fruitless. They were regarded as imposters, and eventually famine swept Xhosa territory, claiming the lives of many thousands of starving families.

On their return to headquarters most of the officials blamed Kreli, and a few Umhlakaza for misleading the people. Brownlee blamed Moshesh. The old chief intended invading the Free State in September, he told Sir George Grey, so by planting the seeds of chaos in Xhosa country, he believed the British would become too involved in the plight of the people to give aid to the Boers.

Brownlee's accusations were based entirely on conjecture. True, from time to time, Basotho envoys had been seen in Kreli's kraal, but they had also visited other chiefs, including Mpande, King of the Zulu. Moshesh was also known to have exchanged cattle and horses with Kreli for grain and leopard skins, but he had exchanged similar items with several other chiefs. This was his way of creating or maintaining goodwill with other tribal rulers. The old chief resented Brownlee's accusations, and it grieved him to learn that these had been endorsed by the High Commissioner.

'I beseech Your Excellency not to credit the reports of men who take advantage of my name to spread such false words,' he wrote to Grey, 'and I beseech Your Excellency not to render my position as a chief still more complicated by mixing me up in a business that doesn't concern me. I already find myself sufficiently embarrassed, occupied as I am in endeavouring to settle satisfactorily the question now pending between me and the Free State.'

During the first half of Summer, exceptionally heavy and prolonged rains fell over central South Africa. Cattle-raiding therefore came to a standstill, easing the tension between Basotho and the Boers. After the visit of Coleman and Viljoen the old chief had sent parties of horsemen from kraal to kraal to search for stolen cattle. Whatever beasts were found he sent to Smithfield, hoping that this would convince the Boers of his integrity and his desire for peace.

The rains ceased in January 1857, and no sooner had the Caledon river returned to its normal strength, than it was crossed night and day, month in and month out, by marauders bound for republican farms and villages. Indeed, to this day, 1857 is remembered as The Year of Endless Plunder.

Kraal-heads everywhere possessed at least one stolen beast, horse or sheep.

Fearing an attack by the Boers, Moshesh continued to send stolen cattle he had retrieved back to the republic. Many of his chiefs ridiculed him, and Letsie called him a weakling. The Boers complained that the beasts he sent were invariably old, emaciated or diseased, and he had not returned a horse in months. The fact was that his subjects refused to part with horses, fearing they would be used by the Boers to invade the Lesotho.

At the beginning of 1858 Moshesh was obsessed with the belief that the republic was preparing for war.

'Have pity on me,' he wrote to the *volksraad*, 'let there be peace.' But he could not really have expected peace to prevail while his subjects continued to plunder Boer farms. By February, for example, Poshuli's commandos had overrun the Smithfield district, driving the Boers into laager and 'wantonly destroying ... game, leaving large numbers of them to rot in heaps'. They also drove vast herds of Boer cattle down to the Orange, exchanging them there with white smugglers for merchandise. Others bands of Basotho had been 'forcibly taking possession of farms' near Winburg, Harrismith and along the lower reaches of the Caledon river. The Boers viewed developments with deep concern. Before the end of the month they had mustered the Winburg, Smithfield, Fauresmith and Bloemfontein commandos, and were ready for war.

An ultimatum signed by Boshof reached Thaba Bosiu on 12 March. It demanded, among other things, that Poshuli be removed from the Vechtkop area, and that Moshesh should undertake to prevent his subjects from entering the republic.

'I request that your answers ... may be candid and without evasions,' Boshof warned Moshesh, 'as upon them will depend peace or war between us.'

After a week had passed without word from Moshesh, the *volksraad* declared war on the Lesotho. Two large commandos were sent to the Caledon river, one from the north and the other from the south.

Fighting broke out on the 23rd, when a commando under

Johannes Sauer, *landdrost* of Smithfield, pounced on the
Barolong of Beersheba and occupied the mission station.
Two days later a Boer patrol, locating the forces of Mopeli
and Moletstane near presentday Ficksburg, drove them into
the hills with heavy losses. Then on the 27th Comdt.-
General Weber, supported by the marauder Letele, who had
by now deserted Moshesh and come over to the Boers, engaged and dispersed the combined commandos of Sekhonyana and Poshuli at Vechtkop. After looting Poshuli's great
kraal, the Boers burnt it to the ground.

Fighting ceased during the following week. While the
Boers held councils of war to consider strategy, the Basotho
hustled their womenfolk, children and herds into the highlands. Thousands of warriors flocked to Thaba Bosiu in
response to a call to arms. Commandos took up vantage
points in the surrounding hills, and a great force under
Letsie moved westward along the banks of the Caledon.

At sunrise on 3 April a Boer patrol under Field-cornet
Pienaar crossed the Caledon into the Lesotho. Suddenly
hordes of Basotho appeared on every side, muskets firing,
assegais clattering shaft upon shaft—a whooping, whistling
mass sent into battle by Letsie himself. Finding themselves
in the claws of an ambush the Boers formed up in close
order, opened fire and, blasting a gap through the nearest
wall of warriors, charged to safety. Casualties were heavy—
thirty wounded and sixteen dead.

Nine days passed before the Basotho and the Boers again
came to grips. At dawn on the 12th, six thousand of Moshesh's best horsemen quietly surrounded a force under
Commandants Senekal and Pretorius, who were encamped
near the Phuthiastana river, on the very spot used by Cathcart in 1852. Formed up in a huge circle, they watched the
Boers all day from their saddles hoping they would come
out and fight.

'On the 13th the enemy come upon us from all sides,'
Senekal and Pretorius reported later '... but was prevented
from forcing an entrance.' Next day at sunrise the Basotho
attacked again, converging on the Boers under cover of a
heavy fusillade. But before they had covered two hundred
paces, they were forced back by a devastating barrage of
gunfire, punctuated with the thunder of cannon. The un-

daunted Basotho beleaguered the Boers hoping to penetrate
their powerful defences. The fight continued 'for four hours
... then at last the Basotho began to retreat in all directions', and were pursued by the Boers.

During the afternoon the Boers broke camp and moved
on. Senekal and Pretorius had planned to hold this strategic
position for at least a fortnight longer, but now this was
impossible. The surroundings were strewn with Basotho
corpses, and soon the stench would be unbearable. Review-
ing the events of the day, Senekal considered the Basotho
hopeless marksmen. Before long Moshesh would be captured and his stronghold destroyed.

Senekal and Pretorius linked up with Weber's commandos at Jammersberg Drift, and on 25 April the entire Boer
force set out for Morija. Reaching the hills overlooking
the mission station three days later Senekal, newly elected
commandant-general in the place of Weber who was indisposed, gave orders for Chief Letsie's settlement to be encircled quickly and quietly. News had reached them an
hour before that the notorious Poshuli and four thousand
men were inside the settlement.

But the Boers were unable to surround the Basotho. Detected earlier by the chief's spies, they were relentlessly
harried by snipers as they advanced. Meanwhile the two
chiefs and their followers had fled across the plains north of
Morija, and were heading for Thaba Bosiu. Arbousset, together with the people of the mission station, had taken
refuge in the hills. Only Maeder, his assistant, remained
behind.[1] The Boers drove off the snipers in the afternoon,
and entered the deserted settlement. They were jubilant
now, singing triumphantly, but entirely unaware of the
'ghastly scene of inhuman savagery'[2] awaiting them.

Reaching Letsie's hut the Boers received a dreadful shock
—they came suddenly upon the mutilated bodies of their
comrades killed in battle on 3 April. Some of the corpses
had been scalped, some dismembered and others impaled.

[1] Among the refugees who accompanied Arbousset were six
traders who had been living at Morija. They were: J. Pullenger,
I. Blake, F. Pickard, R. Hamilton, T. Smith and J. Allington.

[2] Report from the Secretary of the Council of War, to the
Magistrate of Smithfield: Theal, *BR* ii.

The Boers were dumbfounded as they gathered around the unsightly spectacle, then suddenly 'burning with fury' they razed the settlement—every hut, granary and cattlefold. Later they sacked the mission station, sparing only the church and a simple shack occupied by Maeder.

Letsie and Poshuli reached Thaba Bosiu on the 29th, and climbed the hill to report the previous day's events to Moshesh. Two days later Basotho scouts found the Boers heading northwards, in solid formation, midway between Morija and Thaba Bosiu. The next phase of the invasion— an attack on Moshesh's stronghold—was at hand.

At about midday on 5 May, Moshesh and his people, looking over the distant plains and valleys, caught sight of the Boers. In the afternoon and until well after sunset they watched the invaders pitch camp near the Khubelu pass. The Boers, they told themselves, would attack on the morrow.

Precisely at eleven next morning Thaba Bosiu was rocked by an explosion of cannon- and rifle-fire. The Boers were climbing the Khubelu pass! Within moments hundreds of Basotho, concealed behind the ramparts and in crannies and caves, opened fire. 'Bullets came down the hill like rain',[1] compelling the Boers to take shelter among the rocks. An hour later as the Boers inched their way up the slope, a Basotho commando came charging round the south-eastern limb of the hill. With muskets belching, it bore down on the foot of the Khubelu pass threatening to cut the Boer invaders off from their camp.

A skirmish broke out near Rafutho's kraal, and continued until late afternoon when the Basotho commando, buckling slightly before the onslaught of Boer guns, turned tail and headed for the Phuthiastana river. The Boers were not unduly concerned about the run of the day's events. But as the sun set and they studied the gigantic cliffs cresting Moshesh's hill, they became aware of the magnitude of the task before them. Their force was too small, they told themselves, and it required at least another three or four cannon.

That night at a council of war held in Senekal's tent the Boers decided to postpone operations and return to their

[1] Eye-witness account by J. A. Roosema: Theal, *BR* ii.

farms. When next they invaded the Lesotho, they would
take Thaba Bosiu first and the other settlements afterwards.

It is said that when he was told the Boers had broken
camp and were heading homewards, Moshesh wept for joy.
Later at a meeting of the councillors and army commanders
in the *kgotla* he chuckled derisively, recalling that the white
men had sworn to continue the war 'till one of the two
nations were rooted out of the face of the earth'. Lifting his
voice in praise of the spirits, he reminded the dignitaries
that Thaba Bosiu was more than a flat-topped hill, and far
more than an impregnable stronghold. Thaba Bosiu was his
mother. It was the mother of all Basotho.

CHAPTER TWENTY-FOUR

AN UNEASY PEACE

*President Boshof slates his fellow-countrymen for
withdrawing from Thaba Bosiu—He is belittled by
Moshesh—Moshesh snubs Sir George Grey and a
party of Boer dignitaries—He signs a treaty against his
better judgment—He seeks and finds solace in the spirit
cult—He meets M. W. Pretorius at Wonderkop farm*

THE abortive assault on Thaba Bosiu caused Boshof concern and embarrassment.

'The Boers, by their unaccountable sudden break up,' he
wrote on 20 May 1858 to John Burnet, resident magistrate
of Aliwal North, 'have brought me in such a fix as I never
yet was in all my life.' He surmised he would be sacked by
the *volksraad*, or asked to resign. Not that he minded, for
now the Basotho would be less likely to come to terms with
the republic and, more important, the Boers, 'poor fools',
assuming an air of false security, had disbanded the commandos. They seemed to believe they had given 'Moshesh
such a licking that he would keep quiet for many a day'.
Boshof could see little future for the Free State republic
unless, of course, the Boers went hat in hand to the old
chief and tried to win back what little of his friendship they
had previously enjoyed.

As a preliminary to reopening negotiations with the
Basotho, Boshof wrote Moshesh a letter asking him to receive a Boer deputation at Thaba Bosiu. He also mentioned
that Martinus Wessels Pretorius, president of the Transvaal
Boers, intended visiting the Free State and, if necessary,
would act as arbitrator between the republic and Lesotho.
As a devout Christian Boshof was heartsore at the misery
suffered by the Basotho and Boers during April. He begged
Moshesh to forget the past, and look again upon the Whites
of the republic as friends.

Moshesh's reply reflects his frame of mind during those
troubled times—a smugness foreign to his nature. He was

surprised, he let Boshof know, that the mighty president should seek to end a war which, as far as the Basotho were concerned, had not yet begun.

'I have not fought any battle yet,' he added caustically.

Moshesh said he had never taken Boshof's threats seriously, and had therefore restrained his commandos from destroying the Boers. But learning of the sacking of Morija and, later, the arrival of the Boer commandos at the foot of Thaba Bosiu, he had boiled with indignation. 'I am a dog,' he had told himself, 'and if my master Boshof beats me I shall bite him.'

But, continued the chief, if Boshof really wanted peace, he could have it. If he wished he could send both his deputation and President Pretorius to Thaba Bosiu. Not that this could serve much purpose, for surely there was no need for mediation. The object of a mediator was 'to part two adversaries who were fighting against each other'. Only one nation had waged war. And that nation was not the Basotho.

It is unlikely that a man of Moshesh's gentle nature could have gloated over Boshof's predicament for long. He might even have considered overlooking past events. But during the second week in May he received news that shattered his faith in the Boers. A convoy of wagons from the Colony stacked with rifles, powder, ammunition and even some cannons had been seen crossing the Orange, bound for Bloemfontein. Boshof, cried the chief, was a hypocrite. His overtures for peace had been no more than idle words!

A Boer deputation consisting of L. P. Papenfus, W. G. Every and St. P. O'Brien visited Thaba Bosiu on 24 May. After a week's discussion with Moshesh and his councillors, an armistice was signed. The chief also agreed to attend a further meeting, but this time under the chairmanship of Sir George Grey who was due shortly to visit the republic.

Moshesh wrote to Grey in July expressing delight at his impending visit, and asking him to bring powder and ammunition. They agreed to meet on 15 September at the Beersheba mission station. The High Commissioner would also invite the Boers.

Grey reached Beersheba on the appointed day, and was

welcomed by a large party of Boers. Moshesh, however, failed to turn up. Sir George was furious. He sent a letter to the chief demanding an immediate explanation. Two days later a reply arrived that Moshesh was ill and too old to travel so far. If the white men still wished to confer with him, he would meet them within the next few days at Morija.

Grey and the Boers set out for the burnt-down mission station where they found Moshesh and some of his sons and councillors awaiting them. The chief was in an ugly mood. He said he had come not to bargain with the Boers but to demand compensation, firstly for the damage they had done to the homes of his people, and secondly for the misery they had spread throughout the Lesotho. Presenting Grey with a list of conditions demanded by himself and his tribe, Moshesh suggested bluntly that the white men should study it carefully before attempting to negotiate with the Basotho.

Grey and the Boers required only a glance at the document to realize there was no point in prolonging discussions with Moshesh. They suggested that the meeting be postponed. Moshesh agreed, but assured them he himself would not attend next time. He would be represented by councillors.

The next meeting took place at Aliwal North on 27 September, and three days later a treaty drawn up by Grey was signed by the Boer and Basotho delegates. In no way did it meet with Moshesh's demands. In future a portion of the lower Caledon River district, including Vechtkop and Koesberg would be surrendered for reoccupation by the Boers. The High Commissioner himself would have the boundaries marked out with beacons. Basotho plunderers would have to be punished by Moshesh or, failing this, by the republican authorities. Indeed, the Boers would 'be at liberty to attack ... such delinquent chief or chiefs without Moshesh's interference'.[1] Finally, the boundary line drawn up originally by Warden would not be altered. In future it would be strictly enforced.

On 11 October the treaty was taken to Moshesh by

[1] Article X of the Treaty.

22

Burnet, the magistrate. The chief seemed willing to sign it
at first, but suddenly he flew into a rage, demanding that the
terms be altered to those he had presented to Sir George at
Morija. 'The regulations about thieving', caused him great
concern, and he rejected them as ridiculous. The whole
world, he cried, was plagued with thieves; how was he to
prohibit his subjects from stealing?

Moshesh and Burnet haggled and bickered all day, but
when the sun set and no progress had been made, the
magistrate, usually a patient and cool-headed man, jumped
angrily to his feet.

'It is nearly dark,' he barked, and 'we are just where we
began.' He said he had not visited Moshesh 'to wrangle or
to argue with him', and as far as he was concerned the chief
could 'ratify the treaty or leave it'. He would spend the
night with the missionaries and return home on the morrow.

Moshesh was calm now. He had never seen John Burnet
in a mood like this. Reaching for a newly made *kaross* that
lay beside him, he gave it to the white man with a reminder
that they were not enemies but friends. There was no need
for anger, he asserted, no need for hasty words.

'I will sign the treaty,' the old chief said, 'I will come
tomorrow and do so at the missionary's house.' He was
tired of unhappiness. If he 'finished the business', perhaps
his mind would be at rest.

Next morning, as promised, Moshesh signed the document placed before him by Burnet. But he considered the
treaty no more binding than the paper on which it was
written.

The treaty did much to ease the political tension north
of the Orange, and during the Spring and early Summer
Moshesh found and enjoyed the peace of mind he had
craved so long. Although he often yearned for the company
of his sons, in 1858 only Sekhonyana and Mayara visited
him daily in the stone house. They loved their father,
attending to his comforts and keeping him informed of
family and tribal matters. In return he gave them poultry,
skins, calves and, on one occasion, a musket each which he
had bought from an itinerant trader. He often said jokingly

that he regarded those two sons as the leaders of his
ploughing span. Unlike their brothers who tended to ignore
and even defy him, these two were ever at his side vying
with each other to please him.

Looking back on his turbulent life, it would seem that
Moshesh was fated to enjoy no more than the briefest spells
of happiness. Now in December 1858 he was on the brink of
misfortune. His mind was about to be numbed with grief.

For Mayara died suddenly on the 3rd, and scarcely a
fortnight later Sekhonyana decided to leave Thaba Bosiu
and settle with a small group of followers to the immediate
east of the Drakensberg, in the hilly region known today as
Griqualand East. Although he was begged by the elders of
Thaba Bosiu to remain at the side of his distracted father,
Sekhonyana refused. He said he had long been fledged, and
had earned the right to settle in a land of his own, and rule
independently over his own clan. In any case, by moving
away he would free himself of the annoying interference of
his brothers, and especially the man he hated most in all the
Lesotho—Letsie.

In the days following Sekhonyana's departure Moshesh
pined, turning now to his councillors for comfort and not to
his sons Tladi, Sophonia and Tseleko. One day he sent for
Letsie and Molapo, insisting that they stay with him until
his anguished heart had healed. But they began quarrelling
as soon as they arrived. Letsie accused his younger brother
of aspiring to the chieftaincy of the tribe, and Molapo retaliated with a barrage of insults and curses. Before long the
rest of the brothers were taking sides, most of them supporting Molapo. And all the while Moshesh looked on, his
mind pummelled by ever increasing despondency. One day
he told the missionary, Jousse, that he wished he could die.
Only in the spirit world would he find permanent peace of
mind.

It seems strange that in spite of his close association with
the French missionaries, and the solace he derived from
their friendship in times of trouble Moshesh resisted con-
version to Christianity. Over the years he had been fascinated by the biblical philosophies expounded by Casalis,
Arbousset, Dyke and Jousse. He acknowledged and
admired the spiritual magnitude of Jesus Christ, but he

would not believe that His holy spirit could better serve the
needs of black men than the sacred spirits of departed
ancestors. Over the years he had seen a handful of his subjects forsake the age-old spirit cult for the worship of the
white man's God. They had become spiritually elevated,
and for a time were filled with joy. But sooner or later most
of them had reverted to the traditional mode of worship,
often ridiculing Christian orthodoxy and especially the
missionaries' attitude to morality.

Moshesh had never lost contact with his spirit guides,
and in the months following the Boer invasion he had relied
on them, as never before, for advice. By February 1859 the
gloom had lifted from his mind, and he delighted in the
thought that he and his people were blessed not only by the
omnipresent shades of the tribe, but by the Supreme Spirit
Himself—God, the Molmo.

An almost uncanny quiet pervaded central South Africa
in 1859. Moshesh's dealings with the Boers dwindled to
occasional friendly visits by government officials. Boshof
resigned in February, and many months later when he was
succeeded by Martinus Wessels Pretorius, President of the
Transvaal Republic, Moshesh and his councillors pondered
the likely developments awaiting the Basotho.

In April 1860 Pretorius invited Moshesh to a meeting at
Wonderkop, a farm on the outskirts of Winburg. Told that
the old chief was agreeable, the president, accompanied by
twenty horsemen set off, reaching the appointed place on
the 29th. He found Makwayane, Mopeli, Tladi, Tseleko and
Masupha awaiting him at the farm house. Moshesh and a
commando of six thousand were encamped a few miles to
the south. A meeting with Moshesh was arranged for the
1st of May. Thereafter the Basotho, raising their hands in
salutation, took leave of Pretorius. Suddenly they galloped
away and firing their muskets into the air, disappeared
through some trees beyond the homestead.

On the morning of 1 May, Moshesh arrived for the
meeting accompanied by about seventy followers, one of
whom carried a huge white flag. The old man was cordially
welcomed by the Boers, and he 'shook hands very warmly'
with Pretorius. Moshesh proceeded to the spot where the

meeting was to be held, and sat down in a chair. Rising
suddenly, he called the gathering to order.

In an atmosphere of intense silence Moshesh recounted
the history of his people, and to the chagrin of the Boers
delivered 'an oration of three hours continuous'. When at
last he had finished, 'he was followed by several of his
chiefs in the same strain'. It was already late in the afternoon when Pretorius rose to speak.

'Great Chief, Father Moshesh, and chiefs of the Basuto
nation,' began the President, 'you have brought with you a
white flag, so have I. These flags are emblematic of peace. I
have come to establish a peace, not a hollow peace, but a
substantial and everlasting peace. I have come to place you
Moshesh, Captains and people of the Basuto nation, in my
arms and there you shall all rest in security, lovingly.'

Pretorius paused, his ears drumming with tumultuous
applause. Moshesh, he noticed, was grinning and clapping
his hands delightedly.

Moshesh, continued the President, was known to the
Boers as a wise and honourable man whose aim had always
been to foster friendly relations between races, irrespective
of colour. The Boers admired him; admired the fatherly
manner in which he had striven to guide the Basotho, his
children, towards a secure, happy way of life. Sometimes he
had succeeded, but generally his efforts had ended in failure. The reason was that peace could not prevail in a
country where thieves and brigands abounded.

'You Moshesh and your Captains must assist me in
maintaining peace between our nations!' exclaimed Pretorius, 'and that can only be by your assisting me to put
down thieves!'

'We will,' replied Moshesh, 'there are bad people among
us; they must be put down.'

'Remember what you were not many years ago, a poor,
helpless tribe. Who made you what you are now?' asked the
president.

'The Boers, they lifted us up from the ground,' clamoured the chief and his followers.

'Who gave you food when you were starving?'

'The Boers!'

'Well then,' continued Pretorius, 'I have now come again

to lift you up from the ground upon which you are now lying morally prostrate, by reason of your thieving and encroachment on the white man's land. My object in coming here is to restore your character as a nation of Basutos. To take away from you the reproach of being a nation of thieves.... We must establish authorities, police and laws to put down theft and aggression.'

Rising suddenly, Moshesh stepped forward, and snatching up the flag promised to assist the President 'to the utmost'. The Basotho and the Boers, he continued, must never forget the flag he now held in his hand. It was a symbol of everlasting peace.

On the following day Pretorius and Moshesh agreed to establish a tribunal of Basotho and Boers. It would meet regularly at the Merumetsu mission station to be known in future as *Makhotso*—the Mother of Peace. They also agreed to post some two hundred police at selected points along the borders.

Meanwhile a freezing wind had sprung up and rain started falling. Fearing the Caledon would come down in flood and cut the Basotho off from Thaba Bosiu, Moshesh decided to leave for home. But Pretorius insisted he should remain until the following day. The Boers had arranged a party in his honour.

The merrymaking began soon afterwards and continued well into the night. The old chief, unaccustomed to late hours, retired soon after dusk to Pretorius's tent where a bed had been prepared for him. Next morning he and the President rose early to inspect the six thousand horsemen who had accompanied the chief to Wonderkop farm. Led by Moshesh the Basotho then entertained the Boers to a display of dancing, and when this was over, they bade their hosts farewell and left for home.

Martinus Pretorius was pleased with the outcome of the meeting, and was especially impressed by 'the high civilization exhibited' by Moshesh and his dignitaries. He believed he had won their friendship, and could count on them as allies of the republic. He and Moshesh had buried the proverbial hatchet forever.

CHAPTER TWENTY-FIVE

MOSHESH'S TORMENT

*Moshesh is accused of currying favour with the Boers,
and is defied by Poshuli—He meets Prince Albert, son
of Queen Victoria—He is deserted by another of his
sons—Adele Casalis returns to the Lesotho—Moshesh
is warned by his seers to keep away from the missionaries—Some of his vassal chiefs are said to be plotting
his overthrow—J. J. Venter is elected President of the
Free State republic—The Busotho rampage through the
Winburg and Harrismith districts*

AT the first sitting of the *kgotla,* on his return to Thaba
Bosiu, Moshesh was confronted by a body of chiefs and
elders led by Poshuli, who accused him of currying favour
with the Boers at Wonderkop. Why had he not demanded
compensation for the havoc wrought by the Boers on
Basotho kraals, asked Poshuli, and why had Moshesh
accepted Pretorius's hand of friendship? It was as impossible to live in harmony with the Free State republic, as it
would be a snake to mate with a mongoose. The white men
were a treacherous and merciless foe, continued Poshuli,
and unless kept in check would destroy the Basotho at the
first opportunity. Moshesh weathered the storm of criticism
with courage and dignity. He said there was no reason to
fear the Boers provided, of course, they were left in peace.

Considering how little control Moshesh now had over
Poshuli and other leaders of the tribe, he could not have
expected the newly found peace to last for long. Murmurs
of discontent were heard everywhere, from Thaba Bosiu to
Vechtkop. Some of the men who had attended the meeting
at Wonderkop farm predicted a Boer invasion in the Spring.
They scoffed at the idea of a joint tribunal at *Makhotso*—
Mother of Peace, and warned Moshesh that Poshuli had
pledged to kill any policeman found near his territory.

In June Poshuli sent a commando supported by a party
of Bushmen to plunder Boer farms in the Koesberg area.

Carrying off cattle, horses and sheep, the marauders were
challenged by a farmer named Hefer. First they flogged him
and then killed his son and critically wounded five other
members of his household.

A commando of four hundred Boers set out in pursuit of
Poshuli's men, killing six and routing the rest. In July when
complaints reached Thaba Bosiu from Bloemfontein, Moshesh promised half-heartedly to send Letsie to punish Poshuli. But, in fact, there was little he could do to prevent any
further outbreaks of violence. Several of his chiefs, including his brother Mopeli, were as determined as Poshuli to
continue the struggle with the Boers.

At the end of July Moshesh received a letter from Sir
George Grey informing him that Prince Albert, son of
Queen Victoria, had arrived at the Cape. The prince had
asked to be taken to Moshesh and other important chiefs of
South Africa. Although usually a reluctant traveller the old
chief agreed to meet Prince Albert at whatever venue the
High Commissioner selected. 'Everybody would be flocking
to the Sun,' he said, and he 'the oldest of Her Majesty's
servants and subjects' in central South Africa also wished
'to enjoy its light'.

During the third week in August, after further communi-
cation with Grey, Moshesh set out for Aliwal North to
meet Prince Albert. Brought before the royal visitor he
beamed with childlike joy, expressing profound loyalty to
the Queen and complaining that he had been forgotten by
the British since the abandonment of the Sovereignty. Once
he had been counted among the Queen's servants, and he
asked to be reinstated to this privileged position. Above all,
he wanted Britain as his ally and protector.

Albert promised to deliver the message to his mother.
During the following four days he conferred with numerous other chiefs who had come to meet him. Not one of
them was as pleasant or as devoted to the Crown as this
wise old chief of the Basotho—Moshesh.

Moshesh found the visit to Aliwal North a pleasant but
exacting experience, and on returning to Thaba Bosiu he
remained in bed for several days. A strange feeling of

gloom crept over him, presumably as a result of yet another clash he had had with Poshuli and some of the councillors. Much of Moshesh's trouble stemmed from loneliness. In past months he had craved the companionship of those whom he knew loved him. But so many of his dearest friends and relatives were no longer at Thaba Bosiu. They had either moved away from the Lesotho or passed on to the spirit world. Casalis, for example, had gone forever, and it was said Arbousset would be returning to France before the close of the year. The old chief's circle of loved ones was shrinking fast, and more were destined to desert him in the gathering twilight of his life.

One night in 1861 Moshesh was wakened by Makwanyane and Ratsiu with news that the chief's young son, Tseleko, had run away from Thaba Bosiu, taking with him a party of followers and hundreds of horses and cattle. Moshesh was stunned. What could have come over the boy, he asked bewildered and weeping softly. Tseleko was far too young and inexperienced to face the hardships of life without the help of a father. Later, learning that his son had settled unlawfully in the Colony, Moshesh wrote Burnet a letter begging to protect him from harm.

'Notwithstanding his ... misconduct which has caused me much pain,' he wrote, 'Tseleko is still my son whom I love, and I beg Mr. Burnet to deal with him gently and neither to send him back or [sic] put him in prison, but rather to leave him alone free to do as he likes and go where he pleases as long as he does not break the laws of the Colony. I could not bear to hear that evil should happen to him.'

Although for many months the old man pined for his son, he was convinced that he would repent and come back. After several months of wandering and intense hardship Tseleko did return to Thaba Bosiu. And like the legendary prodigal son he was warmly welcomed by his father, now tearful but jubilant, and fêted at a celebration arranged in his honour.

A regular visitor to Thaba Bosiu in 1861 was Adele Casalis. Five years before, she had returned with her father to Paris where she met and married a young missionary

named Adolphe Mabille. She and her husband came to
South Africa, eventually replacing Thomas Arbousset at
Morija. Moshesh derived unbounded pleasure from the
Mabilles' company. Now twenty-four, Delly, as he called
her, reflected the gentleness of her mother, the wisdom of
her father and the kindly disposition of both. Moshesh
often told his councillors he was grateful to God for
sending Casalis's daughter back to the Lesotho. She was
among the few who knew how to cheer him when he was
downcast or troubled.

Moshesh was so 'depressed in spirits' in January 1862,
that for a while not even Adele could comfort him. Yet
another white man, a farmer named Venter, had been murdered, and the Boers, retaliating swiftly, had killed nine of
a party of Basotho said to have been responsible for the
crime. The south-western border seethed with discontent
and threats of war.

In the meantime Poshuli had attacked Chief Letele's clan
capturing thousands of cattle. Aware that Letele was an
ally of the Boers, the Basotho living in the vicinity of
Beersheba had fled in fear of reprisal. 'Old women and children hobbling and crying under their bundles', followed by
'sheep, goats, oxen, horses and wagons', and finally by
'armed and mounted men', streamed tardily into the Lesotho. Warned that the Boers were about to attack Poshuli,
Moshesh sent Tseleko and a nephew of Letsie to Bloemfontein with orders to hand themselves over to Pretorius as
hostages. They were to ask the President to accept them on
behalf of Moshesh, the 'friendly chief', who had not a
'hostile act or thought in his heart'. By this gesture they
would serve as a reminder that the Basotho were determined to settle the recent 'commotion' peaceably.

Pretorius was impressed with Moshesh's farsightedness
and told him so. He also informed the chief that, on in-
vestigation, the Boers were satisfied Letele was as much to
blame as Poshuli for the unrest in the Caledon district. It
had therefore been decided to place the recalcitrant chief in
the charge of a government superintendent named Daniel
Foley. This would be a vital step towards maintaining peace
along the border especially as Letele, grandson of the illus-

trious seer, Mohlomi, refused to acknowledge Moshesh's authority on the grounds of the old chief's inferior birth. Kept in check by Foley for a while, Letele eventually crossed the Drakensberg with his followers and settled in Griqualand East.

A Boer deputation reached Thaba Bosiu on 14 March seeking an interview with Moshesh. When the chief was told that the white men had come to discuss Venter's murder, he refused to see them. He said they had come to the wrong place for neither he nor any resident of Thaba Bosiu had committed the murder. After keeping the Boers waiting six days, Moshesh condescended to talk to them. But he was so obstinate and ill-tempered, that they cut the interview short and returned home.

Pretorius was annoyed when informed of the rebuff received by the delegation. Some days before he had been offended when Sir Philip Wodehouse, newly appointed High Commissioner in the place of Grey, had suggested relations between the Boers and Busotho were dominated by 'a chronic state of ill-feeling'. Now, considering Moshesh's changeable nature he admitted that the remark was not as farfetched as he had thought. The future was unpredictable.

As has been mentioned, much of the gloom that beset Moshesh's mind from time to time stemmed from the quarrels he had with his sons, councillors and vassal chiefs. He and Letsie clashed regularly during the Winter of 1862. Letsie was drinking heavily—John Burnet considered him a 'drunken fool'—and was invariably unreasonable and bitterly critical of all his father did. He accused Moshesh of treating him like a child, scolding him in company, or questioning his decisions in tribal affairs. Nursing a badly injured hand following a shooting accident, Letsie tried to keep out of his father's way. He looked upon Moshesh as a pitiable old man tormentd by an incessant fear of imaginary enemies. He complained that Moshesh had become so impulsive in his old age that only the sycophants of the kraal could tolerate his company for long.

Had Eugene Casalis been there to advise and comfort him in 1862, perhaps Moshesh would have felt less unwanted, inadequate and insecure. He derived some comfort

from the visits of Jousse and the youthful Mabille, but they
lacked Casalis's force and personality and his ability to uplift the old chief when he needed it most.

Moshesh relied far more on the prophecies and philosophies of his seers and diviners than on advice received
from the missionaries. In recent months two seers in particular had been playing an important rôle in his life. They
were Mantshupa Makhetha the woman, and Katsi, a blind
man. They were said to possess extraordinary powers of
healing, and warriors who drank their special decoctions
were believed to become invulnerable to white men's bullets.

What interested Moshesh most was the seers' attitude to
some of the missionaries' teachings. Unlike Mantshupa and
Katsi, the Frenchmen could not make direct contact with
the spirit world, and had to rely on books for their knowledge. This, according to the seers, accounted for the white
men's ridiculous attitude to most aspects of Basotho life.
Polygamy, for example, was considered a sin by the missionaries, but in the eyes of the Molimo it was a thing of
beauty. There were times when the seers' disembodied souls
travelled to the realm of spirits, and found the ancestors of
the tribe 'rejoicing themselves on beer or beef ... marrying
many wives and doing everything the missionaries say is
wrong'.

Much to Moshesh's concern Mantshupa and Katsi predicted that the Boers would invade and destroy the Lesotho
before the end of the year. They warned him to disassociate
himself not only from the missionaries, but also from the
tribesmen who attended their services. 'Such people' were
'lost' and were 'enemies' of the tribe. Moshesh was told to
command his subjects, and especially the converts to turn
their backs on Christianity. There was no better religion
than the worship of ancestral spirits. It was they and not
Jesus Christ who came to the aid of the black men in times
of need and sorrow.

A merciless drought besieged the Lesotho in the Summer
of 1862, and although the spirits were begged for help, they
refused to send even the briefest shower. The land remained
untilled and unplanted, fountains died, waterholes turned
into dustbowls, and the Caledon dwindled into a struggling

trickle. Faced with the horror of famine, thousands of Basotho stole into the Free State in search of food. First they confined themselves to hunting, but later they turned on the Boers, ransacking their homes, polluting wells and fountains and shooting down whoever opposed them.

'This state of things cannot last long,' wrote the *Friend of the Free State*, 'the Boers will either have to trek or fight.'[1] And as the drought persisted the raids increased. By the beginning of 1863 the Boers and Basotho were on the brink of war. Summoning Mantshupa, the seer, Moshesh ordered her to call upon the spirits for rain. All her efforts failed and she was condemned by Moshesh as a charlatan, and driven by Letsie across the Orange into exile.

The first rains fell in February, but by then the planting season had passed. Winter was just around the corner, and the dreaded famine skulked in the vicinity of the kraals. During the Autumn and Spring stock-theft was so rife in the Winburg and Harrismith districts that the *volksraad* appointed a land commission to fix a boundary line in the area and mark it with beacons. Moshesh refused an invitation to accompany the commission, but later, after the Boers and Sir Philip Wodehouse had pleaded with him, he sent Mopeli and Molapo in his place. But when at length the job was done, the chief refused to recognize the line. He was surprised that the Boers should expect him to do so, when they knew he had not been present to supervise the erecting of beacons.

Throughout the Summer, in spite of regular appeals by the Boers, Moshesh refused to change his mind. In May 1863, while spending a few days at Morija, he was visited by a Boer deputation headed by W. G. Every. Asked again to endorse the line Moshesh became angry, saying he would never do so as he believed the Boers were solely to blame for the unrest in the Winburg and Harrismith districts.

In the meantime Pretorius had resigned as President of the Free State republic, and had returned to the Transvaal in March. After three years in office he had become disillusioned, believing that Moshesh was too old to regain control over his unruly tribe. Pretorius was succeeded by a senior

[1] 24 October 1862.

member of the *volksraad*—Acting-President Jacobus Johannes Venter.

Venter had known Moshesh, his sons and councillors for many years. Addressing the *volksraad* in September, he predicted that the old chief would soon be overthrown by conspirators. The protagonists in the plot were Mopeli and Molapo. They had become powerful chiefs, and their commandos comprised not only their own subjects, but the most notorious desperadoes of central South Africa and runaway criminals from the Colony and Free State. Mopeli and Molapo were also known to be plotting Letsie's death, and had pledged to clear the republic of white men. According to Venter, another of his sons, Sophonia, had also become a threat to Moshesh's power. In August he and about a thousand of his people, together with pack-oxen, horses and wagons had overrun the farm of Andries Visagie near the Vet river. Apart from the damage done, they also put the farmer and his family to flight. Venter doubted whether Moshesh was aware of the activities of his vassal chiefs and sons.

The situation in the Winburg and Harrismith districts became critical towards the end of September and Venter, determined to prevent an outbreak of war, sent an urgent plea for Moshesh to meet him at Platberg on 23 May. To his delight Moshesh agreed to come.

Face to face with the old chief on the appointed day, Venter noticed that he and his retinue were aloof and sullen. In actual fact Moshesh was ill. His body aching, his face drawn, he could barely muster a nod in response to Venter's friendly greeting. Mopeli, mounted on a pied stallion, came forward and explained that the Basotho had come to settle finally the boundary dispute in the Winburg and Harrismith district. But discussion would have to be postponed until the following day, as Moshesh was unwell and needed rest.

When the Boers emerged from their camp next morning, they were amazed to find Moshesh and his retinue preparing to leave. Asked why, most of them merely shrugged their shoulders or mumbled inarticulately. Venter begged

Moshesh to wait, but he refused, and mounting his horse handed the President a piece of paper on which was listed the landmarks demanded by the Basotho for the boundary line. Raising a hand in farewell, Moshesh led his followers out of Platberg and headed homewards.

Moshesh's claims were ridiculous, for the line he wanted passed through the heart of the Winburg and Harrismith districts, cutting off over two hundred and fifty Boer farms from the republic. Venter threw up his arms in despair. The old chief was too obstinate for the Boers to handle alone. They would have to call upon Sir Philip Wodehouse to act as mediator.

CHAPTER TWENTY-SIX

THE SECOND BOER INVASION

*Jan Hendrik Brand becomes President of the Free State
—Moshesh charms Sir Philip Wodehouse—Moshesh
uses a Union Jack as a talisman Wodehouse changes
his opinion of Moshesh—Moshesh weeps as his dignitaries clamour for war—The Basotho are forced to
evacuate the Winburg and Harrismith districts—War
breaks out*

THE Free State Boers held a general election in February
1864, and President Venter was replaced by forty-one-year-
old Jan Hendrik Brand, son of the speaker of the Colonial
parliament. A barrister by profession, Brand had enjoyed a
distinguished career in Cape Town, where he headed a
flourishing practice. He had also lectured in law at the
South African College, later to become the University of
Cape Town. Popular and highly respected, he was a courte-
ous, patient and farsighted man—an excellent choice for
the arduous task awaiting him north of the Orange. Brand
reached Bloemfontein in March, and met by a welcoming
party of Boers 'on horseback, in carts and waggons', he was
escorted through the streets, amidst cheering farmers and
the booming of cannon at the fort.

For over a week the Boers fêted their new president, and
at nights they thronged the streets which were 'ablaze with
illuminations, transparencies, mottoes, blazing tar-barrels,
fire-balls and Chinese lanterns'. The moment the celebrations were over, and he was sworn in by the *volksraad*,
Brand wrote to Moshesh. His aim, he said among other
things, was to promote 'justice and equity' and 'good
understanding between the Boers and Basuto'. Should the
Boers transgress he would punish them, but he also expected Moshesh to exercise the strictest control over the
Basotho and especially the marauders.

'By so doing,' concluded Brand, 'our people will be satisfied, happy and prosperous.'

In reply Moshesh said he was happy to know that the new president 'was desirous of doing justice to all'. It seemed that at last the future augured well for both the Basotho and the Boers.

Shortly after his arrival in Bloemfontein Brand invited Sir Philip Wodehouse to act as arbitrator in the highly contentious boundary dispute. Crossing the Orange with his retinue in the early Autumn the High Commissioner called on the President at Bloemfontein and after a brief discussion headed for Thaba Bosiu. He was given a hearty welcome by the Basotho, and found Moshesh so charming and understanding that when eventually he left Thaba Bosiu bound for the Colony, he believed he could settle the dispute without difficulty.

Wodehouse sent Brand a note describing his enjoyable and fruitful visit to the Basotho stronghold. Not only the chief, he wrote, but also his sons and councillors had promised 'to abstain from any acts calculated to cause annoyance with the Free State'. And more important, they had agreed 'to accept, unconditionally, such a decision respecting the boundary as he, Sir Philip, might think fair after proper hearing and examination'. All that remained was for the Boers to cooperate.

The High Commissioner had barely crossed the Orange on his way home, when Molapo and Moletstane heading ten Basotho commandos, burst into the Winburg district on a spree of destruction. Threatened with annihilation the Boers fled, taking their families into laager in a bushy, hill-studded area near presentday Clarens. The Boers retaliated, and joined by a posse of republican police under Sub-Inspector Thornton, they put the marauders to flight. A week later they crossed the Caledon near Butha-Buthe, fanned out over the Lesotho lowlands and moved slowly westwards.

The presence of the Boers troubled Moshesh and infuriated his sons and councillors. There was talk of war everywhere, Molapo and Moletstane were said to be preparing to ambush the intruders. But just when emotions were reaching fever pitch, the Boers were driven out of the Lesotho, not by Moshesh's warriors, but by the fiercest snowstorm to have swept the country in years. The Basotho believed that the spirits in their infinite wisdom, had snatched the Boers from the claws of death. Next time nothing would save the white men. They would be massacred!

In September messengers arrived at Thaba Bosiu with a note from Wodehouse. The High Commissioner had arranged to meet a Boer delegation at Jammersberg Drift on 6 October and wanted Moshesh and his advisers to attend.

Two days before the appointed time Moshesh, accompanied by a retinue of dignitaries, set out for the meeting place in a cold, misty drizzle. Finding the Caledon in flood, Moshesh and his party borrowed 'an old half worn out boat' from a farmer, and crossed the river in relays. This was a terrifying experience for the chief. Throughout the crossing he nursed a strip of bunting—'part of an old British Union Jack' said to have powerful protective qualities. The party reached Jammersberg Drift on the 6th and was welcomed by the High Commissioner, his wife, Lady Wodehouse and Sir Walter Currie, commandant of the Frontier Army and Colonial Police. President Brand had also just arrived.

Brand was the first to address the gathering, and he 'read a very well written and carefully prepared statement of the claims and grievances of the Free State. Moshesh replied at some length in his usual eloquent style on the Basuto side of the question'. Six long hours had passed by the time the chief had finished. Wodehouse, looking weary and bewildered, spoke for no more than a minute or two. He said he had decided to inspect the Winburg and Harrismith districts himself, and would release his decision on the boundary line at the first opportunity.

Moshesh was so 'worn and ill'[1] on his return to Thaba Bosiu, that he spent three weeks in bed. One morning he was visited by the Rev. Maitin, missionary-in-charge of Berea, with a message from Wodehouse. The High Commissioner, after his tour of inspection, had ruled in favour of the Boers! Indeed, according to Wodehouse, the Basotho

[1] Letter from Orpen to Burnet: Theal, *BR* iii.

had 'established villages, cultivated large tracts of land and introduced large quantities of cattle' on properties of farmers they had put to flight. No fair-minded person could condone a 'lawless system of appropriation' such as this. Moshesh would have to move his subjects back into the Lesotho.

A few days later a field-cornet named Steyn arrived on the hill-top and reported that Brand had given the Basotho until 30 November to leave Free State soil. If they refused they would be driven out by Boer commandos. Moshesh was alarmed, for he knew the Basotho could never prepare adequate shelter for their families in so short a time. And what of the crops they had planted, he asked Steyn, were these to be left unharvested?

A great *pitso* was held at Thaba Bosiu on 14 November, and among the scores of dignitaries present all except Moshesh and Letsie 'spoke in favour of war'. Molapo and Mopeli proposed that the Basotho accused by Wodehouse of squatting on Boer farms should refuse to budge on the 30th. It would be better to defy the white men and die honourably, than creep like curs across the Caledon, tails between the legs, and survive in humiliation.

'Moshesh,' cried one of the dignitaries, 'if you wish to sell us as slaves to the Boers ... please consent to their making war upon us and let us be beaten. Then we should become obedient servants.' 'Tax us, take our cattle, sheep, anything,' bellowed another, 'but don't let us be slaves of the Boers.'

Makwanyane called for the immediate invasion of the Winburg and Harrismith districts, and seeing Moshesh shake his head in disagreement, suggested sarcastically that the Basotho should surrender without lifting a weapon in defence of their rights. Again the dignitaries 'cried for war ... and every passionate speech ... was loudly applauded'.

At this stage Moshesh addressed the *pitso*. He said he would not permit a single drop of blood to be spilt over the boundary dispute for the Basotho although superior to the Boers in numbers, were inferior as horsemen and marksmen. He was not asking his people to cower and cringe at the feet of the white men like mangy mongrels. He merely wanted to spare them the horror of war. They were therefore to move well in time. Tears were streaming over the old chief's cheeks. There was to be no more fighting, he repeated, no more bloodshed!

The dignitaries, seeing the old man weep, shook their heads in amazement. Now suddenly they agreed with him, but they stressed one important point. As the move could not be accomplished in a week or even a month, Moshesh would have to appeal to Brand for an extension of time.

Moshesh wrote to the President as soon as the *pitso* was over, but two weeks later when no reply had come he gave orders for the exodus to begin. The perplexed and disgruntled Winburg and Harrismith Basotho collected their belongings, packing sleeping mats, *karosses* and household utensils onto pack-oxen and horses. Their heavier possessions, such as stamping blocks, grinding stones, crates of poultry and granaries they loaded onto carts and wagons. After a few days' trek news arrived from Brand. The *volksraad* had agreed to extend the deadline to 31 January. Some of the Basotho, mindful of the crops they had left behind, turned back, but the majority moved on. During early December the banks of the Caledon teemed with tribesmen, their families and stock. Some of the missionaries accompanied by Orpen arrived to help them across the river. Later Moshesh turned up, and exhorted them to have patience and courage.

Barely was the crossing complete than the Basotho were attacked by a band of *banditti* led by Chief Letele. And they had not progressed many miles, when news arrived that clouds of locusts, drifting inland from the desert in the west, had descended upon the crops they had left behind. Even more devastating had been a fierce and enduring hail storm, which had swept the Winburg and Harrismith districts. Deprived of their grain supply, the Basotho appealed to Moshesh for help. Many of the younger men, growing impatient, formed themselves into brigand bands, and scoured the Tlotsi area robbing kraals and cattlefolds. Moshesh sent a commando to round them up, but the brigands escaped and joined forces with Letele's marauders. By the beginning of 1865 most of the trekking Basotho had settled temporarily with relatives. President Brand was pleased with the way things had turned out, and he sent envoys to thank Moshesh for his cooperation.

In the middle of January 1865 a commando under Chief Lesawana, Moshesh's nephew, raided Boer farms in the Bethlehem area, and challenged by a small Boer patrol, opened fire wounding two of its members. Brand demanded seventy-two cattle as compensation from Moshesh, and he promised to annihilate Lesawana and his followers should they trespass again on Boer territory. Moshesh sent apologies to Brand and a message to Lesawana begging him to make peace with the Boers. Just then Poshuli and Moorosi, leading a huge force of horsemen, began raiding farms near the Wittenberg range, and before long plundering broke out in all parts of the republic. Mopeli captured three farmers, Van Rooyen, Pelser and Muller, north of the Caledon, and after having them tortured and thrashed released them with a warning that should they venture near the Lesotho again he would kill them.

Brand wrote to Moshesh demanding that 'the perpetrators of these acts of hostility' should be delivered to Bloemfontein, together with a fine of fifty cattle. This had to be done by 8 June, or otherwise war would be declared on the Basotho.

Moshesh ignored the President's letter. His people wanted war! At the end of May the chiefs of the tribe met on the hill-top and were given a report on the strength of the army by military commanders Molapo, Masupha, Mopeli, Moletstane and Leritholi, son of Letsie. The Basotho, they were told, could field at least ten thousand horsemen armed with muskets, and about as many warriors bearing assegais and battle-axes. Warned by Moshesh and Makwanyane that the Boers were far more powerful than was generally believed, the commanders became angry, and retorted that the chiefs should return to the kraals and muster their fighting men. Shortly afterwards the meeting broke up in an outburst of wild excitement. The Basotho were going to war!

During the first week in June, while the warriors gathered and were ritually prepared by the witchdoctors for battle, the noncombatants moved into the hills with the cattle and sheep. Messengers hurried southwards with orders for Po-

shuli and Moorosi to patrol the border along the Caledon
River district. Poshuli was to take command in the south,
but he was to keep out of the Free State until he received
further orders.

When no word was received from Moshesh on 6 June,
the Boers held a council of war at Leeukop. Three days
later Brand declared war on the Lesotho. On the 13th, a
huge force led by Jan Fick, the commander-in-chief, and
officered by Commandants Roos, de Villiers, Malan, Joubert, Bester, Wessels and Louw Wepener, advanced on
Mabolela, Chief Mopeli's capital kraal, fifteen miles west of
presentday Ficksburg. Reaching the nearby hills, the Boers
were faced by thousands of Basotho horsemen and warriors
under the command of Molapo, Masupha. Mopeli, Moletstane and Lerotholi. The Boers halted, and splitting up into
several small commandos waited for the enemy to act. Suddenly with a yell, the Basotho charged, brandishing their
muskets, whooping and whistling, but just beyond range of
the white men's guns they drew up, spreading out quickly
into long disjointed lines. Now the Boers came galloping
towards them, firing relentlessly through a cloud of smoke.
After a short skirmish the Basotho fell back, and then galloped away in a disorderly flight. Mopeli's commando
headed for Mabolela.

During the late afternoon the Boers pitched camp on a
hill close by. Next morning saddling their mounts before
dawn, they set out quietly for Mopeli's kraal. It was a grey,
misty morning, and as they approached a gap in the hills,
they found it blocked by a Basotho army ten times larger
than their own. And the slopes above them swarmed with
snipers.

Jan Fick called a halt. He had not anticipated opposition
from Chief Mopeli, let alone from the bulk of Moshesh's
army. With the backing of all his officers except Wepener,
he ordered the Boers to retrace their steps towards the
camp. The assault on Mabolela would have to wait.

The Basotho were puzzled at first, believing the enemy
was hoping to entice them into the open. However, an hour
later, learning from scouts that the Boers were heading for

home, they set out for Mabolela to celebrate what they considered the first victory of the war.

Meanwhile Poshuli and Moorosi had joined forces and were encamped with a commando, two thousand strong, near the Caledon's confluence with the Wilgebosch stream. At dawn on 20 June, they crossed into the Free State, and turning westwards, rampaged through the Smithfield district. Finding farms deserted or in the care of servants—for the Boers were on commando, and their families in laager on the Smithfield commonage—the Basotho quickly rounded up twenty thousand cattle and five times that number of sheep.

On the evening of the same day the Basotho came upon a patrol of fifteen Boers which they surrounded, killing twelve and wounding the remaining three. Challenged later by some eighty Boers, they fled, abandoning almost half of the booty cattle. When night fell they headed for the Caledon, crossing it in the light of a full moon. By sunrise next morning they had progressed deep into the Lesotho together with their valuable haul.

Only sporadic fighting took place during the following weeks. Skirmishes broke out in the Bloemfontein, Winburg and Harrismith districts, and a colony of Bastards was wiped out by Masupha's commando at Platberg. Lesawana's followers, coming upon a convoy of transport wagons from Natal, killed the owner, Pieter Pretorius, his wife and five children, a friend called Andries Smit, seven coloured servants and an Indian coolie.

So far, not many Basotho had been slain. The Boers seemed strangely inactive. Many considered them afraid, and unlikely to continue the war much longer. But not Moshesh. He had reason to fear the Boers more than ever. Recently he had recalled Mantshupa, the seer, from exile and had sought her guidance. According to her the Basotho were on the brink of a great disaster.

CHAPTER TWENTY-SEVEN

THE DEATH OF A HERO

Louw Wepener destroys Poshuli's settlements—The Boers shell Thaba Bosiu—They advance up the Khubelu pass, and are repulsed—Wepener is killed in action

THE Boers invaded the Lesotho in mid-July 1865, one commando under Louw Wepener advancing from the south, and another under Fick from the north. The combined force consisted roughly of two thousand burghers and one thousand non-white auxiliaries. Wepener's first encounter with the Basotho took place near the Koesberg range, when he attacked and dispersed a commando under Chief Lebenya, one of Moshesh's less powerful vassals. Moving on Wepener first destroyed Poshuli's settlement at Vechtkop and then, six miles east of Morija, occupied Letsie's new village—Matsieng, the Place of Locusts. He also proclaimed a vast portion of the Lesotho, west of the mission station, Free State territory.

Fick, meanwhile, had marched again on Mopeli's kraal, and finding it deserted had crossed the Caledon and captured Masupha's stronghold on Berea hill. Towards the end of July he and Wepener linked up south-west of Thaba Bosiu. They immediately began planning the assault on Moshesh's stronghold.

Moshesh suddenly fell ill soon after the arrival of the Boers, and for three days he refused to budge from his bed. According to Lautre, a missionary doctor recently arrived in the Lesotho, the old chief was suffering from intense fatigue. The invasion had caused him so much anguish that in a week he had barely closed an eye, and not a morsel of food had passed his lips. Moshesh was afraid, and he was lonely, for apparently few of the dignitaries could find time to visit him. Only Makwanyane kept him informed of developments.

Of all the passes leading to the hill-top, the Khubelu was the most strongly fortified, firstly because it was so near Moshesh's village, and secondly because experience had revealed that invaders considered it easiest to negotiate. The Boers were certainly unlikely to attempt any of the other passes.

At daybreak on 8 August Thaba Bosiu was rocked by a bombardment of shells fired from Ntolokholo hill in the south. Next moment two parties of Boers were reported climbing the southern slopes—one under Louw Wepener, along the Raebe pass, and the other along a goat-track below Mokhachane's kraal. Panic broke out, and Moshesh, emerging from his home, gave orders for the cattle to be driven to the top of the pass and stampeded onto the advancing enemy. In the meantime Wepener and his men had decided to retrace their steps down the hill. The Raebe was too treacherous. Only eight of the Boers had managed to reach the summit, but seeing the cattle approaching had turned about and scrambled after their comrades. The second party of Boers had also decided to abandon the climb, and were filing slowly down the goat track to the base of the hill.

Not a further shot was fired by the Boers during the following week. On the 15th the Basotho caught sight of the Boers' non-white contingent taking up positions at the foot of Ntlokholo hill, and on a rise near the mission station. A little later two-thirds of the Boers moved southwards on horseback, leaving about six hundred in camp. After riding right round the base of Thaba Bosiu, in a show of strength, the Boers dismounted near Rafutho's kraal. They sat down on the grass in groups while Fick and his officers met for discussion.

A little after eleven o'clock Wepener, supported by Wessels, Bester, Senekal and three hundred men moved up the Rafutho pass to the 'gutter' as the Boers called the Khubelu pass. Covering their left flank was part of the non-white contingent which had stormed and taken the mission station an hour before. To the right, sheltered among rocks was a small party of Boers, and from the bottom of the hill the artillery 'commanded a severe fire of shot and shell on the face of the summit of the hill'.

Terror-stricken by the fierce bombardment, the Basotho manning the nearest ramparts scurried away into the crannies of brush along the southern lip of the pass. Wepener and his comrades continued to climb, each step carefully calculated, backs hugging the walls of the pass or squeezed into crevices. Occasionally they would pause to fire, reload and inch on through a gathering cloud of stagnant gunsmoke. Taking up positions in an outcrop of rocks, Bester and a small party of burghers covered Wepener's advance with a curtain of musket fire.

The resistance offered by the Basotho was ineffective, firstly because they were generally incompetent marksmen, and secondly because the Boers were only visible for a second or two at a time as they darted in and out of the rocks. At about midday the van of Wepener's party moved into a narrow, stone-strewn fissure which meanders upwards along the cliffs forming the northern wall of the pass. Moshesh's sons, Masupha, Molapo and Tladi who commanded the topmost ramparts had been waiting for this moment to come. They ordered their men to hold fire until the fissure was full of Boers.

Cautiously the white men moved upwards, step by step, and when Wepener reached the top of the fissure, he climbed onto a narrow ledge and edged himself into a gap in the cliff. Just below him crouched his coloured afterrider, for many years his trusted servant and constant companion.

Suddenly a burst of gunfire tore through the fissure, cutting down six of the burghers. The rest scampered away followed by a rush of boulders rolled over the cliffs by Masupha's men. Five minutes later the firing ceased, and when the dust lifted out of the pass, Wepener sent an urgent appeal to Fick for reinforcements. A fight had broken out a little higher up, and to the right of the pass. He could hear the opposing sides cursing and taunting each other. Looking down the 'gutter' Wepener beheld several of his men conveying wounded burghers, including Wessels, to safety. The situation, he remarked to his afterrider, would become utterly hopeless unless help came soon from Fick.

Learning of Wepener's dilemma General Fick acted

swiftly. He sent an aide to summon Commandants Joubert, Malan, Roos and de Villiers, intending to send them with reinforcements up the hill. As they were nowhere to be found, the general called upon a young commandant named Smit to hasten to Wepener's aid. But he refused, complaining that his men considered the risk too great. Only in the late afternoon could Fick raise a relief party, consisting of Boers and Batlokwa. He himself led it up the pass.

Meanwhile Wepener, fearing that reinforcements would not reach him before sunset, had decided to press on alone. He had crept along the ledge in full view of the Basotho manning the ramparts above, and began climbing up the pass. Masupha's men opened fire, hurling Wepener backwards on to the ledge.

'I am mortally wounded,'[1] he cried, and sprawling partly over the edge of the ledge, he died. A shout of triumph rose from the ramparts and cliffs. The Basotho had been waiting to see this white man killed.

While Masupha's men reloaded, they fixed their eyes on the pass below, straining to pick out shapes and forms emerging from the haze of the rising smoke. It was then that they caught sight of Louw Wepener's afterrider. He was kneeling beside his master's corpse and struggled to move it from the ledge into the fissure. Next moment a krantz above him swarmed with Molapo's warriors, and they sent a jumble of boulders crashing upon him. Like his master, Wepener's afterrider died bravely and almost instantaneously.

By this time Fick and the relief party had climbed to a point about forty paces below the ledge. But they could move no farther, for each time they tried, they were given 'a smart peppering from the summit'. They were discussing tactics when pandemonium broke out high up in the pass— 'a rushing noise like a thousand horsemen in full charge', accompanied by 'tremendous yells and screams' and the rattle of musket fire. The Basotho were charging!

Fick and his men turned and fled 'at a frightening pace down the mountain, dislodging the stones in their hurry

[1] According to an eye-witness, Christiaan du Rand, see F. D. J. Wepener, *Louw Wepener*, p. 64.

and falling over each other in their frantic haste'. They reached the foot of the hill within minutes and rejoined the rest of the force near Rafutho's place.

But the Basotho charged no farther than the lowest rampart, and by sunset they had returned to their positions. When night fell, and silence returned again to Thaba Bosiu, the defenders of the hill collected their dead, and took the wounded to Moshesh's kraal for treatment by the chief's medicine men. Casualties had not been as heavy as Moshesh had feared, and as far as his own family was concerned, Mopeli had been shot in the arm and Tladi in the groin. The rest of his sons and brothers had come out of the encounter unscathed. Boer casualties were also light— eleven killed, nine seriously wounded and about twenty lightly.

In the gloomy grey light of a half-moon, two of Louw Wepener's followers, Chris du Rand and Carl Mathey, crept up the fissure. Reaching the ledge, they lifted Wepener's body and carried it to the opposite side of the pass where they laid it to rest in a shallow trench, beside the corpse of a comrade, Adam Raubenheimer. After a short prayer the two men slid silently down the pass and hurried back to camp. Among the many who crowded around them for news of the gallant commandant's fate was Dick, Louw Wepener's son. They could offer him little solace, but gave him a watch they had removed from his father's waistcoat pocket.

CHAPTER TWENTY-EIGHT

SURRENDER

Moshesh praises the defenders of Thaba Bosiu—His plea for peace is rejected by Brand—The Boers shell Moshesh's kraal—The blockade of Thaba Bosiu—Hundreds of cattle perish on the hill-top—The Boers swoop on Basotho commandos in outlying areas—Louw Wepener's skeleton is brought down from Thaba Bosiu —The Basotho chiefs surrender

A LITTLE before midnight, in an atmosphere of tense silence, some of the dignitaries and warriors met in Moshesh's kraal to offer sacrifices and prayers of thanksgiving to Molimo, the Supreme Spirit. Moshesh did not attend, for apparently he preferred to be alone with his thoughts in the stone house. He could hear the Boers singing at worship in their camp below the hill. He must have pondered on the events the morrow would bring.

All next day the Basotho watched and waited for the Boers to attack, but when night fell without incident, most of them concluded that Fick had abandoned the assault on the hill, and was resting his men before leading them home. When yet another day passed and the Boers remained cooped up in camp, Molapo had three oxen slaughtered and invited Moshesh, the councillors and military commanders to a feast in the *kgotla*. Asked to address the gathering the old chief said he was as proud of the defenders of the hill as he had been of their fathers, in years gone by, when they had repulsed the conquerors, Shaka, Mzilikazi and Matiwane. But the Boers, he continued, had not yet left, and remained encamped at the foot of the hill. They were not to be considered vanquished until every one of them had left the Lesotho.

A week later the Boers were still at Thaba Bosiu and showed not the slightest intention of renewing operations. Moshesh was baffled, and contrary to the advice of his councillors he decided to sue for peace. In a letter to Brand

he begged that the Boers should be removed from Thaba
Bosiu, and he suggested that a meeting of opposing leaders
be convened by Sir Philip Wodehouse as soon as possible.

'It is my profound wish,' he added, 'that peace should be
restored between us.'

A reply from Brand reached Thaba Bosiu on the same
day. The President said the Boers were determined to crush
the Basotho, no matter how long this took or how many
lives it cost. The present struggle, he added, had come about
as a result of the many injustices suffered by innocent
people, both black and white, at the hands of the Basotho.
Brand asked Moshesh to cast his mind back to the crimes
committed by Poshuli and other Basotho brigands. Could
the chief recall the ruthless torture and slaughter of Boer,
Bastard and Barolong families? Most of these atrocities
stemmed from the 'sheer hypocrisy of Moshesh', for he was
'constantly talking of peace', but had done little or nothing
towards 'securing its blessing'.

'You have allowed your sons, your brothers and your
people to rob and plunder,' continued Brand, 'instead of
compelling them to earn the fruits of honest labour.' But
the Boers were not unreasonable. They were prepared to
cease hostilities provided Moshesh undertook to honour the
following terms:

He would have to remove himself and his subjects from
Thaba Bosiu, and hand over all arms and ammunition to
the Boers. He would have to deliver, within four days, ten
thousand head of cattle and five thousand horses, 'in satis-
faction of the expenses of the war'. Moshesh would have to
pay an additional fine, also 'within the said four days',
namely sixty thousand sheep and thirty thousand head of
cattle 'as compensation for the robberies and damage done
by his people both before and after the war'. Finally, he
would have to cede all Basotho lands, overrun in recent
weeks by Fick and Wepener to the Free State. Should Moshesh agree to the terms, he was to send a written reply
preferably with two of his senior sons whom the Boers
would hold hostage until a peace treaty had been signed.

Brand waited impatiently for word from Moshesh, but
three days later when no reply had come, he instructed Fick
to capture Basotho herds in the vicinity and send them to

Winburg. The round up of cattle began on the morning of 25 August and was watched from the hill-top by Moshesh and his people. The Boers found some two thousand beasts in the surrounding hills, not realizing that only a week before fifteen thousand animals belonging to Moshesh himself had been taken to a valley in the Maluti foothills. The old chief was on tenterhooks all day. After sunset he called his herdsmen together and sent them under escort to bring his herd on to Thaba Bosiu.

Next morning at dawn, scarcely had the last of Moshesh's beasts reached the hill-top than the Boers broke camp and formed a chain of small but well fortified laagers around Thaba Bosiu. According to an eye-witness Moshesh's stronghold was soon 'completely surrounded . . . with Boer camps', some of which were 'perched' on the surrounding heights. During the afternoon Boer artillery, positioned 'on a promontory of the Berea, exactly opposite the southern point of Thaba Bosigo [sic]' pounded the hill-top with shells, and continued to do so day after day.

By the 31st there was chaos on the hill, much of Moshesh's village, including his stone house was razed to the ground, and droves of cattle tormented by thirst and hunger surged noisily backwards and forwards, from one edge of the summit to the other. Moshesh should never have brought his herd onto the hill-top. There was now scarcely food and grazing for five hundred beasts, let alone fifteen thousand.

The old chief took shelter in a herdsman's tumble-down hut, his mind dark with gloom, his worn out body trembling with fear. Moving to a cavern in the western slopes, he found himself almost deserted by his subjects, and he was beset with loneliness. Often he would break down, whimpering softly to himself, and covering his ears with his hands in an effort to shut out the booming of the guns and woeful lowing of the cattle.

During the first week in September hundreds of beasts died on the summit and the slopes became strewn with blown-up, fly-ridden carcasses. Huge flights of vultures came sliding down from the skies. At nights the hill crawled with hyenas and jackals. In an effort to save his animals from a slow, dreadful death, Moshesh had thousands driven

down the Raebe pass into the valley, although knowing full
well they would fall into the hands of the Boers. His tribe
was doomed. Soon the rains would come, but there could be
no tilling or planting, for even the lands were patrolled by
enemy horsemen. The granaries were almost empty. Famine bestrode the horizons.

Dejected beyond comfort Moshesh emerged from his
cavern and roamed the hill-top, now quarrelling with his
councillors, now hurling insults at his commanders and
warriors or blaming his unruly sons and brothers for the
dilemma facing the tribe. If only the British would come to
his rescue, the Boers would have to withdraw across the
Caledon or face destruction. He would write to Sir Philip
Wodehouse asking him to annex the Lesotho on behalf of
Britain.

On 17 September a British envoy named William Reed
arrived at the foot of the Ramaseli pass with a letter for
Moshesh from Wodehouse. Fetched by a dignitary he was
taken to the *kgotla* where Moshesh and the councillors
awaited him. It was an unusually cold day, and the chief
was dressed in a voluminous *kaross* and a lofty fur headdress. After a short while five hundred warriors 'all in
carosses [*sic*]' and armed with assegais and guns escorted
Moshesh and Reed to a cave just below the summit.

Wodehouse's letter filled Moshesh's wearied mind with
anguish. The High Commissioner said nothing of Moshesh's proposal, but demanded ten thousand cattle or fifty
thousand sheep as compensation for losses suffered recently
by the British of Natal at the hands of Basotho marauders.
Wodehouse considered the behaviour of Moshesh's subjects
an 'insult to the British Government'.

Moshesh was so disappointed that he told Reed to leave
him, promising to call him again in a day or two. For almost a week the envoy strolled about the hill inspecting
damage done by the Boers or visiting the warriors manning
the defences. He noticed that there were about two thousand people on the hill-top, mostly men, and warriors
guarded not only the passes, but also the upper slopes.
Some of the men manned earthen and stone breastworks
and others shallow rifle pits. There was no shortage of

ammunition. Squads of boys worked from morning till night collecting bullets for smelting and moulding into slugs.

Reed found the stench of decaying carcasses unbearable, and he cursed Moshesh for keeping him waiting so long. The chief was a strange old fellow, he reflected. He seemed to do nothing but grouse and gorge himself with coffee and biscuits.

At last Reed was summoned by Moshesh. The chief looked grave and edgy.

'I have given orders that they (the stolen cattle) shall be restored,' he said curtly, and with a flick of the wrist he dismissed the envoy.

As the blockade of Thaba Bosiu continued Moshesh, fearing the destruction of the tribe was at hand, called constantly on the spirits for help. There were always seers, diviners or witchdoctors at his side to advise and uplift him spiritually. According to John Burnet, the younger dignitaries of the stronghold considered the chief's 'once vigorous mind partially gone', and complained that 'his judgment' was being 'harassed and poisoned by these wretches'.

At the beginning of November, Wessels attacked and defeated Chief Moorosi's clan in the south. A fortnight later Fick dispersed a powerful Basotho commando at Platberg, and Smit heading seven hundred Boers and almost as many tribal levies under a Colonial named Tainton fell upon Matsieng—the Place of Locusts. He put the garrison to flight, killing fifteen of Letsie's best warriors.

During December the Boers hounded Basotho commandos in the vicinity of Modderpoort, Korannaberg, Mekwatleng, Viervoet, and Berea, and in January 1866 they crushed the bulk of Moshesh's force near Winburg. Molapo gave himself up in February, and in March the entire tribe surrendered. The Basotho were hungry, bewildered and broken, and could hold out no longer. Moshesh was indisposed and in bed. Mopeli and Sekhonyana were in charge of affairs at Thaba Bosiu.

On 8 April Dick Wepener, son of the ill-fated Louw Wepener, visited Moshesh with four fellow-boers. They found the old chief sitting hunched up on an ash-heap, among the ramparts cresting the Khubelu pass. Moshesh wore a smoking-cap embroidered in yellow silk, and he was half-draped in a scarlet blanket he had bought some time back from a trader. Rising slowly to greet the strangers, he looked sick and decrepit, and not a day under his seventy-nine years. His once powerful body now hung in pulpy pockets of skin, and his arms and legs were knob-jointed and seemed almost fleshless.

Dick Wepener hated Moshesh, had borne him a festering grudge since the death of the gallant Louw Wepener in the Khubelu pass. He refused to accept a hand of greeting proffered by the old chief, adding brusquely that he considered Moshesh his enemy. He said he had come to the hill-top not to dilly-dally, but to fetch Louw Wepener's remains.

'Ask him where his father is,' cried Moshesh caustically, addressing an interpreter. He was shocked at the white man's insolence, and was offended.

'You killed my father,' retorted Dick, 'you know where he is; how can you ask me? I must ask you where you put him.'

Young Wepener's companions glared at him incredulously. Suddenly Dick felt ashamed and begged the old man's pardon. He had not meant to be rude. Moshesh smiled benevolently. He too had once been young and impulsive, he said, and he asked Dick Wepener to think of him as a friend. Calling Tladi, his son, the chief told him to take the Boers to the spot where Louw Wepener was buried.

'Father and Adam Raubenheimer's grave was situated about twelve paces from where father fell,' Dick narrated in later years. Removing a pile of stones from a shallow trench shown him by Tladi, he had come upon two skeletons bleached white by storm-water and the heat of the Summer sun.

As he packed the bones of the first skeleton into a bag, Dick wondered if they really belonged to his father. But on close inspection of the skull his doubts vanished. It was the identical shape of his father's head. He also recognized the teeth, and especially the incisors which had been worn down at a slant during many years of avid pipe smoking.

Returning to Moshesh's kraal Dick Wepener expressed deep appreciation at the help he had received. Next day he and his friends were back at Constantia, his father's farm, and they laid Louw Wepener's bones to rest in the family graveyard.

Dick had found the visit to Thaba Bosiu an uplifting experience, but a horrifying thought lingered in his mind. He had learnt from Tladi that within an hour of Louw Wepener's death, Moshesh had sent medicine men to cut the heart from the corpse and cook it.[1] He had also decreed that 'each young commander should eat a portion of it, so that they would become as brave as this man [Louw Wepener]'.

The year 1866 marked a further gradual downward slide in Moshesh's already precarious health. It also marked the rapid waning of his influence beyond the confines of his kraal. Much of the burden of chieftainship had already been placed on the somewhat flimsy shoulders of Chief Letsie. But the heir-apparent was in many ways a weak man, and what made matters worse, he knew it. He was also an impulsive man. For example, one minute he would heap gifts or privileges on the sycophants who frequented Mat-sieng, and then suddenly he would sjambok a menial for

[1] It is not impossible that Wepener's heart was removed from the corpse, for it was common practice then as it is still in parts of Southern Africa for human organs to be used in ritual, and especially in the preparation of potent medicines called *diretlo*. John Burnet claimed to have seen Wepener's corpse just before its burial, and this was later corroborated by Tladi. (See *Louw Wepener*, p. 67.) Long after the war Louw Wepener's sister, Mrs. Catherina van Reenen was visited by an elderly tribesman on her farm, Plauen, near Harrismith. This man had taken part in the defence of Thaba Bosiu, and had seen the commandant slain. Recalling the events that followed, he said Louw Wepener's heart had first been hung in a cave and then eaten by the commanders. Moshesh had been present, but had taken no part in the proceedings.

It is worth noting that after Boer leader Piet Retief had been cudgelled to death by the Zulu in 1838, both his heart and liver were removed and presented to King Dingane (see Becker, *Rule of Fear*, p. 225).

interrupting him. One day in the *kgotla* he fired a pistol at a
stock-thief brought before him. Letsie was an expert in the
art of duplicity, and was loyal to no one, not even his own
father. In May he begged the British to annex the Lesotho,
but annoyed soon afterwards by Sir Philip Wodehouse, he
turned to the Boers pleading with them to accept him and
his followers 'as subjects of the Free State'.[1]

In due course Letsie found himself rejected by the Boers,
snubbed by the British and cold-shouldered by his brothers
and the dignitaries of Thaba Bosiu. He was invariably un-
sure of himself, and he became progressively obscure in
character.

The responsibilities thrust upon Letsie by circumstances
weighed heavily upon him. The Lesotho was heading
rapidly for destruction! The people were hungry and insecure, and the younger army commanders cried out
angrily for action against the Boers. Letsie was determined
to prevent a further outbreak of hostilities, but was powerless to do so as most of the fighting men refused to acknowledge his authority.

Matters became critical at the beginning of 1867. The
volksraad decreed that Basotho still resident in the territories conquered recently by the Boers should leave at once
or face expulsion by force of arms. The Basotho appealed
to Brand for an extension of time. After the previous lean
year, they had planted crops which had to be harvested if
the tribe was to survive.

But granted permission by Brand to remain until the
reaping season was over, the Basotho started preparing
immediately for war. It was decided that Moshesh's personal force would continue to man the defences of Thaba
Bosiu. Masupha, Tladi, Lerotholi and others would hold
the flat-topped Qeme hill, and Poshuli Tandjesberg in the
south. It was also decided to store the forthcoming harvest
in the hills, to drive the stock into the Malutis and to
build up stores of firearms and ammunition. Scores
of Colonial traders were known to be heading for the
Lesotho with loads of contraband weapons. When the time
was ripe, the Basotho would rise again and crush the
Boers.

[1] Letter from Chief Letsie to President Brand: Theal, *BR* iii.

Told about the impending uprising by Wild Cat spies, the Boers began sacking kraals and granaries in March. After a day or two heavy rains set in, extinguishing the flames and forcing the Boers to discontinue the operation. Deeply troubled, but grateful to the spirits for their timely intervention, Moshesh sent envoys to confer with Brand. He told them to reassure the President that the Basotho would leave the conquered territory as soon as their crops were reaped. They certainly had no intention of attacking the Boers. Again Brand took pity on Moshesh and stayed the expulsion of his subjects. He warned the envoys that should the Basotho attempt to deceive him, he would order their annihilation.

When the Autumn came little effort was made to harvest the crops. The Basotho openly defied the Boers knowing an attack would soon be made against the republic. Acting on advice from scouts and informers Brand again called out the commandos, and on 16th June launched what was to become known as *Ntwanyana*—the Little War—the final struggle between the Basotho and the Boers.

Crops and kraals were destroyed. Skirmishes broke out everywhere, and hordes of Basotho women and children fled into the hills. Moshesh's chiefs heading commandos large and small streamed into the Free State from all parts of the Lesotho. Spring arrived, and the struggle continued. No new crops were planted in the Summer, except inland in the mountain folds, far removed from the blood-soaked lowland regions.

In March 1867 thousands of hunger-stricken Basotho poured into the Free State in search of food. Some became outlaws, and others said to be veterans of the *difaqane* era, reverted to cannibalism.

Moshesh's health was crumbling now, and the confidence that had always served to fortify him in times of crisis drifted slowly away. Messages of encouragement from the Colony meant little to him, and he showed only fleeting interest in a magnificent case of pistols sent him by Napoleon III. He was often forgetful and confused, and sometimes his conversation was so incoherent as to cause his companions grave concern.

The reaping season had always been a time of good cheer and festivity, and the Winter although hard and bleak was usually a time of plenty. But now disaster followed disaster, and the seasons passed in a shroud of gloom. Letsie and Mopeli surrendered to the Boers in June, and were followed in July by sixteen chiefs, some of them heroes of the tribe whose deeds were legendary throughout central South Africa. The redoubtable Moletstane, chief of the Lion People, once known as Moshesh's right hand, laid down his arms in September, and swore allegiance to the Boers. The cunning Poshuli, most feared of all Basotho brigands, was gone—killed in action near Tandjesberg. Again the shadows of doom were gathering. Soon the sun would cease to shine.

THE END OF AN ERA

Sir Philip Wodehouse arrives at Thaba Bosiu and formally proclaims the Lesotho a British protectorate —Moshesh begs Adele Mabille to pray for him—His health deteriorates further—He and Adele become estranged—Moshesh sends for Adolphe Mabille and Dr. Casalis—He agrees to be baptized—His reconciliation with Adele—Moshesh passes away in his sleep and is buried at Thaba Bosiu

ONE evening towards the end of September, while taking a stroll with Tladi, Masupha and Makwanyane, Moshesh was called by his councillors to the *kgotla*. A British envoy from Sir Philip Wodehouse had arrived and asked to see him. The old chief could barely muster a spark of enthusiasm for the stranger's visit. He was far too weary and downcast and plagued by a mysterious, pulsating sound of buzzing deep within his head. Learning later from the envoy that his plea for British protection had at last been forwarded by Wodehouse to Queen Victoria, Moshesh's eyes sparkled with delight. At last the sun was 'breaking through the clouds', he cried. Before long his 'chiefs and subjects' would be 'glad and happy' again in its comforting warmth.

Four long, anxious months passed without further word from Wodehouse. Then on the afternoon of 26 January 1868, a second envoy arrived on the hill. He announced in the *kgotla* that the Queen had 'graciously' condescended to accept the Basotho 'as subjects of the British Throne'! Moshesh and his subjects became wild with excitement, and as the news spread across the land, the sound of rejoicing rose from every kraal.

Wodehouse's announcement came as a shock to President Brand, for he had not expected the British to interfere in the Boers' dispute with the Basotho. Backed by the *volksraad* he warned Moshesh and Wodehouse that the Boers intended continuing the fight 'with vigour'. They would have no mercy on Moshesh and his tribe of cut-throats.

A proclamation placing the Basotho under the suzerainty of the Queen was issued in Cape Town on 12 March. Two weeks later Sir Walter Currie, arrived in the Lesotho, heading five hundred men, and pitched camp near Korokoro. Sir Philip Wodehouse followed early in April, and on the 15th he and Currie visited Moshesh. At a great *pitso* held on the hill-top the High Commissioner formally proclaimed the Lesotho a British protectorate. After a week with Moshesh he returned to the Cape promising to negotiate a new boundary line in the west with the Boers, and settle the question of the territory they claimed to have conquered in the recent struggle.

From that time on Thaba Bosiu became a refuge for scores of white men, among whom were 'deserters from the Queen's army ... vagabonds, robbers and delinquents of all grades and classes'. The 'very lowest class of traders' also flocked to the territory with stocks of brandy, guns and ammunition, which they sold to the Basotho under cover of darkness. These white men 'had a most downward effect' on the Basotho people, and were a source of unending feuds.

Currie had remained in the Lesotho as British Representative, but after two months had been recalled to the Cape with four hundred of his men. He was succeeded by Commander James Bowker, a subordinate officer.

Negotiations between Wodehouse and the Boers took far longer than Moshesh and the councillors had anticipated. By August the old chief had grown so impatient that he asked Bowker and the Rev. Jousse to investigate. He said his health could not hold out much longer, and he had to feel the joy of mental quietude before his death.

A recent development in Moshesh's indisposition was his inability to keep awake for more than half an hour at a time. For instance, while conferring with Bowker and Jousse he drifted off on two occasions, waking up with a start and rubbing his impassive bloodshot eyes with the back of his hand. Both times he snored vehemently, as only Moshesh could snore.

Often, between snoozes, Moshesh was so talkative that no

one dared interrupt. Adolphe Mabille found him irritating, and during a visit to Thaba Bosiu at the end of 1868, he concluded that the old man was no less muddled than the inveterate *dagga*-smokers found hanging about the *kgotla*.

On 4 February 1869 Wodehouse and the Boers met at Aliwal North, and after a week of haggling they reached agreement on the new boundary line. Henceforth it would follow the Caledon river to Jammersberg Drift, thence to the junction between the Orange and Kornet spruit, and finally to the mouth of the Tees. Beacons were to be erected following Moshesh's approval.

When the meeting was over Wodehouse sent word for Moshesh to meet him on the 22nd, at the Korokoro camp. A few days later a reply arrived from Thaba Bosiu. Moshesh was too frail to risk leaving his kraal for any length of time. He would be unable to reach Rafutho's kraal at the foot of the hill, let alone the British camp ten miles away. He would arrange for a *pitso* at Korokoro on the appointed day, and would send Letsie and other chiefs in his place.

Fully three thousand Basotho, mounted and draped in multi-coloured blankets, attended the *pitso* at Bowker's camp. The British and Basotho dignitaries were seated in the shade of a gigantic rock. On Wodehouse's right were Mabille, Jousse, Maitin and a new missionary named Keck, and on his left, Letsie, Molapo, Masupha and others. In front of the High Commissioner sat Moletstane, Tladi, Sekhonyana, Tseleko and several of the less influential chiefs.

Using Mabille as an interpreter, Wodehouse read the assembly a message of goodwill from the Queen, adding that nations across the seas rejoiced at the news that the Basotho were now under the protective wing of the British. All that now remained was for the tribe to approve the convention held in February at Aliwal North. And the sooner the Basotho ratified the new boundary line, the sooner peace would return permanently to central South Africa.

After a full day's discussion, all the chiefs said they were satisfied that Wodehouse had acted in their interests, and he was loudly hailed as a friend of the Basotho. Moletstane alone seemed dubious. Wodehouse was jubilant, and announced amidst a roar of approval that he intended conferring with Moshesh himself before returning to the Cape.

Wodehouse visited Thaba Bosiu next day, and was taken to a small stone hut where he found Moshesh asleep beneath a pile of skins and blankets. Waking with a jerk the old chief stared blankly at the white man, then suddenly recognizing him, placed a shaky, sinewy hand on his arm. Wodehouse, said Moshesh with a flicker of a smile, was welcome at Thaba Bosiu. On the previous day he had seen a vision of the High Commissioner engulfed in a beautiful glowing light and surrounded by the spirits of the tribe. By this he knew that Wodehouse was a great friend and benefactor, and a worthy servant of the mighty Queen. The chief said he expected to die soon, and was glad now that he knew his people were safe.

These few words reached deep into Wodehouse's heart, and it grieved him to see how frail the old man had become since their previous meeting. At Moshesh's request he began describing the landmarks of the new boundary line, but realizing suddenly that the chief had drifted into a deep, breathy sleep, he padded out of the hut and waited outside with Ratsiu, Makwanyane and other dignitaries.

Moshesh slept off and on throughout the day and seemed oblivious to the High Commissioner's presence. Towards sunset Wodehouse set out for the British camp at Korokoro. Ratsiu would explain the boundary line to Moshesh on the morrow.

A few days later the Mabilles arrived at Thaba Bosiu to spend a week or two with their colleagues. Adele, accompanied by the Rev. Keck, visited Moshesh on the first sabbath, finding him in the same stone hut. In past weeks news of his lingering illness had caused her much anxiety. Often she had gone to the orchard at Morija to meditate, turning her thoughts back to her childhood and the happy moments she had spent in his company. She had recalled his frequent visits to her father's mission station, a heavy, black mantle hanging from his shoulders and a lofty tophat reaching up from his large, fleshy ears. She had always known of his affection for her, and had always striven to please him. But in later years, and especially since her return from France, she had lost a little of the warmth she had once felt for him. Considering the efforts made by her father and other missionaries to convert him to Christianity, she could not understand why he should cling so steadfastly to the traditional worship of spirits. She had never heard him speak disparagingly of the Christian doctrine but neither had she heard him praise it. Moshesh accepted Christ as a spirit, but in no way superior to the spirits of the tribe. This riled Adele. She was determined to impress upon him the Saviour's words to Thomas: 'I am the way, the truth and the life; no man cometh unto the Father, but by me.'

On that Sunday morning while she sat with Moshesh in the stone house, Adele pleaded with him to give his life to Christ before it was too late. At first he looked at her incredulously, then shaking his head he said he could never change now, it was too late. But in any case, continued the chief, the spirits of his forefathers had served him so well, that he could see no reason to forsake them in the Autumn of his life.

Adele grew angry. Why, she cried, was he so stubborn, had he forgotten that Christ alone could prepare a place for him in God's great realm of the spirits? And as angry words continued to pour from her lips, she noticed that the old man was weeping. Suddenly her voice failed her. She, his little Delly, had not intended to cause him sorrow. She had come to help and comfort him.

'Oh my child,' sobbed Moshesh, 'what you say is true. What must I do? What is holding me back? Pray for me.'

And so together they prayed, Moshesh sitting straight up on his bed, his face buried in his huge, bony hands, and Adele kneeling on the floor close by. When the prayer was over, she rose and bade him farewell. The old chief looked happier now. Taking her hand and holding it firmly he wished her 'God speed'.

'Do not forsake me, and do not weary of praying for me,' he quavered, 'perhaps God will answer your prayers.'

The cause of Moshesh's illness seems not to have been recorded by the missionaries, not even by Adele's brother,

Eugene, by now a qualified missionary doctor labouring
among the Basotho. The chiefs and missionaries attributed
Moshesh's condition to advancing senility. He was about
eighty-two now, a considerable age for those arduous times,
and both the missionaries and his medicine men knew he
would be embarking soon on his last journey.

Summer and Autumn passed without any noteworthy
change in Moshesh's condition. He still slept almost con-
tinuously, and with apparent relish. He was no longer interested in intricate political matters, claiming that his mind
had been maimed over the years by an unrelenting deluge of
problems and was therefore now incapable of bearing even
the minutest additional burden. Nothing seemed to excite or
depress him unduly these days, but told one day that the
missionary, Daumas, a Natal lawyer named Buchanan and
Tseleko were planning to visit London and petition the
Queen on the Basotho territory lost to the Boers, he insisted
that they should not go. They believed Her Majesty had the
power to restore the territories conquered by the Boers to
the Basotho, but he predicted that the mission was doomed
to failure.

Since the javelins of war had been set aside, he told them,
and since the roar of gunfire had been replaced by the
laughter of children and the chirping and piping of birds,
the Lesotho had been blessed by the spirits. Peace had come
at last, and would prevail provided both the Boers and the
Basotho purged themselves of the evil influences which had
drawn them together in bloody conflict.[1]

The Winter of 1869 was milder by far than any the
Basotho could recall. Although fanned by a tangy breeze,
Moshesh's sprawling village, now almost entirely rebuilt,
was invariably sun-drenched. Each day, with the help of his
servants, the old chief would find a cosy corner beside his
hut, and snooze or daydream in the soft warmth of the
Winter sun. Spring was heralded by unusually violent rains,
and for several days Moshesh was confined to bed, a
woollen cap pulled over his ears. Not until the sun returned
would he venture out-of-doors again. Seated in an arm-

[1] Daumas, Buchanan and Tseleko did visit England, but were
received unsympathetically by the British government. Disillusioned, they returned to South Africa in 1870.

chair, he would gaze across the infinite landscape in the west, where his subjects toiled in the fields.

In November he was laid low by a stomach disorder and when he recovered he could manage no more than two or three steps at a time unaided. Bowker visited him one morning and found him sprawled half naked on his stomach across the bed. The chief had just recovered from a bout of coughing and was on the verge of collapse. Breathing convulsively, trickles of sweat meandered over his furrowed neck and down his back. His bloated face and bulging eyes reflected his desperation, and he complained that by prolonging his life on earth, the spirits were tormenting him. He had beseeched them to fetch him, he told Bowker, but it seemed they wanted him to suffer a little of the agony endured by Christ before His passing.

The chief said he was grateful for Bowker's visit, but urged him to leave and return some other day. Beside the bed lay a magnificent leopardskin *kaross* which he asked the white man to forward to Queen Victoria on his behalf. This, said Moshesh, had been made specially for Her Majesty. It gladdened his heart to know that now the Basotho were counted among her children.

By December, Moshesh's 'feebleness was so extreme that when he wished to leave his bed, he had to be carried like a child'. Adele and Adolphe Mabille spent a few days with the missionaries at Thaba Bosiu in January 1870. One morning after arranging with the councillors to see the chief, they climbed onto the hill-top taking their baby son, Louis, with them. They were shocked to see the transformation he had undergone since their previous meeting. The rigours of suffering had altered his once noble face. His head seemed to have shrunk; his bush of tousled hair had grown considerably whiter; his eyes had crept deeper into their shadowy sockets and his white-stubbled cheeks were hollowed. Delighted to see them, he tried to lift himself, but could only raise his head. A councillor seated beside him on the bed, 'propped him up in his arms'.

After exchanging a few words of greeting with him and showing him her baby, Adele said she and her husband had come to enquire after his health, and to hold a short service

at his bedside. First Adolphe led them in prayer, and then
he addressed the chief. Moshesh, he said, was not to fear
death for it marked not the termination of life, but the
rebirth of the spirit. The spirit of man was indestructible, he
said, and was destined to live forever either in heaven or
hell. It was therefore essential that Moshesh should come to
terms with God. The time had come to accept Christ, and
Christ alone, as his Saviour.

'Lord,' cried Adolphe, quoting the words of Simeon,
'now lettest Thou thy servant depart in peace, for mine eyes
have seen Thy salvation.'

Taking the old chief's hand, the missionary held it
against his chest.

'Moshesh,' he said, 'I would like to hear you say those
words before you leave this world. Oh Moshesh, will you
also be able to say that you have seen the salvation of
God?'

Suddenly the chief burst into tears, declaring he was
afraid to die. Adele, assuming that at last 'his conscience
was working' recited the opening verses of St. John, Chapter 14, and 'begged him to ask Jesus to prepare a place
(*tulo*) for him in heaven'. Moshesh wiped away his tears,
and asked Adele to write him a prayer on a piece of paper.
But Adolphe objected, saying 'in a low voice' that it was not
the prayer Moshesh wanted, but the paper, for this he
would use for magical purposes.

'Could I tell God of the number of your sins,' Adele
asked the chief, explaining that she was incapable of writing
a prayer to meet all his needs. 'Just pray with all your heart,
and say to God, Have mercy on me for I am a sinner.'

'You are a bad child,' retorted Moshesh, 'who said I am a
sinner? I too shall go to heaven.' He was fuming now. He
assured Adele that when the time for his passing came he
would need neither her help nor her prayers.

Adele and Adolphe decided to leave, and 'with sad
hearts' bade him farewell. One of the councillors observing
their disappointment, tried to comfort them. He said Moshesh was possessed by an evil spirit, and beyond convers-
ion to Christianity. He advised them to try again at a later
date, when the evil spirit had been exorcised.

The Rev. Jousse[1] often saw Moshesh after the departure of Adele and Adolphe. On each occasion he read the portion from St. John, Chapter 14, that Adele had recited to the chief. In due course he persuaded Moshesh to repeat the second part of the sixth verse after him, namely, 'no man cometh unto the Father, but by Me'.

'Son of Mokhachane,' said Jousse one day, 'a home is prepared for you in heaven; believe in Jesus, the Saviour of the world, and you will be saved.'

These words made Moshesh happy. Jousse did not consider him a sinner as Adele had done. When the missionary left, the old chief sent for one of his Christian subjects and made him read the same passage from St. John, over and over. Later he sent a councillor to the mission station to speak to Jousse. He wanted the Frenchman to inform Casalis and Arbousset that Moshesh had 'become a believer'.

At the end of February Moshesh summoned the young missionaries, Mabille and Dr. Casalis to the hill-top. He had a feeling that their presence at his bedside would help to strengthen him. Recalling the highlights of his long life, he told them that the road he had travelled had been long, arduous and invariably fraught with hazards. Now he was approaching the journey's end, he realized how easily he might have fallen out along the way had he not been accompanied by such wise and kindly men as his lifelong friend, Makwanyane, Mohlomi the seer and Eugene Casalis, Arbousset and their successors. He was old and withered now, and yet he was happier than ever before. He had undergone a rebirth since finding peace of mind, and was no older in spirit than Louis, Mabille's baby son.

'Can you certify that what the missionaries have taught is the truth?' he asked Mabille.

'Yes,' replied Adolphe, 'I have that certitude myself; I know it is the truth.'

'I believe so too,' said the chief, smiling broadly.

Moshesh was exhausted, and his eyes were heavy with approaching sleep. Thanking the missionaries for coming, he suggested that Mabille should return to Morija and fetch Adele and Baby Louis.

[1] Jousse's narrative: E. W. Smith, p. 184.

Adele visited Moshesh with her baby at the beginning of March. Entering his hut, she found it thronged with dignitaries.

'Here is the beloved person so longed for [by Moshesh],' she heard one of them say. She felt a surge of joy within her. Her heart had never ceased to ache since her last meeting with the chief.

Moshesh was so happy to see his Delly that he burst into tears, and with trembling hands beckoned her to place the baby in his arms. With tears streaming down his cheeks, he gazed at the tiny face, and smiling softly he turned to Adele.

'My age-mate, my age-mate!' he cried, 'Delly your child is my age-mate.' Pressing the baby against his breast he added: 'Adele, my Adele, you have shown me the way to heaven, I hope I shall enter; I am at peace, sweet peace.' He said he had decided to be baptized by the missionaries, and would summon all subjects to Thaba Bosiu for the occasion.

Moshesh told Adele to hasten back to the missionaries and ask them to prepare for the great event. No sooner had she left than the chief called three of his wives to his side. He told them to hurry after Delly, his daughter, and remind her to pray for him, for he could see the shadows of death creeping closer and closer. He did not want Delly to grieve for him, but rather to rejoice in the knowledge that she had shown him the road to the Saviour, Jesus Christ. His wives were also to tell her that she, her husband and all their missionary friends were to remain in the Lesotho after his passing. They were to take special care of Baby Louis, for he was destined to become a teacher of God and a friend of the Basotho. He would one day walk in the footsteps of his illustrious grandfather, Eugene Casalis.

March the 12th was set aside for Moshesh's baptism, and immediately messengers set out in all directions to summon the people to Thaba Bosiu. Meanwhile the chief's hut was being plastered and whitewashed for the great occasion, and a huge platform built out of soil on the outskirts of the kraal. Moshesh insisted that the ceremony should be clearly seen by all.

The hill-top thronged with visitors two days before the baptism, and thousands more were approaching on foot, on

horseback or in carts and wagons along every track leading
to Thaba Bosiu. But Moshesh slept through all the excitement. Not even Letsie could rouse him. At sunset the
hordes, dividing into groups, squatted in circles round the
fires lit in the late afternoon for their benefit. The drone of
their voices kept the missionaries awake all night.

Waking at daybreak on the 11th, Moshesh called Letsie
and Tladi who slept beside his bed on the floor. His voice
was thin and wheezy and tinged with the breath of death.
He called them repeatedly by name, but as they rose to their
feet, he slipped again behind the veil of sleep. Three hours
passed and still the old chief slept. Just after nine the spirits
came to fetch him. He left peacefully and without a sound.

Moshesh—the Shaver, son of Mokhachane, was laid to
rest on 12 March, the day set aside for his baptism. Early in
the afternoon Letsie and other close relatives fetched the
corpse from the hut, and carried it on a homemade bier to
the burial ground close by. A huge procession of mourners
followed—chiefs, councillors, warriors and servants mute
with grief; wailing women old and young draped in black;
children bunched timidly together and a small party of
white men, including the missionaries, Jousse, Dyke, Maitin, Rolland, Dr. Casalis and others. Adele had come on her
own, for her husband was ill, and confined to bed at Morija.
There were also several strangers in the throng—emissaries
from neighbouring tribal territories who chanced to arrive
on the hill at the time of Moshesh's passing; traders, their
families and servants; five skin-clad Zulu *indunas* from the
royal kraal of King Mpande; renegade Colonials seeking
sanctuary in the Lesotho, and a British envoy who had
come specifically to convey Queen Victoria's gratitude to
Moshesh for the *kaross* he had sent her.

The burial service, conducted by Jousse in the heavy heat
of the Autumn sun, was long and tiring. In addition to the
address and prayer delivered by the missionary, Ratsiu,
Makwanyane, Letsie, Tladi and other renowned orators of
the tribe took turns in extolling the virtues of the departed
chief. While the grave was being filled in, some of the
mourners sang a tribal dirge, and others wept. In the
afternoon a cairnlike mound of rocks was built over the

grave. Towards evening, Letsie placed a simple slab of
stone, hewn from the hillside, at the head of the mound. It
bore a solitary name crudely carved into its chalky surface
—the most honoured name in all the Lesotho—MOSHESH.

BIBLIOGRAPHY

Annual Report of the South African Literary and Scientific Institution. Cape Town, 1835.

ARBOUSSET, T. and DAUMAS, F. *Narrative of the Exploratory Tour to the North-east of the Colony of the Cape of Good Hope.* London, Bishop, 1852.

ASHTON, H. *The Basuto.* London, Oxford University Press, 1952.

BACKHOUSE, JAMES J. A. *A Narrative of a Visit to the Mauritius and South Africa.* London, Hamilton, Adams, 1844.

Basutoland Records (two volumes unpublished).

Basutoland Government Archives.

BECKER, PETER. *Path of Blood—The Rise and Conquests of Mzilikazi Founder of the Matabele.* London, Longmans, 1962.

BECKER, PETER. *Rule of Fear—The Life and Times of Dingane King of the Zulu.* London, Longmans, 1964.

BECKER, PETER. *Sandy Tracks ... to the Kraals.* Johannesburg, Dagbreek, 1956.

Blue Book, Kaffir Tribes. February 1848.

BROADBENT, SAMUEL. *A Narrative of the First Introduction of Christianity amongst the Barolong Tribe of the Bechuanas, South Africa.* London, Wesleyan Mission House, 1865.

BROWNLEE, C. *Reminiscences of Kaffir Life and History.* Lovedale, Mission Press, 1896.

BRYANT, A. T. *Olden Times in Zululand and Natal.* London, Longmans, 1929.

Cape Monthly Magazine. October 1871.

Cape Quarterly Review. 1882.

CASALIS, E. *The Basutos.* London, Nisbet, 1861.

CASALIS, E. *My Life in Basutoland. A Story of Mission Enterprise in South Africa.* London, Religious Tract Society, 1889.

CHASE, J. ST. C. *The Natal Papers: A Reprint of all Notices.* Grahamstown, Godlonton, 1843.

COLLINS, W. W. *Free Statia, or Reminiscences of a Lifetime in the Orange Free State, South Africa.* Bloemfontein, Friend Printing and Publishing Co., 1907.

CORY, G. E. *The Rise of South Africa* (five volumes). London, Longmans, 1910–19.

DU PLESSIS, J. *History of the Christian Missions in South Africa.* London, Longmans, 1911.

ELLENBERGER, D. F. and MACGREGOR, C. J. *History of the Basuto, Ancient and Modern.* London, Caxton Printing Co., 1912.

ELLENBERGER, V. *A Century of Mission Work in Basutoland.* Morija, Morija Press, 1938.

ENGELBRECHT, S. P. *Geschiedenis van die Nederduitsch Hervormde Kerk van Afrika.* Pretoria, de Bussy, 1953.

FREEMAN, J. J. *A Tour in South Africa.* London, John Snow, 1852.

Friend of the Sovereignty, 18 March 1854.

GIBSON, A. G. S. *Reminiscences of the Pondomise War of 1880.* Cape Town, S.A. Electric Printing & Publishing Co., 1900.

GIE, S. F. N. *Geskiedenis van Suid-Afrika of Ons Verlede* (two volumes). Stellenbosch, Pro Ecclesia, 1928–32.

Gospel Work in Basutoland. (Pamphlet.)

Grahamstown Journal, 27 May 1854.

HARRIS, CAPTAIN W. C. *The Wild Sports of Southern Africa.* London, John Murray, 1839.

HERRMAN, L. *Travels and Adventures in Eastern Africa, by Nathaniel Isaacs* (two volumes). Cape Town, Van Riebeeck Society, 1937.

HOOK, D. B. *With Sword and Statute.* Cape Town, Juta & Co., 1906.

ISAACS, NATHANIEL. *Travels and Adventures in Eastern Africa* (two volumes). London, Edward Churtan, 1836.

JONES, G. I., ed. *A Report on the Recent outbreak of 'Diretlu' Murder in Basutoland.* London, H.M.S.O., 1951.

Jaurnal des Missions (1856).

KIRBY, P. R., ed. *The Diary of Andrew Smith, Director of the 'Expedition for Exploring Central Africa', 1834–1836.* Cape Town, Van Riebeeck Society, 1939–1940.

KIRBY, P. R., ed. *Andrew Smith and Natal, Documents Relating to the Early History of that Province.* Cape Town, Van Riebeeck Society, 1955.

LAGDEN, SIR GODFREY. *The Basutos* (two volumes). London, Hutchinson, 1909.

MACGREGOR, J. C. *Basuto Traditions*. Cape Town, Argus Co., 1911.

MALAN, J. H. *Die Opkoms van 'n Republiek ... Die Geskiedenis van die Oranje-Vrystaat Tot die Jaar 1863*. Bloemfontein, Nasionale Pers Bpk, 1929.

METHUEN, H. H. *Life in the Wilderness, or Wanderings in South Africa*. London, Bentley, 1848.

MITRA, S. M. *Life and Letters of Sir John Hall*. London, Longmans, 1911.

MOFFAT, ROBERT. *Missionary Labours and Scenes in Southern Africa*. London, John Snow, 1842.

MOODI, D. C. F. *The History of the Battles of the British, the Boers and the Zulus, etc., in Southern Africa* (two volumes). Cape Town, Murray and St. Leger, 1888.

Ninety Years Work. (Pamphlet.)

ORPEN, J. M. *Reminiscences of Life in South Africa*. Durban, Davis & Sons, 1908.

POTGIETER, C. S. and THEUNISSEN, N. H. *Kommandant-Generaal Hendrik Potgieter*. Johannesburg, Afrikaanse Pers, 1938.

PRELLER, DR. GUSTAV S. *Daglemier in Suid-Afrika*. Wallachs' Bpk, 1937.

PRELLER, GUSTAV S. *Piet Retief, Lewensgeskiedenis van die grote Voortrekker*. Pretoria, Volkstem Drukkery, 1911.

PRELLER, GUSTAV S. *Voortrekkermense, 'n Vyftal oorspronklike Dokumente oor die Geskiedenis van die Voortrek* (six volumes). Cape Town, Nasionale Pers Bpk, 1920.

Public Records Office, C.O., 48/155.

SMITH, EDWIN, W. *The Mabilles of Basutoland*. London, Hodder and Stoughton, 1939.

SMITH, SIR HARRY. *The Autobiography of Lieutenant-General Sir Harry Smith*, ed. G. C. Moore Smith. London, John Murray, 1903.

South African Commercial Advertiser, 21 August and 7 October 1836.

STEEDMAN, A. *Wandering in Southern Africa*. London, Longmans, 1835.

STOW, G. W. *The Native Races of South Africa: a History*

of the Intrusion of the Hottentot and Bantu, etc. London, Swan Sonnenschein, 1905.

THEAL, GEORGE MCCALL. *A Fragment of Basuto History, 1854–1871.* Cape Town, Saul Solomon & Co., 1886.

THEAL, G. M. *History of South Africa, 1792–1872* (five volumes). London, George Allen & Unwin, 1908.

THEAL, G. M. *South Africa.* London, T. Fischer Unwin, 1899.

THEAL, G. M., ed. *Basutoland Records ... Copies of Official Documents of Various Kinds, Accounts of Travellers, etc.* (three volumes). Cape Town, W. A. Richards & Sons, Government Printers, 1883.

TYLDEN, G. *A History of Thaba Bosiu ... A Mountain at Night.* Maseru, Morija Printing Works, 1945.

TYLDEN, G. *The Rise of the Basuto.* Cape Town and Johannesburg, Juta & Co., 1950.

VAN WARMELO, N. J. *History of Matiwane and the Amangwane Tribe.* Pretoria, Government Printers, 1938.

WALKER, ERIC A. *A History of Southern Africa.* London, Longmans, 1957.

WALTON, JAMES. *Villages of the Paramount Chiefs of Basutoland* (Pamphlet). Reprint from *Lesotho*, vol. ii, 1960.

WEPENER, F. D. J. *Louw Wepener.* Pretoria, De Bussy, 1909.

REFERENCES

For full details of books and documents referred to,
see preceding Bibliography.

CHAPTER ONE: THE CALEDON VALLEY
  ORPEN, 5. LAGDEN: i, 18–22, 24. ELLENBERGER, D. F.: 21–6, 29–30, 38–9, 101–6, 109, 120–1. ARBOUSSET: 400. MACGREGOR: 21, 24, 46. THEAL, *History*: i, 462. CASALIS, *The Basutos*: 15–16, 20–33. BECKER, *Path of Blood*: 50–1. TYLDEN, *The Rise*: 5.

CHAPTER TWO: EARLY MANHOOD
  ELLENBERGER, D. F.: 22–4, 53, 77, 90–8, 107–9, 260, 342, 382–4. ARBOUSSET: 377–90, 391–402, 152–6, 312–15. CASALIS, *The Basutos*: 65, 107–8, 124–5, 170–3, 210–33. ASHTON: 158.

CHAPTER THREE: PROPHECY OF DOOM
  CASALIS, *The Basutos*: 17, 181–3, 186–7, 199–201, 215. ASHTON: 62–87. ELLENBERGER, D. F.: 95–7, 104, 108–9, 110, 272–8, 361. ARBOUSSET: 85–6, 373–6, 405. MACGREGOR: 17, 20–2. BRYANT: 62–9, 73–7, 83, 95–100, 119–20, 162–5, 419–20, 421. BECKER, *Path of Blood*: 10–15; *Rule of Fear*: 8–10. GIBSON: 11–19.

CHAPTER FOUR: THE WILD CAT PEOPLE
  MACGREGOR: 17–19, 24–8. ELLENBERGER, D. F.: 110, 121–6, 128–9, 134–42, 143–6, 222, 225. ARBOUSSET: 94, 101, 393–9, 402–4, 405, 425. CASALIS, *The Basutos*: 16–17, 187–9, 284–6. THEAL, *Basutoland Records*: ii, 83. BECKER, *Path of Blood*: 50–61. TYLDEN, *The Rise*: 5, *A History*: 4. THEAL, *History*: ii, 27, 34, 442–3. MOFFAT: 340–1, 346–7, 354–65. *Journal des Missions* (1856): 92–4.

CHAPTER FIVE: EXODUS
  ELLENBERGER, D. F.: 77, 127, 144, 146–50, 181, 227–8, 294–410. THEAL, *Basutoland Records*: i, 604–5. TYLDEN, *The Rise*: 5, 6; *A History*: 3, 6. ARBOUSSET: 88–101, 410–12. MACGREGOR: 19, 26, 53–4, 57. CASALIS, *The Basutos*: 100, 209, 272. BECKER, *Path of Blood*: 59–60; *Sandy*

14–20, 103–7, 110–11, 112–14, 116–19, 123–4, 127. *Andrew Smith and Natal*: 52. *Public Record Office*, Cd 48/55.

CHAPTER TWELVE: THE GREAT TREK

CASALIS, *My Life*: 233–4; *The Basutos*: 59–65, 67, 69. BECKER, *Path of Blood*: 139–43, 155–8, 170–1. THEAL, *Basutoland Records*: i, 8–10, 15–16, 36. KIRBY, *The Diary of Andrew Smith*: i, 103–5, 106–7, 110–14, 116–20; ii, 14, 16–18. METHUEN: 205. THEAL, *South Africa*: 93, 187; *History*: ii, 274–93, 309–10, 318, 353–75, 477–8, 479. WALKER: 196–7, 201, 203–9. MALAN: 10–13, 511, 524, 526. PRELLER, *Voortrekker Mense*: i, 117–20, 122, 124. GIE: 296–331. CHASE: 50, 88, 103, 110, 119, 132. CORY: iii, 396–7, 401. *South African Commercial Advertiser*: 27 August, 7 October 1836. HARRIS: 86, 111. POTGIETER: 52, 54, 57, 61–2. PRELLER, *Piet Retief*: 96, ENGELBRECHT: i, 19–20. MOODI: 137–80, 525.

CHAPTER THIRTEEN: CASALIS MOVES TO THABA BOSIU

CASALIS, *The Basutos*: 73–8, 80–2, 87–91, 100–1, 102, 202–5; *My Life*: 238–9, 241, 243–4, 246–7, 270–1, 275–83, 284. THEAL, *Basutoland Records*: i, 23–4, 25, 27–9, 36, 40–1, 49; *History*: ii, 306, 309–10, 318, 352–6, 357–64, 366–73. SMITH, EDWIN W.: 29–31, 32. WALKER: 203–9, 211. CHASE: 88, 110. MOODI: i, 525. MALAN: 19–20, 28, 526. ELLENBERGER, V.: 25–8. BACKHOUSE: 364, 366–72, 373–6. BECKER, *Path of Blood*: 174–8, 193–5.

CHAPTER FOURTEEN: TREATY WITH THE BRITISH

MALAN: 26–32, 33. BACKHOUSE: 356–8, 418–19, 421–2, 428. THEAL, *Basutoland Records*: i, 36–42, 45–60, 62, 65–76, 77–9; ii, 300–3, 427, 429–30. CASALIS, *The Basutos*: 82–4. SMITH, EDWIN W.: 32, 51–3, 96. THEAL, *History*: i, 503–5; ii, 468–9, 479–81, 483–4. BECKER, *Rule of Fear*: 244. ELLENBERGER, V.: 53–7, 59–60.

CHAPTER FIFTEEN: SIR PERIGRINE MAITLAND

TYLDEN, *The Rise*: 25, 28. WALKER: 222–3, 225. THEAL, *History*: ii, 233–4, 485, 487–93, 494, 498–9. ASHTON: 307. THEAL, *Basutoland Records*: i, 56, 77–9, 81–2, 84–5, 86, 87, 89–90, 92–101, 104–7, 109–11, 113–15, 116, 117, 120–6, 128–30, 131, 133, 134–7, 139–48, 150–4, 156–7, 204, 500–2. MALAN: 43–5, 57, 58, 60, 63–6, 81, 82–3, 84–5, 128. ELLENBERGER, V.: 55–6, 59–62, 64–6, 69. CASALIS,

MALAN: 208–10. ORPEN: 296–9, 300–3, 304, 341, 349, 353. WALKER: 255, 258–9, 362, 367–8. LAGDEN: 179. TYLDEN, *The Rise*: 67, *Friend of the Sovereignty*, 18 March 1854. WALTON: 5.

CHAPTER TWENTY-ONE: THE BOERS TAKE OVER
MALAN: 195–213. WALKER: 259–60. THEAL, *History*: iii, 442–3, 447–51. ORPEN: 338, 344, 350, 353, 354, 356–9, 360–1, 363–8, 455. LAGDEN: i, 182. *Grahamstown Journal*. THEAL, *Basutoland Records*: ii, 112, 116. TYLDEN, *The Rise*: 66–7.

CHAPTER TWENTY-TWO: UNHAPPINESS CROWDS MOSHESH'S LIFE
SMITH, EDWIN W.: 61–2. *The Friend of the Sovereignty*. ORPEN: 269, 298, 455–6, 457, 460, 461. THEAL, *History*: iii, 455–7; *South Africa*: 364–5. WALKER: 199, 217. PRELLER, *Daglemier*: 243–5. COLLINS: 80–90, 138. THEAL, *Basutoland Records*: ii, 118–23, 124–6, 133, 134–5, 136–8, 140–1, 142–3, 149–50, 152–3, 154–9, 162–3, 165, 166, 167–8, 169–70, 171–2, 178–9, 180, 181–2, 185–6, 191, 192–3, 194–5, 196–7, 199–201, 202, 203–4, 205–6, 209–10, 211, 212–14, 215, 216, 223–5, 228–9, 230, 232–6, 237–8, 241–2, 249, 321–2, 445, 457–64.

CHAPTER TWENTY-THREE: THE FIRST BOER–BASOTHO WAR
THEAL, *Basutoland Records*: ii, 203, 204, 205–6, 209–10, 212–13, 214–16, 223–5, 228–9, 230, 232, 233, 234–5, 237–8, 239, 241, 242, 244–6, 248–9, 252, 254–8, 259, 260–2, 267–9, 283–4, 287–90, 291, 292–5, 296, 297–8, 299, 300, 301–3, 305–9, 310–11, 312, 313, 314–15, 317–18, 320, 321–3, 327, 328–9, 331, 333–4, 335, 336, 337, 339–41, 342–4, 345–7, 351, 353, 354, 359, 361–2, 364, 370–1, 374, 375–6, 379–80, 381–2, 387, 388, 390, 398, 407, 411, 412, 414, 416, 423, 426, 427–9, 430, 431–8, 439, 443–53, 474; iii, 123–4. MOODI: ii, 86–7. ELLENBERGER, V.: 100–4. THEAL, *A Fragment*: pp. xxvi, xxxiv. WEPENER: 31–4. MALAN: 275–94, 348–60. THEAL, *History*: iii, 468–82.

CHAPTER TWENTY-FOUR: AN UNEASY PEACE
THEAL, *Basutoland Records*: ii, 353–4, 358–9, 360–5, 368, 370–2, 373, 374, 379, 382, 387–8, 390, 391–3, 395–7, 398–9, 402–3, 408, 409, 410, 411, 415, 418, 438, 440–3, 471, 476–8, 482–3, 484–6, 488–9, 490–6, 506–7; iii, 274. LAGDEN: i, 233–4, 263, 276, 277. MALAN: 368–85. THEAL,

862, 881–2; *A Fragment*: 66, 95–6, 97–8, 108, 110–12, 114–17. ELLENBERGER, V.: 136. WEPENER: 75.

CHAPTER TWENTY-NINE: THE END OF AN ERA

THEAL, *Basutoland Records*: iii, 834–9, 839, 840, 842–3, 844, 846, 847, 851–3, 856–7, 858, 861, 862, 864, 875, 879, 883, 892. *Basutoland Records* (Lesotho Government Archives): iv, part i, 28, 29, 31, 33, 34, 36, 47–8, 49–50, 51, 55, 57–62, 63–8, 69, 87, 88, 98–9, 102–3, 104–5, 112, 113, 114–15, 119, 120, 122, 125, 127, 139, 141, 179–83, 192–3, 194–5, 196–7, 198–201, 208, 212–13, 239–40, 268, 218–83, 284, 285–6, 289–96, 297–8, 301–5, 310–12, 316, 317–19, 320, 321, 322, 328–9, 335, 336, 337, 342, 352, 353–65, 367, 368, 374, 377, 385–94, 421–3, 436, 449, 451, 453–5, 456–63, 465–7, 472–6, 478–9, 483, 489–90, 516, 527, 532–3, 540–2. v, part ii, 282–4, 285, 304–28, 333, 334–5, 336–7, 350, 353, 354, 355–6, 357, 358–9, 360–3, 367–77, 379–82, 387, 393, 395–6, 398, 401–5, 410–11, 416–21, 423–6, 430, 432, 433, 434–5, 436, 437–42, 452, 455. THEAL, *A Fragment*: 122–4, 126–7, 133, 136, 140. SMITH, EDWIN W.: 181–6.

INDEX

304 INDEX